Email
Marketing

Email Marketing

Using Email to Reach Your Target Audience and Build Customer Relationships

Jim Sterne
Anthony Priore

Wiley Computer Publishing

John Wiley & Sons, Inc.

NEW YORK · CHICHESTER · WEINHEIM · BRISBANE · SINGAPORE · TORONTO

Publisher: Robert Ipsen

Editor: Cary Sullivan

Managing Editor: Marnie Wielage

Associate New Media Editor: Brian Snapp

Text Design & Composition: North Market Street Graphics, Lancaster, Pennsylvania

Designations used by companies to distinguish their products are often claimed as trademarks. In all instances where John Wiley & Sons, Inc., is aware of a claim, the product names appear in initial capital or ALL CAPITAL LETTERS. Readers, however, should contact the appropriate companies for more complete information regarding trademarks and registration.

This book is printed on acid-free paper. ⊚

This publication is designed to provide accurate and authoritative information in regard to the subject matter covered. It is sold with the understanding that the publisher is not engaged in professional services. If professional advice or other expert assistance is required, the services of a competent professional person should be sought.

Library of Congress Cataloging-in-Publication Data:
Sterne, Jim, 1955–
    Email marketing using email to reach your target audience and build customer relationships / Jim Sterne, Anthony Priore.
      p. cm.
    "Wiley computer publishing."
    Includes index.
    ISBN 0-471-38309-0 (pbk./website : alk. paper)
    1. Telemarketing.   2. Electronic mail messages.   3. Customer relations.
  I. Priore, Anthony. II. Title.
HF5415.1265 .S7417 2000
658.8'4—dc21

                                      99-086130

Printed in the United States of America.
10 9 8 7 6 5 4 3

CONTENTS

N early 20 years ago, Lester Wunderman, founder of Wunderman, Ricotta and Klein (later Wunderman Cato), predicted a world of one-to-one marketing. Over the years, he and others have spoken about the wastefulness of a direct marketing world in which 98 percent of the mail is *not* responded to, and yet the 2 percent was often profitable in the long term.

> *By the end of the century, one-third of all retail sales will take place in a non-store environment.*
> **Stanley Marcus, Chairman Emeritus, Neiman Marcus**

While Marcus's estimate of the time and percentage may not be accurate, it does not diminish the trend that he saw years before others . . . for he made this statement before the invention of the personal computer and before the emergence of the online world, which we now take for granted.

Now, more than ever before, we marketers live in a world where the promise of true one-to-one marketing is upon us. It is made possible by the development of the personal computer and the software that can identify, like never before, the real interests and behaviors of people we want to reach.

But that is just the beginning. For in this new and growing world of Internet marketing comes a new concept. A concept that is both consumer-friendly and consumer-driven. A concept that is to marketing in the new millennium what attitudinal advertising and mass marketing was to a significant part of the twentieth century.

That concept is *permission-based (opt-in) email advertising.*

Those of us with some gray in our hair remember the words that created the great direct marketing companies: *responsible persuasion.* This meant using art and copy to persuade a consumer to seriously consider our offer. It worked. And it still works in many, but not all, instances. Today's consumers are too smart, too savvy, and too overwhelmed with media options to have much patience for advertising (in any form) that is not relevant to them and their lifestyles.

And that is where permission-based advertising represents the single most important new trend in Internet marketing.

Why? Because at its core it recognizes that the Internet is consumer-driven and that consumers, with their ultimate control over what they see and how long they are engaged, depend on the relevance of an offer. When they participate in an opt-in program, they have chosen to do so. In that simple action they have indicated a willingness to consider products and services, which is a strategy that is 180 degrees different from all of the past marketing efforts to which they are accustomed.

But as with all things new, new skills are needed, and that is where building customer relationships with email marketing comes into play. A centering in direct marketing is crucial for success as an e-commerce marketer. But new skills and new knowledge are required, and this book does a terrific job of providing that new information.

Its content is both familiar and new. It illustrates what makes email different from both traditional direct mail and other direct response media forms. It also highlights how to make the most of this new medium, and by providing that understanding many of you will find your own new breakthroughs.

This is a terrific time for smart marketers who know about taking responsible risks and are willing to find new ways to reach new customers. And this book can make the process even more fun and more successful.

I hope you find that success.

Jerry I. Reitman
Executive Vice President (retired), Leo Burnett Company
Author of *Beyond 2000: The Future of Direct Marketing* (NTC Books)
JIReitman@juno.com

I'd like to thank Jerry Reitman, direct marketing veteran and author of *Beyond 2000: The Future of Direct Marketing* (NTC Books), and Tom Collinger, professor of direct marketing at Northwestern University, for their generous support and for sharing their vast knowledge of direct marketing with me over the years. I'd also like to thank Harvey John Morris, Director of Brand Marketing at yesmail.com, for his tireless assistance in assembling this book. Thanks to the Direct Marketing Association (DMA) and the Association of Interactive Media (AIM) for being invaluable sources of information. And, finally, special thanks to Dave Tolmie, CEO of yesmail.com, for his marketing vision and enthusiastic encouragement to develop this book.

—*Tony Priore*

I'd like to thank Mark Swanson from eShare, as well as Andy Bourland and Richard Hoy from the ClickZ Network, for sharing their stories. The same to Michael Tchong from and for *Iconocast* and thanks to Rick Bruner from IMT Strategies for sharing some early results from their email marketing survey. Special thanks go to Ron Richards from ResultsLab for his breakthroughs and insights. Finally, thanks to all the people at YesMail who provided hard evidence, moral support, and very fast answers.

—*Jim Sterne*

CHAPTER 1

Introduction

I'm a big believer in email. I firmly believe that for any client, it's got to be part of the marketing mix.

CINDY DALE, VP, BBDO

You've Got Mail! And so does everybody else. It's everywhere. Web sites may have been the first wonder of the Internet. Banner advertising may have astonished marketing mavens around the world. Streaming media might someday give us the video phones we were promised at the New York World's Fair in 1964.

But the most powerful tool for marketing, the most powerful tool for branding, the most powerful tool for direct response, and the most powerful tool for building customer relationships turns out to be plain old, ordinary email. It's cheap, it's easy, and everybody on the Internet has an address.

Why then is so much of the email you get so bad?

Because it's so cheap and so easy, and reaching everybody on the Internet is as simple as hitting the Send button.

Bad email is the bane of our existence. We hate it because we love our email. A PricewaterhouseCoopers survey found 83 percent of Internet users felt email was their primary reason for using the Internet. Given the choice, an overwhelming majority turned down books, radios, and televisions in favor of an Internet connection with email on a desert island.

In their report *Opt-in Email Gets Personal* Forrester Research (www.forrester.com) said opt-in email "will spread like wildfire." They believe using opt-in email for marketing "will explode" because companies will be lured by high response rates, low costs, and the ease with which any firm, large or small, can get started.

As for wildfires, in an April 1999 Forrester survey of 47 marketing managers 77 percent said email marketing was crucial to their marketing plans, having found it as effective as affiliate programs, but much less expensive. An August 1999 study by IMT Strategies, a research and advisory firm focused on sales and marketing technology trends, preliminarily showed signing people up to receive email announcements sat at the top of their priority list. Why?

IDG List Services (www.idglist.com) provides a succinct answer in their "10 Benefits of Emailing" in the media kit for renting *The Industry Standard* email list:

Quick Lead Generation. Email has quick output and quick response for lead generation.

Selectivity. Email offers the same list selectivity as traditional list rental.

Media Reinforcement. Email can be an adjunct to any media to quickly reinforce a message, product announcement, seminar date or trade show.

Cost Effective. Email is extremely cost effective on a cost per contact basis for customer acquisition.

Higher Response. Overall responses may be higher as only relevant materials will be sent which assures a more receptive audience to the offer.

Lower Costs. There are no production paper, or postage costs—only the cost of the Email server companies.

Privacy Issues. Subscribers choose to receive Email solicitation through a negative option given upon subscribing. Subscribers are also aware of the source of their name and are always given the choice to opt out. This addresses the privacy issue directly and again assures a responsive audience.

Customer Dialogue. As an interactive medium, Email establishes a dialogue with new and present customers. Repeated messages can create an effective brand awareness or a continued response from and conversation with the customer.

Trackable. Email is also a trackable medium, as you can direct responders to answer through many types of response vehicles.

No Postal Undeliverables. Undeliverables are quickly identified and an effort is made to correct them and resend.

Ask a different research company and you will get a different answer for the average response rate of opt-in email campaigns. Jupiter Communications (www.jup.com) will tell you 5 to 15 percent. Forrester will tell you 14 to 22 percent. Ask a different email marketer and get a different answer. Some are getting only 3 percent and some are getting 40 percent. But they all agree on three things: It's not very expensive, it's not very hard, and it's got a better return on investment than other marketing and advertising techniques.

That would explain why Microsoft sends out more than 20 million email marketing pieces every month.

What Does It Take?

The truth is, a step-by-step approach to email marketing might just be the least expensive, most effective way to reach your audience. Whether you're looking for people to buy a product or service, vote for a candidate, sign a petition, or join a club, email is proving to be cheap, fast, and measurable. Response happens fast online as well. Marketers enjoy having 80 percent of all responses show up within two to three days of distribution.

A step-by-step approach works and the real magic is that you don't have to be a VP of anything or work for a major corporation in order to fund an email marketing effort.

Who Is This Book For?

This book is *not* for people who are running email servers or writing email system code. This is decidedly *not* a technical book.

If you have a product or a service to sell, this book is for you.

If you have a product announcement to distribute, this book is for you.

If you have revenue goals to achieve, this book is for you.

If you have excess inventory on hand, this book is for you.

If you have a time-critical or event-oriented sale to make, this book is for you.

If you run your own company out of the spare bedroom of your home and are searching for the best way to reach the most people with the least expense, this book is for you.

If you are a member of a huge team spinning off a brand-new company with millions of dollars to spend on branding and awareness, this book is for you.

If you are the vice president of marketing, the director of promotions, the public relations manager, the marketing communications executive, or any of the people who are responsible for carrying out the plans created by those people, this book is for you.

If you have a master plan for finding new prospects, turning them into customers, building a learning relationship with them, and engaging in some serious customer relationship management to put your theories of lifetime customer value to work, this book is *definitely* for you.

If you think sending email to everybody on a CD of addresses you bought online for $29.95 is a good way to do marketing, immediately wipe your fingerprints off this book as you put it back on the shelf. This book is *not* for you!

As the authors of this book, we have paid very close attention to what works and what doesn't. As entrepreneurs and consultants, we have succeeded in the world of Internet marketing by staying far away from what doesn't work. Spam doesn't work. If you agree, you can skip the whole second chapter.

However, if you're faced with a client, a boss, or a board of directors who just don't quite understand why this method is not the best thing since infomercials on late-night cable, then Chapter 2, "Spam: The Email We Love to Hate," can help you help them stay out of trouble—out of trouble with customers, out of trouble with the press, and out of trouble with the law.

Email Is Bigger than You Thought

The January 21, 1999, edition of the *Iconocast,* an electronic marketing newsletter by Michael Tchong (www.iconocast.com), indicated that marketing is not going to get easier.

> It's faster than a speeding bullet. It's able to leap over tall assistants with a single click. It's THE champion for truth, justice and the e-galitarian way. Yes, it's email. In 2000, more than 7 trillion emails will be sent in the U.S. alone, up from a "trifling" 4 trillion last year. If you think your inbox is full now, read on! Email is already firmly in second place on the hit parade of communication tools. A remarkable achievement given the fact that the telephone, invented in 1876, preceded email by 96 years (which appeared with Arpanet in 1972). A study by Institute of the Future found that email trails total phone and voicemail use by some 42 messages per day. But unlike the phone, email is also a publishing tool, or one-way medium. And while phone companies scramble for more numbers due to a sharp rise in cell phone use, the email system has had little trouble scaling up to the 263 million email boxes now found worldwide, according to newsletter "Electronic Mail & Messaging Systems."

It's a loser's game to publish a book that states how many people are on the Internet. While the ink is drying, the number of people online is swelling. If you assume there are hundreds of millions of people with Internet access, you are right. If you *really* need to know, check out one of the sites that tries to keep up with such things:

Nua Surveys: www.nua.ie/surveys/how_many_online/index.html

Estats: www.estats.com

AllNetResearch: www.allnetresearch.com

According to Forrester Research, almost 50 percent of the U.S. population will communicate via email by 2001. Quick, check your calendar. To reach all these people and to reach them in a meaningful way, it's very important to understand the finer points of customer consent before you start cranking out the messages.

Permission Email: Opt-out versus Opt-in

A sharp line divides real email marketing and spam. Spam is unsolicited. That means the recipient never asked for it.

Once you start haggling over *how* a recipient asks, that sharp line starts to blur. There is a difference between opt-in and opt-out. There is a difference between requesting a white paper and agreeing to a lifetime supply of monthly newsletters. There is a difference between sending messages that are well received and messages that spell harassment.

The modern marketer takes acceptable practices on the Internet very seriously. While the differences between spam, opt-in, and opt-out sound like a quarrel over shades of gray and splitting hairs, it's really a question of brand management and customer respect. We'll be up front. We believe in a well-defined, hard line that says opt-in is where it's at. Anything less is asking for trouble.

Anatomy of a Permission Email Campaign

Once the rules of engagement have been laid down, it's time to start planning. Your plan may be a romantic daydream. "Let's send out some emails and see what happens." Or it might be a sophisticated program of analysis, design, and development and a process of rapid, continual improvement.

Create a campaign that has a start, a middle, and ongoing enhancements built in. Don't waste your money—or your time—on ill-conceived efforts that do not add up. Strategy counts. Clear objectives are crucial. You need to plan differently for how you'll use email in different segments of the sale cycle.

A repeatable process of planning the scope, scale, and timing of your campaigns will allow you to create better and better marketing programs, achieve better and better results, and establish better and better relationships with prospects and customers. Crafting a good plan is more than half the battle. It separates the marketers from the master marketers.

Setting Your Sights: Targeting Your Message

The Internet is not a mass medium. It is a medium chock full of tiny niche markets. People gather in small groups of common interest. People choose to sign up for newsletters and announcements about ever more specific subjects. If you're looking to reach Northern Ireland motorcycle enthusiasts, people writing screenplays, or folks using PowerPoint on Macintoshes, they're out there.

Renting an opt-in email list from a major vendor allows you to tightly target your message. Choose the right list, get the best results. The best result is adding new names to your growing database. This is the heart of your marketing program. This is where you are going to make the most of one-to-one marketing and practice electronic customer relationship management. Email marketing is the most effective way to start these relationships and your ability to provide personalization through data mining is the most effecive way to ensure customer satisfaction and increase loyalty.

Start with a clear understanding of how list selection works, then make sure you choose a list vendor with the skills, experience, and tracking tools you'll need.

Then all it takes is killer creative.

Writing an Email Masterpiece

There are dozens of books written about writing compelling direct mail. This is the first book to recognize email as a different medium. It's as different from postal mail as Web sites are from printed brochures.

Writing a winning email message requires attention to format and style, of course, but little things suddenly mean a world of difference. What do you put in the Subject: line? Each word makes a critical difference in whether your message is opened at all. Once it's opened, you only have seconds to capture the reader's imagination. You have to grab their attention and keep it.

Deliver value with every email, pay heed to layout, design, and personalization, and you will be rewarded with the most effortless call to action a marketer ever had to offer: Click Here. The success of your campaign has multiple break points. It hinges on whether recipients open the message and whether they click. But it doesn't stop there.

The success of your email marketing campaign is going to depend a great deal on what happens *after* that click. Do you send them to your homepage? That's a start. How about taking them to a personalized, focused, and carefully crafted landing page to make the sale? Otherwise, you might be leaving them to hunt down that special offer on their own.

E-Newsletters, E-Promotions, Viral Marketing

Reaching out to new customers works very well through email, but the power comes when you start sending out periodical messages to a growing list of interested prospects and customers.

Newsletters keep people informed. They keep your name top-of-mind and they give you a monthly opportunity to sell something. Spend some time formatting your newsletter so it's readable. Make sure your newsletter is a *news*letter and not just a sales letter. Make sure it provides value. Then try out a multitude of ways of getting people to subscribe. Encourage them to get others to sign up.

Besides the *Company Times,* it turns out a lot of people really *do* like straight sales pitches. What's the next special of the week? What's on sale? What contests or sweepstakes can they win? While these are powerful tools, they can cut both ways. You could end up with a database full of nonqualified nonprospects. Above all, confirming consent is critical. Do it well, and you can move up the chain of customer communication to *viral* marketing.

Viral marketing is good old word of mouth on steroids. When people can communicate at the speed of light all over the world, marketers have the opportunity to fuel their discussion with something worth repeating. Everything from free email accounts to virtual gift baskets have a way of spreading the word about you in the most credible way of all, because the customer is the one doing the spreading.

Some companies are doing such a good job at viral marketing that they offer advertising space on *their* email. Newsgroup discussions, email list discussions, reminder services, e-coupons, and e-games are all available for promoting your products and services. You want to use every means possible to bring people to your Web site, where you can give them your brand message, get them to sign up for your newsletter, and sell them.

The smallest change in the way you write your ad can have a huge effect on how they perceive your Web site once they show up, so properly setting expectations and creating a proper context becomes a fine art.

Testing Your Talent, Reckoning Your Response, Managing Your Mail

Do all of your direct marketing pieces fit into a standard number 10 envelope? Or do you use a straight postcard? Or do you go for the three-fold, four-color glossy with a perforated business reply card? Maybe you're willing to try a combination. Email may seem tame by comparison, but there are still a variety of choices, and not all of them work in all cases. The only way you're going to know if a particular message, formatted in a particular way and with a particular subject line, is going to work on a particular audience is to test it.

The number of testing variables is daunting. What? In plain, old, boring email? If you're producing a television commercial, the variables are astronomical. So much so, that testing everything is actually impossible. What if the actress were wearing a green dress instead of blue? What if there were clouds in the sky? What if the kid next door walked by and looked longingly at the new product in her neighbor's yard?

But with email, the testing is very possible. Daunting, but possible. Just be aware of the various variables, and set up systems so you can isolate those variables and record them properly.

Analyzing the response from each trail takes skill, patience, and a little help from the technical side. How many people actually opened the email? How many clicked on the link? How many made it all the way to the landing page without bailing out? How many made it all the way to checkout with a full shopping cart? How many of them had a question or two for you along the way?

A complete email marketing plan means being completely ready to answer questions and solve problems. They'll contact you about the trouble they encounter on your site. They'll want to know if they can exchange the sweepstakes prize if they win. They'll want to know if they can get a discount by buying in bulk. They are your customers. Be ready to roll out the red email carpet and treat them like the valued customers they are.

Stories from the Front Lines

Theory and practice are often different. We present logical reasons for our advice and we back it up with research where available, but there's just nothing like getting the word from the horse's mouth.

The industry is young. The stories are rare. Those who are doing very well are anxious that their secret marketing weapon not be shared with too many others, and those who are not doing it well are keeping their heads down. But a few brave souls are willing to share what they have experienced and we're all better off for their generosity.

A Look toward the Future

This industry is in its infancy and just learning to walk without falling down too many times. Soon, its legs will be stronger, its balance more keenly developed, and it will break into a run.

There are a number of possibilities on the horizon. Some of these trends are obvious: Email will grow as a communication tool; personalization databases will get more precise; digital signatures will allow us to include more transactive content. Other trends can only be guessed at. We took our best shot.

What's Your Take?

We invite you to participate in the development of this industry. Come to www.yesmail.com/book.html and share what you learn along the way. There are not many of us today and we can all use your help.

> *They always say time changes things, but you actually have to change them yourself.*
> **Andy Warhol**

CHAPTER 2

Spam: The Email We Love to Hate

To understand why spam is so despised, you have to understand something about email. Yes, you already use it all day long, but it's worth a moment to dig into the subject. It helps to examine your own attitude about email in general and the messages you receive in particular.

It's also worth knowing something about how spam can tarnish your brand and get you in closer contact with the judicial system than you might care to be.

The Psychology of Email

Email is most wonderful because it is convenient. We send messages when it's convenient for us and you read them when you have time. You can reply at two o'clock in the morning and it doesn't bother us in the least. You're a night owl and we're morning people. Doesn't matter. But there is another reason that email is so wonderful. It's solitary.

You are alone with your thoughts. You have your back turned to the rest of the world and you could easily be thought of as working. Are you planning a family feast with your sister-in-law or a camping trip with your nephew? Reading about the latest movie release or a sale at the local department store? Nobody can tell. But they *can* tell that you are focused on something and should probably be left alone. You are safe inside your Busy Cloak.

A Private Affair

With the emailer comfortably cut off from interruption, she focuses on her writing. She waxes eloquent. She lets them have a piece of her mind. She surfs the Web a little for just the right reference to describe how she felt when her boss gave her that raise or her dog finally learned that trick. She goes on for as long or as little as she chooses because there are no interruptions. When she feels her message is complete—Send!

During her flight of literary fancy, she is not stymied by a look of misunderstanding on the person with whom she is communicating. She does not have to acquiesce to another person who wants to get their two cents in. She does not suffer the rejection of others in the room who are looking at their fingernails, absently sifting through papers on their desk, or simply falling asleep.

In his "Email Communication and Relationships" (www.rider.edu/users/suler/psycyber/emailrel.html), John Suler, Ph.D., said:

> Unlike face-to-face encounters, which are synchronous, email discussions do not require you to respond on-the-spot to what the other has said. You have time to think, evaluate, and compose your reply. Some people take advantage of this convenient "zone for reflection." Some do not. When I receive a message that emotionally stirs me up, I apply my "Hold On!" rule of thumb. I compose a reply without sending it (or write nothing), wait 24 hours, then go back to reread the other person's message and my unsent reply. Very often, I interpret the other person's message differently—usually less emotionally—the second time around. Very often, the reply I do send off is very different (much more rational and mature) than the one I would have sent the day before. The "Hold On!" rule of thumb has saved me from unnecessary misunderstandings and arguments (see the section called "Transference: Seeing the Other Clearly").

While engrossed in the act of composition, the author is in total control and may weave an argument to the best of her ability and to the level of her liking. Reading email is just a little different.

Incoming

Getting notes in school. Getting a postcard in the mailroom at the dormitory. Receiving a letter from home while out on military patrol at the far ends of the earth. These are the things that make postal mail so romantic. We love getting notes, cards, packages, and messages that are just for us. We love being singled out as important enough to rate the time and effort it takes to send a letter.

It takes about 20 years for that excitement of getting mail to wear thin. Where we used to stand at the mailbox, Charlie Brown-style, and wait for a valentine, we now trudge toward the mailbox, knowing it will be filled with circulars, come-ons, and bills. But the hope still glimmers that, someday, there will be something special. Something just for us.

Reading email has now become the same as that trip to the mailbox. There are department-wide memos and invitations to softball games that were mailed to everybody in the company. When we come across that personal message, that message that really is just for us and really is something we want to read, it's all the more precious.

But when it is spam, it's an insult.

According to the good Dr. Suler, "Inevitably, email users are subjected to the 'spam' of unrequested messages designed to sell an idea or a product. Junk mail. To Internet old-timers, spam is anathema. It's the apocalyptic sign of the commercialization of cyber-space. People subjectively experience email as a personal space in which they interact with friends and colleagues. Spam is the commercial that pops up in your face, intrud-ing on that private zone. In the list of incoming mail, it stands out like a wart."

If you have been in business for a while, you may have tried at least one conventional postal direct mail campaign to promote your business. Conventional mass mailing is probably the most-used selling technique. Even with a response rate of only about 1 percent, it can be effective and profitable. Mass mailings are also one of the more eco-nomical ways of advertising a business. A one-time mailing (one-page letter and tri-fold brochure) can cost less than $1.00 per person, depending upon the cost of the brochure. Larger, more complex mailings cost substantially more.

The temptation to send the same message electronically is overwhelming. Push a but-ton and blast your message to millions for only pennies. But hold fast. Direct email should only be sent to persons who request information.

In the middle of 1998, Novell commissioned a survey about the effect of spam on business in England. The study calculated that it might be costing businesses in Britain and Ireland as much as $8.2 billion per year in lost productivity, maintenance, and system upgrades to accommodate the unwanted email traffic. Want to guess what that number might be in the States?

Spam Defined

Here's a definition from Whatis.com, an Internet glossary at www.whatis.com/email-wds.htm#spam:

> Spam is unwanted email, typically sent unsolicited to large numbers of recipients. Most typically, spam is created and sent by companies seeking to increase their business through the use of bulk email programs, but spam can also be sent by an individual. No one likes receiving spam, and it's therefore considered rude to send it. The rule is this: if you're sending unsolicited email to a bunch of people, you're spamming—stop.

Let's make it even clearer than that. Spam is unsolicited bulk email.

First, it's unsolicited. That means it comes when not called. It shows up exactly like junk mail in your mailbox. Often people define spam as commercial email. While that's fine for here and now, since we're here to talk about marketing and commerce, spam can also be a message asking for a donation to a nonprofit organization. It may be a notification of an upcoming bond issue. It may be campaign literature, an announcement of a free concert, or a plea to all sinners to repent their ways. It doesn't have to be commercial at all to be spam.

Britain's biggest charity found out the hard way, as reported by ZDNet (www.zdnet.com/zdnn/stories/news/0,4586,2245399,00.html).

Oxfam Nixes Kosovo 'Spam' Campaign

Britain's largest relief agency opts out of a plan to raise money for Kosovo refugees via email.

Britain's largest foreign aid charity, Oxfam, had planned to experiment with direct email canvassing for the first time, using 10,000 email addresses from users of British Telecom's Talk21, a free email service, and Auto Trader magazine's Web sites, alongside a banner-ad campaign. Nonetheless, when a report on Excite's UK news service said Oxfam was considering "spam in a good cause," the news quickly circulated around several anti-spam mailing lists and the news.admin.net-abuse.email newsgroup.

The anti-spammers were not charitably disposed toward Oxfam's idea. "Oxfam could go around robbing banks to support their relief effort, too, but that doesn't mean we should stand back and let them," said Julian Haight, creator of the Spamcop Web site.

"I recently received a request from a Mexican elementary school asking for donations for a computer lab—again, a very good cause, but still spam—and I reported it to the ISP."

Added Haight: "Oxfam should prepare for a PR black eye if it pursues this course. They may garner some donations, but the vast majority of the recipients will simply delete the mail—but also file Oxfam in a category with pornographers, scam artists and other sleaze."

COMPLAINING TO OXFAM

Among the activists who contacted Oxfam through its Web site was Steve Harris, who wrote the "Spamicide" program.

He said a woman he contacted on the site had not heard of the email campaign and was "horrified." A few hours later, a statement appeared on Oxfam's site announcing that, "after consideration, Oxfam GB decided not to pursue this option."

Matthew Eccles, managing director of WWAV Rapp Collins, the direct marketing group that worked on the campaign, was quite upset at the reaction of the anti-spammers.

"What has happened is an absolute tragedy—not just for Oxfam but the people of Kosovo," he said.

Eccles declined to say how much money Oxfam thought it might have raised via the email campaign.

He noted that the banner ad campaign on BT, Auto Trader and UK Web sites began only Tuesday, and no figures were in on how well it had done. The sites posting banner ads did so free of charge.

Aversion to spamming "When you come down to it," he said, "the problem arose because of references to spamming, which was not what we wanted to do. What we were doing was contacting people who said they are happy to receive third-party emails."

In fact, in both cases, users who submitted their email addresses in order to receive services would automatically be eligible to receive email from third parties unless they selected otherwise.

"I would have no qualms about suggesting such a campaign again to any fund-raising client in future," Eccles added.

In the end, the campaign has gone ahead, but without the email component.

Julian Haight is relieved—"I'm just glad they decided against it—it restores my faith in Oxfam. I always thought of them as one of the good guys."

Next, it's bulk. That's usually easy to tell when you're on the receiving end because the To: address is something absurd or the ever-so-clever (such as "Recipient List Suppressed"). But sometimes they come right to your address and they look almost like somebody is trying to communicate to you. Here's where the line starts to get fuzzy.

Splitting Hairs

If we told you not to send *any* unsolicited email, then you would be constrained from sending a message to the principal of your child's school, asking for a meeting. Even if you had 400 children and sent the same message, in bulk, to all of the principals of all of their schools, it wouldn't be spam.

That's because you have a preexisting relationship with those principals. It can be argued that anybody who ever asked for information about your windshield wiper fluid would naturally be interested in your fine array of high-quality wipers. In the world of postal mail, you'd be right. Send them a postcard. Send them a poster. Send them a bouquet of flowers and a coupon for 15 percent off. Fine! But email doesn't work that way.

The Illogic of It All

You say you *like* getting email? You *like* learning about great new offers? You feel others would, too? Then think for just a moment about the impact on the network if every company in the United States (let alone the world) decided to send out one little email a year to everybody. Only one. Only once per year.

Given some 12 million companies in the United States and 365 days a year, you have to ask yourself if getting 1370 email messages *every hour* is your idea of fun. And if you are at all technically inclined, imagine the bandwidth needed to support such transmissions.

The most frightening part is how easy it all is. You want the addresses of everybody who subscribes to a newsgroup on dogs? Take a look at what Floodgate (www.floodgate.com) used to offer:

> The Floodgate Bulk Email Loader imports simple text files that anyone can down load from CompuServe, Prodigy, Delphi Genie, or the Internet. Test [sic] files contain ads, forum messages, or data from the member directory. Each of these files is filled with email addresses. Floodgate is designed to read these files and strip out the email addresses. It then sorts the addresses, removes any duplicates, and formats them into an output file, with 10, 20, 30 addresses per line. This is all done in one simple step. Just point and click.

A recent trip back to www.floodgate.com shows they are no longer offering this software package. Instead, they are offering rentals of the lists they have harvested off the Internet using their own tools. Maybe they learned the same lesson learned by the people from CherryPicker (www.cherrypicker.com). See Figure 2.1.

We're starting to see more and more offerings like Spam Hater (www.cix.co.uk/~net-services/spam/spam_hater.htm):

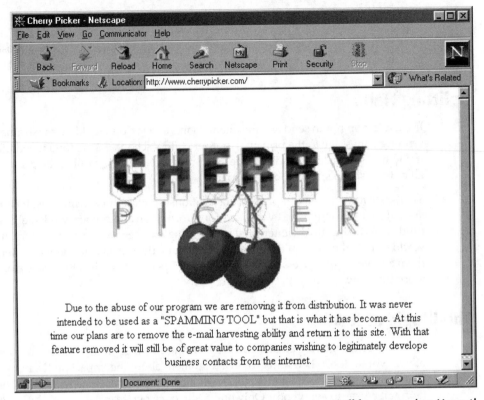

Figure 2.1 Gosh, we never thought anybody would use our stuff for *spamming*. Honest!
Sure.

Get lots of email offering you get-rich-quick schemes? Want to hit back? "Spam Hater" is
free Windows software that helps you respond effectively and makes it hot for these people.

Analyses the Spam

Extracts a list of addresses of relevant Postmasters, etc.

Prepares a reply

Choice of legal threats, insults or your own message

Appends a copy of the Spam if required

Puts it in a mail window ready for sending

Tool to help keep you out of spammers databases

Analyses Usenet spam

Context sensitive help—right mouse click on the item concerned

Shows a sample of the spam it's analysing

Generates a "WHOIS" query to help track the perpetrator

Generates a "TRACEROUTE" query to help track the perpetrator's upstream provider
    (Now offers this on-line if your system supports it)

Spam Hater V2.09 works with lots of popular email programs directly—without cutting and
pasting. Almost all other Windows mailers/news programs can access it via the Clipboard.

The Definitive Treatise

Robert Raisch was deep into the heart of the Internet long before it was cool. After all, he was the one who originally registered his company's domain name as "internet.com." You don't snag that one if you show up after the party is in full swing. He is founder of The Internet Company, cofounder and creator of The Electronic Newsstand, and was instrumental in the initial design and implementation of the Global Network Navigator, which was purchased by America Online.

Besides all that and more, Rob wrote the definitive work on unsolicited email at the end of 1994. It is reprinted here with his permission.

Postage-Due Marketing

An Internet Company White Paper by Robert Raisch

EXECUTIVE OVERVIEW

In recent months, a number of online marketing efforts have shown the failure of traditional direct marketing practices on the global Internet.

By exercising significant limitations in the Internet's technology, these efforts have sought to use the distributed news and mail technologies of the Internet as an inexpensive way to deliver commercial messages directly into the hands of consumers.

The Internet community has dubbed this practice as "spamming"—after a popular British television sketch where a restaurant patron orders a commercially available pink luncheon meat repeatedly, well past the point of absurdity.

While the media have chosen to characterize this as a cultural issue, the truth is that these ill-considered marketing efforts cost each person reading the distributed advertisements a measurable fee for their receipt.

For this reason alone, this style of marketing is both ineffectual and potentially very damaging to the marketer.

INTERNET "DIRECT MARKETING"

Arizona "Green Card" lawyers, Laurence Canter and Martha Siegel, used the global Internet's second most popular information delivery service, Usenet News, as a direct marketing channel in a manner which initially appears to be very similar to traditional direct mail. By "posting" an advertisement for legal services to thousands of separate discussion forums, Canter and Siegel succeeded in placing their message in the hands of hundreds of thousands of consumers for very little apparent cost.

But Canter and Siegel submitted their commercial solicitation in every newsgroup available without any concern for the topic of discussion in those newsgroups. They posted a message about their service to help foreign students fill out federal immigration forms into discussions about the Information Superhighway, cultural issues of Tamil Indians, Microsoft Windows™ development tools, and thousands of other discussions—few of which had any interest in issues of American immigration.

Continues

Postage-Due Marketing *(Continued)*

While some point to the minimal cost of this marketing effort and the huge return it generated as proof that Canter & Siegel have discovered the holy grail of direct marketing—cheap, effective information distribution—this assumption ignores the real costs incurred, not by the marketer, but by the consumer. As most professional marketers realize, effective marketing is never cheap nor easy.

The media has chosen to paint this as an issue of culture clash between the idealistic Internet old guard and a pragmatic new breed of online marketeer without understanding the economic or social realities of the situation. Upon a little research, this characterization lacks any real substance.

In essence, Canter and Siegel's actions were economically irresponsible, demanding that the public shoulder the cost of their marketing tactics—without any possibility of refusal.

THE USENET NEWS SERVICE

Usenet News is a collection of user-written messages or articles placed in separate categories or newsgroups based upon topic. These articles are then shipped from computer to computer to hundreds of thousands of Internet participants. For example, an article about bicycling might end up in the newsgroup called "rec.bicycles.mountain" or an inquiry for employment opportunities may show up in "misc.jobs.wanted."

The programs that accept or reject these articles do so based upon the newsgroup in which they appear—e.g., if a subscriber has an interest in bicycling and the article is labeled as a member of a "rec.bicycles" newsgroup, the computer will accept receipt of the article and save it in local storage. Suppose someone were to post a news article that talked about the sanctity of human life and how the author believed that all abortion must be considered murder. This would be the author's opinion and an example of the freedom of expression that the Internet technologies support so well. However, for the sake of argument, suppose that this article was labeled as an appropriate member of the "rec.bicycling" newsgroup.

Since the subscriber has instructed the programs that receive these articles to accept anything in this newsgroup, the computer blindly accepts this inappropriate or "off-topic" article. Once the article has been received by the computer, the subscriber's money has been spent and resources consumed without any opportunity to refuse the article. This is how it must be, because to judge whether an article is appropriate to the subscriber's needs, it must first be retrieved and read.

POSTAGE-DUE MARKETING

Using the global Internet as a direct marketing vehicle to distribute messages to users with little concern for their topical appropriateness or the costs involved in their distribution is called Postage-Due Marketing.

In the physical world, advertisers bear the entire cost of distributing messages to the consumer. The only cost the consumer shoulders is the time it takes to consider a solicitation and either embrace or discard it.

In the online world, the costs of distribution are shared between advertiser and consumer. Consumers pay a measurable fee to receive information via the global Internet—from a shell or SLIP account to a highspeed dedicated connection. Some pay hourly charges for information and some pay per message, but each Internet subscriber pays in some way for the information they receive.

To fully appreciate why Postage-Due Marketing raises the ire of the global Internet community, ask yourself whether you would accept a collect call from a telemarketer or an advertising circular that arrived postage due. Or, if you spent an entire evening consumed with calls from telemarketers while you waited for an important call.

SIGNAL TO NOISE RATIO

Most Usenet newsgroups have a charter or stated purpose for their existence. This charter may be a written document which can be retrieved from online archives or those more active members of the discussion or it may be a simple social consensus, agreed upon by the members of the group.

Consider what might happen should Postage-Due Marketing proceed unchecked on Usenet. Participants in discussion will spend the majority of their time sifting through those commercial solicitations which find their way into the conversation and the truly valuable, on-topic responses.

In measuring the value of any communications medium, we talk in terms of the difference or ratio between the amount of valuable information (the signal) and any noise which might degrade the quality of that information.

Once the signal to noise ratio of a Usenet newsgroup falls below a certain level—measured by each participant, each day—the conversation no longer holds enough value to prove useful.

This phenomenon can be witnessed on many of the commercial online services, like America Online and CompuServe, who have set aside special message areas for advertising only.

These areas are often filled each day by many marketing messages, each vying for the attention of the consumer. Once this process begins, each marketer attempts to keep their own message as fresh and as new as possible in the mind of the consumer.

Unfortunately, while this might seem to be an effective marketing strategy, it really means that each marketer must post a new copy of their solicitation each day and more often than not, more than once each day. Soon the discussion vanishes under the weight of the marketer's message.

Sadly, a large number of useful Usenet newsgroups are already burdened by this off-topic commercial effluvia. Many have remarked that this kind of intrusion is similar to the boorish salesman who, when attending a social function, feels the urge to turn polite conversation into a sales opportunity.

SOCIAL COMPACTS

All members of a society live by certain rules which make it possible to co-exist and communicate effectively with their peers. We do not lie, cheat or steal from those around us. We do not drive on the wrong side of the highway. And we do not use our neighbor's property without their permission.

Simple rules like these allow us to function effectively as a society. Some are important enough to require protection by law while others are part of the social compact we all observe for the benefit and support of human community.

Continues

Postage-Due Marketing *(Continued)*

Engaging in Postage-Due Marketing ignores the single most important truth of the global Internet: above all else, the global Internet is a community—and like any community, participation in it implies certain rules and obligations.

EFFECTIVE ONLINE MARKETING?
In their own way, Laurence Canter & Martha Siegel have been very successful. They have leveraged a dangerous misinterpretation of the online world into global media visibility and a potential best-selling marketing book that instructs others to freely tread on the flowerbeds of the public common. But at what cost?
The cost can be a summons in some places.

Spam and the Law

You should know that there are several laws on the books about sending unsolicited faxes. The reasoning is that you are using other people's resources: paper and electricity. The Telephone Consumer Protection Act of 1991 describes faxes loosely enough to be applied to email:

> The term "telephone facsimile machine" means equipment which has the capacity (A) to transcribe text or images, or both, from paper into an electronic signal and to transmit that signal over a regular telephone line, or (B) to transcribe text or images (or both) from an electronic signal received over a regular telephone line onto paper.

Local Law

But now, each state in the union is creating its own rules and regulations about email in particular.

California Assembly Bill 1629 suggests that you are trespassing when you spam people, because you are sending messages through the network of an Internet service provider (ISP) without permission. Legislators in California feel that the equipment is owned by an ISP, and they, therefore, may determine who's allowed to use it and for what purposes. Once the ISP has published their no-spam policy, they can sue the miscreant for $50 per message, up to $25,000 per day.

Some states are only protecting people from fraud, as in the case of a Washington state law that allows the recipient to sue the offending party for $500 per fraudulent message. The plaintiff must also show that the spammer knew the recipient was a Washington resident. Not a very helpful law when the point is to limit the amount of junk mail.

But more and more states are jumping into the fray and crafting laws that help protect their constituents from the evils of unsolicited mail. To keep up to date, stay tuned to MSNBC's State Spam Legislation page (http://msnbc.com/modules/spam/data/state.htm). See Figure 2.2.

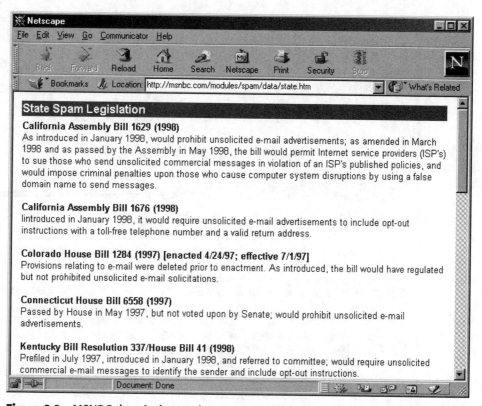

Figure 2.2 MSNBC does its best to keep on top of the state of state spam legislation.

Federal Law

While the U.S. government has taken its time to figure out what to do about email, there is some snail-paced legislation winding its way through Congress. Some of these bills allow spam under certain circumstances, such as the ability to opt out or be removed from a spammer's list. We can only hope that these brain-dead approaches are killed before they multiply. (There's a lot more about that in Chapter 3, "Defining Opt-in.")

Other bills are aimed at amending the fax regulations to clearly identify email as unlawful use of recipients' resources. As you might guess, MSNBC is trying to keep watch on that as well at http://msnbc.com/modules/spam/data/federal.htm.

Another fine resource for keeping your eyes on the spam scene is Junkbusters (www.junkbusters.com). See Figure 2.3.

Jason Catlett spends his time focusing on privacy. The spam fighters of the world benefit from his attention. His site includes good advice on how to minimize the amount of spam you get and how to deal directly with spammers.

For a detailed diatribe, check out Death to Spam at www.mindworkshop.com/alchemy/nospam.html. There are also organizations that are going after spammers

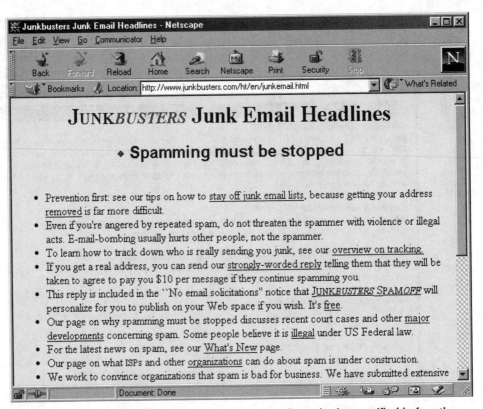

Figure 2.3 The man behind Junkbusters is Jason Catlett, who has testified before the Federal Trade Commission.

with technology. SpamCops (http://spamcop.net) has created a system for spam reporting and another for spam filtering (see Figure 2.4) and Bright Light technologies is "committed to enhancing the quality of Internet email. Our first product, Bright Mail, fights unsolicited bulk email—otherwise known as 'spam'—which is one of the biggest obstacles to the continued evolution of the Net. Bright Mail's unique combination of people and technology can detect and block spam before it reaches ISPs, corporate servers, and user mailboxes."

But legal problems are going to be the least of your worries. The biggest problem you face, should you decide to go this route, is the tarnishing of your brand.

Spam and Your Brand

You spend a lot of money over a long period of time to create a strong brand. You want a brand that people look up to, trust, and recommend to their friends. In these times of information overload, branding becomes ever more important.

As Steve Hayden (part of the Apple "1984" television commercial team) said in an article in *Advertising Age* (November 11, 1996):

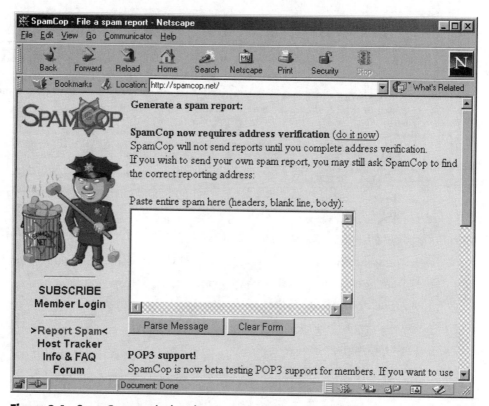

Figure 2.4   SpamCops.net is the place to go for help in filtering the spam you get today.

In a world of information overload, brands become ever more important. Icons with virtual memory, brands save time. I may have intelligent agents that can go out and assemble pages of reports on every camcorder on the market, but I don't have time to read them. I'll buy Sony. With so many choices of content, and with such an assortment of sources, people will depend more and more on the feelings of trust they hold for the companies they do business with. If you already have a strong brand, you now have a new place to make it stronger. If you don't, you have a momentary opportunity to get out there on the Net ahead of the competition and establish yourself.

In a nutshell, you want to be careful to do everything in your power to stay on the good side of as many people as possible. Sending unsolicited email is one of the quickest ways to show up in print in an unsightly way as OnSale found out (see Figure 2.5).

But let's go one step beyond the nasty press you might get and right into the psyche of the millions of people on the receiving end of your marketing message. It tells them with one push of the Send key, that you are in league with scam artists and pornographers.

Running with the Wrong Crowd

Spam is instantly and always associated with the following types of messages.

From *What Makes People Click: Advertising on the Web*

Your brand isn't just what you want people to think of you. It's what they actually think of you.

A brand is something that lives apart from what the company plans, because it is the culmination of all of the interactions a marketplace has with the firm.

A person sees an ad and has an impression.

She looks up information on the Web, she has an impression.

She calls the firm and talks to the receptionist and the impression changes.

She is put on hold and hears the music and "Your call is important to us."

She talks to a sales rep.

She waits for the materials to arrive.

She reads the materials.

She talks to her colleagues about the product.

She reads about the firm in the financial pages.

She reads product reviews.

She makes the purchase.

She sees and feels the product packing.

She tries to use the product.

She calls customer service.

She talks to her friends about her experience.

If you take the sum total of how she feels and thinks about all of her interactions with the company and how well they met her expectations and lived up to the promise—and you multiply that by the thousands or millions of people who have also read about, talked about and interfaced with the company and the product—you have a brand. You want that brand to be a positive sentiment.

You want the public to know, deep in their heart of hearts, that your company stands for confidence, your logo implies trust and your products mean dependability. Or, you want them to think of you as young, hip and fun-loving. Either way, you want them to think of you in these terms for all of the days of their lives.

Get Rich Quick

```
To: jsterne@targeting.com
From: "friend@prodigy" <griffin@prodigy.net>
Date: Fri, 30 Jul 99 10:06:13 -0400
Subject: read carefully important info!!!!
```

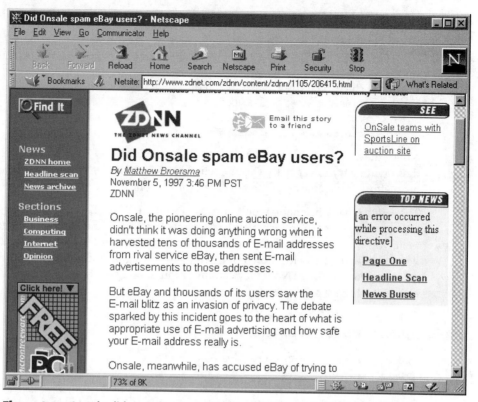

Figure 2.5 OnSale didn't realize how bad the publicity could be for spamming.

```
Let me show you how to turn $20.00 into $50,000 in 90 days!!! this is
totally legal and consists of 5 reports to also help you in your own
bussiness.Tricks to bulk email, becoming a millionaire on the internet
and more email me and i will send you full report on how to do it!!!
```

If we had a nickel for every one of these we get, we'd be rich already!

Too Good to Be True and a Gotcha!

```
From: <junior957@beer.com>
To: <jsterne@targeting.com>
Date: Tue, 27 Jul 1999 16:24:57
Subject: GET YOUR OWN WEB SITE NOW FOR ONLY $9.95 PER MONTH!

GET YOUR OWN 5 MEG WEBSITE FOR ONLY $9.95 PER MONTH TODAY!
STOP PAYING $19.95 or more PER MONTH OR MORE TODAY for your web site!
DO YOU ALREADY HAVE A WEBSITE? ALL YOU HAVE TO DO IS TRANSFER THE DOMAIN
TO OUR SERVERS AND UPLOAD YOUR DATA AND YOU ARE READY TO GO! YOUR NEW
WEB SPACE CAN BE CREATED INSTANTLY WITH JUST A SIMPLE PHONE CALL OUR
OFFICE.
```

```
ALL OUR WEBSITES USE FRONT PAGE '98. YOU CAN CHANGE YOUR SITE AS MUCH AS
YOU WANT!
WE OFFER ALL THE LATEST FEATURES LIKE REAL AUDIO,CYBERCASH, SECURE
SERVERS, SEARCH ENGINE SUBMISSION and MERCHANT INTERNET CREDIT CARD PRO-
CESSING ACCOUNTS. WITH COMPLETE WEB DESIGN AT REASONABLE RATES. A SET UP
FEE OF $40.00 APPLIES for FIRST TIME CUSTOMERS.
FOR DETAILS CALL 1 877 213 XXXX
THANK YOU
to be removed email junior957@beer.com
```

Notice the all-caps "shouting." Notice the prices that are too good to be true. Notice the way they try to verify that your email address is valid by enticing you to respond in an effort to be removed. Don't ever fall for that one.

The savvy email aficionado won't unsubscribe at all. Why? Because so many spam messages are ruses to confirm valid addresses. If you click the Reply button and tell them you want no more of their attention, either it bounces because they don't want you to know their real location or it merely sends a signal back to their server and validates your address. Now they can turn around and sell their "cleansed" list to others at a higher price.

Spamming for Spammers

```
To: BizAdvertisers@alltheworld.net
Date: Fri, 30 Jul 99 18:54:05 EST
From: profitnow8@yahoo.com
Subject: TARGETED EMAILS ON CD-'TARGETED' = MORE SALES!!


* * * * * * * * * * * * * * * * * * * * * * * * * *
* * * * * * * * * TARGET EMAIL 2000 * * * * * * * * * * *
* * * * * * * * * * * * * * * * * * * * * * * * * *
             H A L F   P R I C E   S A L E!!
                  LIMITED TIME ONLY
-----------------------------------------------------------------
What is TARGET EMAIL 2000?
-----------------------------------------------------------------
          SIMPLY THE BEST TARGETED EMAIL LISTS ON ONE
CD-ROM AVAILABLE.....when you purchase
TARGET EMAIL 2000 CD-ROM
YOU ALSO GET F R E E BULKMAIL SOFTWARE
& UTILITIES WORTH APPROXIMATELY $800 ....
........TOTALLY FREE.!!!

Target Email 2000 contains the highest quality targeted lists on the
market, reasonably priced and guaranteed to generate leads for your
business.
```

The only thing targeted about the people on this list is that there is nothing they can do to get untargeted. These sorts of lists get passed along and along and along. Once on a spammer's list, always on a spammer's list.

This one actually made us wince. It went on for pages, but was sprinkled with gems (and spelling mistakes):

```
Date: Sun, 25 Jul 1999 13:42:14 +0100
From: xxx@abnet.or.jp
To: zsbotkrwag@msn.com
Subject: Controverial Marketing Techniques That Works!!!
```

My name is XXXX XXXXXX and I am one of the few who have managed to make
a very comfortable living marketing products on the Internet. My methods
and techniques have been quoted in newspapers and highly acclaimed magazines such as Computer Edge.
I have marketed everything on the Internet from Personalized Baby Calen-
dars to Information and have made money with everything.
I AM LIVIING PROOF that with the proper techniques and information
sources at hand anyone can turn the Internet into their own personal
GOLD MINE.
Internet Marketing when done successfully can make you more money than
you dare to dream., but it must be learned and done professionally or it
will produce nothing but headaches and the depletion of your hard earned
cash.
So my offer to you is this. You send me $39 bucks I will mail You my
Email Marketing Kit CD Disk containing the following information and
software.
*******The Internet Marketing Kit Will Supply You With*******
<> The Internet Marketing Kit E-book Containing the following informa-
tion.
Chapter 1...The Bulk Email Handbook
This Section is a complete guide to Bulk mailing, the subject content
covers, a) How to Make a Fortune With Bulk email b) Finding A Product.
c) How To Write Killer Sales Letters. d) How To Collect Addresses From
The Internet and d) The Fulfillment Of orders.
Chapter 2...How To Make Money With Junk Email
A complete overview of techniques used by successful Bulk mailers that
are making a fortune with Bulk email
Chapter 3...Cloaking (The Truths and Myths About Cloaking Software)
Chapter 4...$10,000 a week with classifieds
This is For Real!! Pass it up lightly and you'll be making one of the
biggest mistakes of your life! If it's big money your after take a seat
and read this section very carefully.
Chapter 10...4000 Places To Promote Your Web Site
Need places to promote your site, these 4000 sites are the answer to
your problem.
<> As if this wasn't enough, hold on to your seat, I am even going to
give you absolutely FREE the following software:
1.) A copy of CHECKER CHECKS BY FAX SOFTWARE...
This is a fully functional program not a crippled demo. Now you can take
payment from your customers by Fax, Phone or Email simply by taking
their Checking account information.
2.) A copy of smtp lookup software that will find you foreign mail
servers you can use to send your mail completely undetected. This Software will test mail through hundreds of servers an hour. I will even
Supply you with a list of 16000 foreign domains to insert into your
testing.

```
And I will throw in 500,000 Fresh Email addresses. If you are selling a
product or service these are the addresses you want.
Just mail your check or money order made out to XXXXX XXXXX to:
XXXXX XXXXX
xxxxxxxxxxx Street
xxxx, xxxxxx, 12345

Check here if you would like to receive information
about our other products ( )
Thank you for your time If you have any questions
don't hesitate to contact us at
Tel: (123) 345-6789
Fax: (123) 345-6789

To be removed from our mailing list just click on the link below
mailto:xxx@saigon.vnn.vn?subject=Remove-Now-K
```

Yes, we felt compelled to remove the contact information. Some of you may have been persuaded by this marketer's less than stellar technique. In any case, please note that the From: address is out of Japan and the "to be removed" address is on a mail system in Vietnam. You really don't want to get involved.

Honest! We Wouldn't Lie to You!

```
Date: Wed, 04 Aug 99 11:40:23 EST
From: IRC@hkj.gov.jo
To: Friend@public.com
Subject: HOW TO PURCHASE YOUR "DREAM HOME" WITH NO CREDIT!

NOTE: THIS IS NOT SPAM!! This is a one time mailing. When you visited
one of our webpages you indicated that you would be interested in this
information, if not please excuse the intrusion and simply delete this
message. THANK YOU
```

We just love spams that start out, "This is not a spam." These people have been look-ing at too many René Magritte paintings (www.rh.cc.ca.us/online/art/treachery_images.htm).

Straight to the Point

```
To: <rne@targeting.com>
From: <babpo@vol.vnn.vn>
Subject: LIVE HOT PHONE SEX !!!
Date: Sat, 24 Jul 1999

LIVE HOT PHONE SEX!
NO CREDIT CARD NEEDED!
NO 1-900 FEES!
```

```
CALL NOW!!!
1-473-407-7173
```

Straight to the XXX Site with a Bit of Deception

```
From: larry laffer <mom@www.jiangnan.com.cn>
Date: Fri, 16 Jul 1999 17:07:31 -0400 (EDT)
Subject: hi forgot about that password


hey john,
i told you i'd send it—this site kicks ass. check it out.
http://www.mujweb.cz/www/tvrdy_porno/link.htm
i wouldn't tell too many people though, it might get all jammed like the
other porn sites.
keep in touch
larry
```

Messages with a subject line about passwords tend to get read. This one had no To: in it. We couldn't see if it was from a suppressed list or not, because the entire entry about the recipient was missing. However, it is obvious that these folks wrote a routine that reads email names and makes a good guess as to what your first name must be. In this case, the email address is jsterne@targeting.com. So this software saw the "j" and assumed that the majority of people whose names start with "J" are named John. It's a lot of trouble to go through to promote a porn site.

You Know It When You See It

The next time somebody asks you for a serious answer about why spam is bad, and they don't understand that it's simply evil, point them to Mark Gibbs's masterpiece, so they can see what sort of crowd they'd be running with.

Offers, Rumors, and Exclamations!!! It's True!!

By Mark Gibbs

Network World, 07/12/99
www.nwfusion.com/archive/1999b/0712gibbs.html

Don't read this column. Oh well, it's probably too late anyway. Opening Network World to the back page automatically unleashes a deadly computer virus that will ultimately melt your monitor and email the contents of your refrigerator to every entry in your address book. It will also send a message to your congressman saying you are in favor of the forthcoming modem tax. Can you believe it? A tax on modems is being quietly slipped into legislation alongside the tax on email. You haven't heard of the tax on email either?

Continues

Offers, Rumors, and Exclamations!!! It's True!! *(Continued)*

Congress wants to tax your modem and charge you 5 cents for every email you send!!! And they can check every email whether it's encrypted or not! That's right, the CIA and the NSA keep copies of all email you send in a vault under Area 51. It's true!! The trouble is you're not informed! That's because your Web site isn't getting enough exposure. For only $9.95, we can guarantee that your Web site gets a higher ranking in every search engine and Web site list on this and every other planet in this arm of the Milky Way. And we have an easy way to advertise your Web site or product. We have spent the past 18 hours gathering information on Web sites that will give you free or almost free advertising. While others are paying $25 billion per advertisement, you can advertise your product, service or site, without having to pay anything. Almost. There aren't any catches or requirements, and you don't have to lift a finger. All you do is give us full administrative access to your Web site, and we'll do the rest. Oh yeah, and your social security number, the deeds to your house and the registration for your car. We'll send 'em right back, honest! Without any work on your part, we'll ensure you get more visibility than Yahoo or AOL. Your Web site will take off, and your profits will go sky high! Incredible!!! Really! Honest! Then you'll start to see the big bucks!!! The sky's the limit!!! It's true! Yes, that's right, working from home for only 27 seconds every three weeks, you can have an income of $5,000, $750,000 or even a quarter trillion dollars per month. That's more money than you can make chairing the FCC!

That's right! $500,000 to a quarter of a trillion dollars and that could be tax-free! Just let us register your domain for you, and we'll ensure your personal tax haven is secured. And do you know that the government can't legally tax you? You didn't? It's true!

For only $39.95, we'll email you a report on how Congress has never ratified the levying of taxes and how to build an atomic bomb. For only $10.95 more, we'll send you 10,000 Internet money-making pyramid schemes that are perfectly legal, honest!

Just send $5 to the 2,000 people at the top of the list and when your name reaches the top, you'll get $20,000,000, and the kidney that was stolen from you when you got drunk in Las Vegas will be returned. And you'll get to see the hottest teens around. No kidding! They're really just barely legal despite the fact that they look like construction workers.

We've got free accounts with no strings attached! It is all paid for by the modem tax! The column is never sent unsolicited. Your name was given by a friend or you visited our Web site and clicked on the "send me any old crap" link.

If you would prefer not to receive information or special offers from us, please reply to this column at nwcolumn@gibbs.com with "Unsubscribe" as the subject line and you'll never hear from us again!!! Honest. It's true!!!!!

What They Really Mean

Spam is easier to understand if you have a handy translation guide. Nicolas Petreley gives us a few hints to help out.

Down to the Wire

By Nicholas Petreley, editorial director of LinuxWorld
www.linuxworld.com

What do you get when misbehaving children never grow up? Spam.

Have you ever had a 5-year-old lie to you? Yes, it's sad in one respect, but I find it almost amusing in another. Young kids usually have no idea how easy it is for adults to know when they're lying. That's not surprising, since children have so little experience. What amazes me, however, is that some of these kids never learn. I'm talking about those kids who grow up to work in public relations or marketing. One gets the impression that they still don't realize we know when they're lying.

That set me to wondering what the world would be like if everyone were legally bound to tell the truth, the whole truth, and nothing but the truth. It would certainly change the nature of email marketing, wouldn't it?

I waded through my spam folder and tried to imagine what it would be like if the authors of these messages had to be honest about their motives and tactics.

SUBJECT: HOW TO MEET BEAUTIFUL WOMEN

We are a bunch of lowlife racketeers who would be in some other line of work if we actually had a clue how to meet beautiful women. So we're hoping that some of you are stupid enough to think we can increase your chances of getting a date if you respond to this email advertisement. If you are, please call (900) 555-5555. My 62-year-old Aunt Martha will answer the phone as the flirtatious "Desiree" and will gladly build up false hopes for only $2.99 per minute.

We apologize if you are so gullible that you actually believe you received this solicitation by mistake. If you want us to remove you from this list, please send us email with the word "unsubscribe" in the subject line. We won't actually remove your name. But your response will flag your email address as valid, which makes it possible to sell your email address to others for a higher price.

SUBJECT: SLEAZE-COMMERCE SERVER IS NOW FEATURE COMPLETE!

Congratulations! You are among the first million people we handpicked to pay for an early look at a beta product we're calling "feature complete" because it includes only those features we've been able to complete.

We're way behind schedule and way over budget on this product, so it is imperative that we raise some extra cash on this thing now, even if it's not ready.

Fortunately, we started the hype on this product way before we had even agreed on the basic design. We're hoping that you're probably so impatient to get something in your hands by now that you can be suckered out of your hard-earned cash.

So if you are looking for something to distract you from important duties like making sure your business is running year-2000-compliant software, send us $60 for the latest build of SleazE-Commerce server, and we'll send you a copy as soon as we can get it to compile without errors.

Continues

Down to the Wire *(Continued)*

SUBJECT: INCREASE YOUR BUSINESS PROFITS!

If you could accept credit cards, would your Internet-commerce business benefit? Did you know that 99 percent of all Internet transactions in the past year were credit card transactions? If this painfully obvious fact surprises you, we want you as our customer now!

SUBJECT: HELP DEFEND OUR RIGHT TO INNOVATE

We are writing to our customers in a last-ditch effort to get someone to help us defend our right to innovate new and devious ways to protect our monopoly. Your name was specially chosen because we are confident that you will want to participate. If you really knew the difference between innovation and Shinola, you probably wouldn't be buying our products.

We understand that it is difficult to write letters supporting our company because one must write about the occasional threats to our monopoly as if their existence implies that we do not control the market. This is a particularly challenging task, since you must avoid at all costs the details of how we respond to those threats. And you must never use the word "monopoly" in your argument.

That's why we have created the brand-new program ActiveTurf 4.0. ActiveTurf is an application that automatically generates and mails letters of support. Get your beta copy of ActiveTurf 4.0 now by sending $60 to the following address. . . .

Copyright July 19, 1999, by InfoWorld Media Group., a subsidiary of IDG Communications, Inc. Reprinted from InfoWorld, 155 Bovet Road, San Mateo, CA 94402. Further reproduction is prohibited.

The point is that you would probably *not* like your company associated with those that offer Barely Legal Teen Debutants [*sic*] and Utterly Taboo Animal XXX Hardcore. Why? It'll hurt your brand image. Of course, it can hurt you in more ways than that.

The Penalty for Misbehavior

In 1994, Laurence Canter and Martha Siegel (the "Green Card Lawyers") were the first to use spam to promote their legal services. They decided to send the same message offering to help noncitizens fill out applications for the Green Card Lottery to every Usenet newsgroup. The wrath they incurred and the price they paid are lessons to all of us. They were warned, they were cautioned, and still they ridiculed Internet customs.

In their book, *How to Make a Fortune on the Information Superhighway,* Canter and Siegel describe how they started off on the right foot by participating in the alt.visa.us newsgroup. People had specific questions and they knew the answers. They were willing to share their knowledge and the result was great. "Within a day or so our electronic mailbox overflowed with individual immigration inquiries," they maintained. "People we had never met wanted to hire us as lawyers."

Then they tried an experiment. They posted an ad for their services in about a hundred alt.culture. (country) groups. In their own words:

> Hundreds of requests for additional information poured in. . . . We also received our first "flames." . . . A few individuals did not like the fact that we had posted our notices to a number of newsgroups. We were informed that when you post to newsgroups, you must post only on the topic of the group. "What," someone wanted to know, "does the Green Card Lottery have to do with atl.culture.japan?" Others advised us to look into "Netiquette," the informal code of behavior certain people believe must be observed when you operate in Cyberspace. Still others were not so polite.

Undeterred by this negative response, Canter and Siegel posted to 1000 newsgroups and then to 6000. Each time they were met with flames and ill will. Each time they ignored the signals and shrugged it off. You'd almost expect these people to walk gladly through a Japanese home in their hiking boots, raise their voices when their host could not understand them, and insist vehemently that their host bring them a knife and fork for their dinner—even having been told that these are contrary to local customs and good manners.

It doesn't matter if you think your actions are proper, it matters what your clients think. You must respect the culture of whatever country you're in, even if it's that newly founded realm called cyberspace.

The result of their continued breach of netiquette harmed them and others around them.

> Call after call came complaining about what we had done. . . . The amount of (electronic) mail was particularly staggering because a number of protesters decided to do more than just apply bad language to the situation. Instead, they sent mailbombs, huge electronic files of junk designed to clog up our computer by their sheer size.

This "clogging" overflowed the computers at Canter and Siegel's Internet provider, shutting them down. The system operators rebooted the system only to find thousands of additional flames waiting. This actually happened several times. The access provider terminated Canter and Siegel's account. Canter and Siegel went elsewhere and experienced the same situation. The sad part is that many others were using those access providers as well and had their service interrupted for days on end.

Stories circulated that some annoyed recipient wrote a program that dialed Canter's pager every 20 minutes between the hours of 1:00 a.m. and 5:00 a.m. Net lore is often spurious, but it is also indicative. In a population this large, there are sure to be those with an equal-but-opposite sense of right and wrong. They may also possess the ability and desire to carry out such acts of revenge.

In this day and age of hacking, you might worry about an annoyed net-nerd reaching out and touching you in ways you don't wish. But the truth is that one posting to a list about your spamming behavior might do a lot more damage to your reputation.

Accepted Practices

Take a lesson from the American Marketing Association Code of Ethics for Marketing on the Internet (www.ama.org/about/ama/ethcode.asp). See Figure 2.6.

PREAMBLE

The Internet, including online computer communications, has become increasingly important to marketers' activities, as they provide exchanges and access to markets worldwide. The ability to interact with stakeholders has created new marketing opportunities and risks that are not currently specifically addressed in the American Marketing Association Code of Ethics. The American Marketing Association Code of Ethics for Internet marketing provides additional guidance and direction for ethical responsibility in this dynamic area of marketing. The American Marketing Association is committed to ethical professional conduct and has adopted these principles for using the Internet, including on-line marketing activities utilizing network computers.

GENERAL RESPONSIBILITIES

Internet marketers must assess the risks and take responsibility for the consequences of their activities. Internet marketers' professional conduct must be guided by:

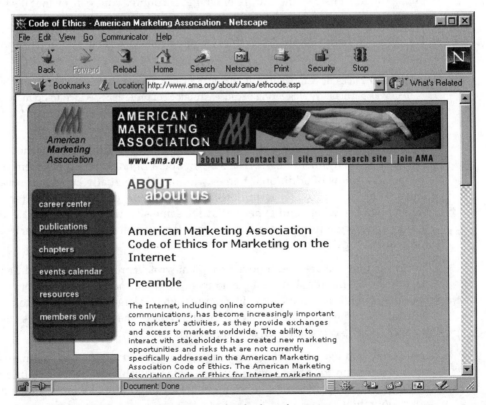

Figure 2.6 The AMA sees things more clearly than the DMA.

1. Support of professional ethics to avoid harm by protecting the rights of privacy, ownership and access. 2. Adherence to all applicable laws and regulations with no use of Internet marketing that would be illegal, if conducted by mail, telephone, fax or other media. 3. Awareness of changes in regulations related to Internet marketing. 4. Effective communication to organizational members on risks and policies related to Internet marketing, when appropriate. 5. Organizational commitment to ethical Internet practices communicated to employees, customers and relevant stakeholders.

PRIVACY

Information collected from customers should be confidential and used only for expressed purposes. All data, especially confidential customer data, should be safeguarded against unauthorized access. The expressed wishes of others should be respected with regard to the receipt of unsolicited email messages.

OWNERSHIP

Information obtained from the Internet sources should be properly authorized and documented. Information ownership should be safeguarded and respected. Marketers should respect the integrity and ownership of computer and network systems.

ACCESS

Marketers should treat access to accounts, passwords, and other information as confidential, and only examine or disclose content when authorized by a responsible party. The integrity of others' information systems should be respected with regard to placement of information, advertising or messages.

"The expressed wishes of others should be respected with regard to the receipt of unsolicited email messages." Enough said.

The Critical Rules of Unsolicited Email

1. Don't do it.

2. If you're thinking of trying it just once, see rule number 1.

So if sending unsolicited email is verboten, how do you get your message out to the world? You use something called *permission* email, or *opt-in* email.

Lots of companies are doing it. Lots of them are being very successful.

CHAPTER 3

Defining Opt-in

E-commerce is opting in to opt-in marketing. In a big way.

> *Despite the fact that opt-in email has been a part of companies' communication strategies for less than two years, over 70% of respondents already see it as "important" or "very important."*
>
> **Opt-In Email Gets Personal, Forrester Research, March 1999**

> *While spammers have given email a bad rap, one thing is for sure: The volume of solicited commercial email will climb steadily. Forrester Research projects that some 250 billion SCE (solicited commercial email) messages will be sent by 2002, creating a $1 billion market. A survey of 60 leading marketers by New York-based Gruppo, Levey & Co. found that 40% currently conduct email direct marketing campaigns, while another 37% plan to do so in the near future.*
>
> **Iconocast, January 21, 1999**

Every time you turn around, there's another opportunity to enter your email address on some company's Web site. That's because it works so well. You'll find companies as diverse as Hewlett-Packard (see Figure 3.1), Ben & Jerry's Ice Cream (see Figure 3.2), and Kinnard's Pharmacy (see Figure 3.3).

Why are they opting in to this new type of marketing? Well, it's not very expensive, it's not hard to test, and the results are significant.

A recent PricewaterhouseCoopers survey found people spending 84 percent of their time on the Internet for email. With email playing that large of a role for Internet

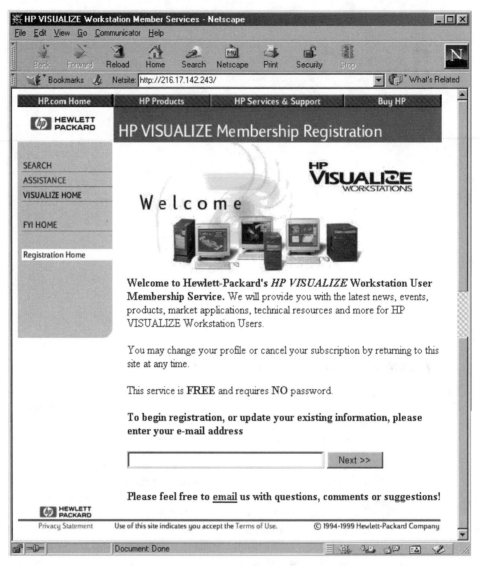

Figure 3.1 Hewlett-Packard publishes "news, events, products, market applications, technical resources and more for HP VISUALIZE Workstation Users."

usage, marketers cannot ignore the potential power of an effective opt-in direct email campaign.

A lot more time and ink could be spent describing how fast this marketing tool is being adopted, or we can just get to the point about how to do it well. If you need the numbers, look to the research companies like Forrester Research (www.forrester.com) and Jupiter Communications (www.jup.com).

Just don't blink. This trend is taking off.

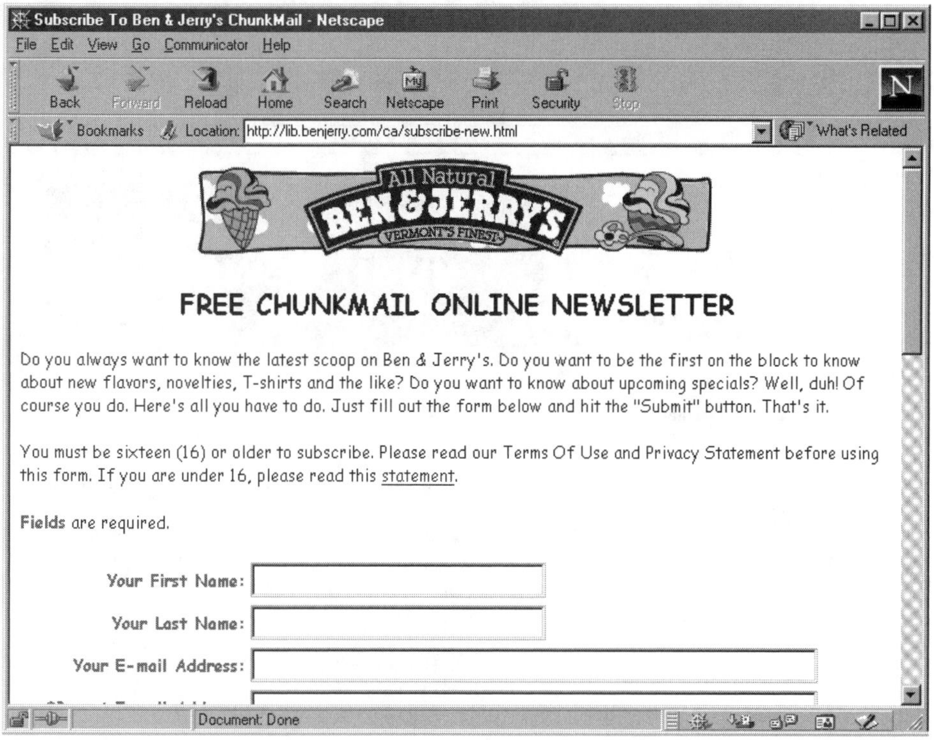

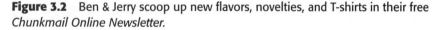

Figure 3.2   Ben & Jerry scoop up new flavors, novelties, and T-shirts in their free *Chunkmail Online Newsletter.*

Understanding Opt-in by Understanding Opt-out

Solicited email is easy to identify: The customer asked for it.

No, we don't mean the customer was looking at your wristwatch.html and clicked on a link that said, "Email me my discount coupon for 20 percent if I buy today." That's giving you permission to send them one specific email. If you want to continue sending them updates, announcements, or additional offers, you need explicit approval.

If you thought we were splitting hairs when we talked about spam, hold on to your hat. There is an even finer distinction between varieties of solicited email, but the overall distinctions are even more important. Why? Because if you do it wrong, it looks just like spam.

Occasionally, you find yourself on a mailing list for certain types of information that you never requested, even though the senders insist you did. Why? Chances are, you were placed on this list because you visited a site and/or tried a free service. You may even have entered an online drawing or contest to win a free trip to Jamaica. Because you expressed your interest in travel, the Caribbean, your name goes onto those lists as somebody who is genuinely interested in learning more about such matters.

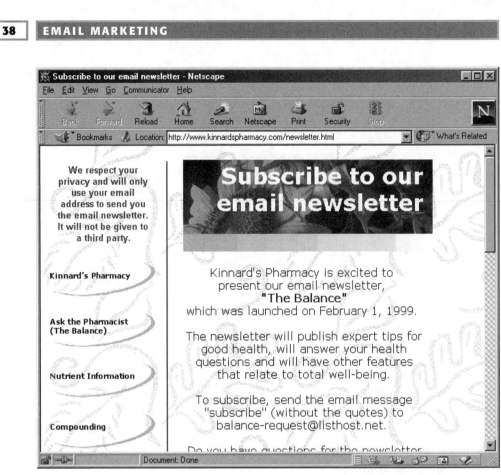

Figure 3.3 Kinnard's Pharmacy publishes expert tips for good health and answers your health questions.

Though many such services are legitimate, many are used strictly to build email lists for mass mailings or spamming. We'll leave the spammers to their own special place in the netherworld, and focus on those opt-out folks who are merely misguided rather than evil.

Opt-outers believe that sending a targeted message to people who have shown interest in a specific topic is an ideal mode of marketing. It works just great with postal mail. In order to show that they are not Satan's spawn, they offer a way to get your name off their list and never be bothered again.

In order to get your name removed from these lists, you have to "unsubscribe" (even though you never intentionally subscribed in the first place). This is *opt-out*. It places the need for action on you to unsubscribe. Since these lists sometimes sell your name and address to other lists, you may end up having to unsubscribe any number of times. The owners of the list are betting that you, like many people, will not take the time or make the effort to unsubscribe. They assume your silence is your consent.

What purpose do these lists serve and why do these site owners want to add your name to a mailing list you did not request? Usually because they sell classified advertising space in their emails. If they can claim to have a mailing list of 25,000, they can attract more business owners willing to pay for ad space. Or, perhaps, they are willing to risk annoying 99 percent of the people who receive their emails for the 1 percent who will read about (and maybe buy) the products they are selling. They are trapped in the direct postal mail business model and it doesn't work online.

Cliff Kurtzman, CEO of The Tenagra Corporation, explained the downside of opt-out in his eloquent article on ClickZ in May 1998 (www.searchz.com/clickz/051598 .shtml):

> Tenagra sends a newsletter out every two months or so, and it's both an extremely productive as well as inexpensive way to stay in the mindshare of current and potential clients, along with other users of our web site.
>
> This technique is often called "opt-in email marketing" because each person joining the mailing list "opts" to do so themselves. Mailing lists can be so successful that we sometimes suggest to our clients that they put at least as much attention into their newsletters as they do in their web site.
>
> But problems can develop when people cross the line from email marketing into "spamming." It doesn't matter if the sender tells the recipient how to get off the list—it is still spam if sent in an opt-out manner. There are three main reasons why:
>
> 1) Many people feel uncomfortable responding to such unsubscribe instructions on a spam list, knowing that many spammers use unsubscribe requests simply as a signal to confirm that the recipient is reading the email and should therefore be sent even more spam.
>
> 2) Some recipients have many email aliases under different domain names, and won't know which one they have been involuntarily subscribed to the list under.
>
> 3) It is unfair to the recipient for them to have to spend their time removing themselves from a mailing list that they never wanted to be on in the first place. Many people and businesses bill for their time, and making these people waste their time trying to get off a list that they did not subscribe to is essentially the same as stealing from them.
>
> Someone who adds others to their mailing list without first getting their permission may not quite be in the same category as the adult-oriented services and MLMers (Multi Level Marketers) that are known for sending spam.
>
> However, each time they send out an email to their list, those recipients that were subscribed involuntarily will think of the sender as rude for not having first asked them whether or not they wanted to be on the list. The sender has transformed their newsletter from an opportunity for them to reinforce their mindshare in a positive way into a negative experience. All because they were too lazy to simply ask if the recipient wanted to get onto their list in the first place.

Microsoft played both ends of the game in their offering to Office 2000 preview consumers (see Figure 3.4).

They start brilliantly by allowing recipients to enter an email address and a zip code, while signing up to receive information on Microsoft Office 2000 events in their neighborhood. Not only do subscribers get information on a specific topic, but they get it tailored to a specific location. This is a great way for customers to get what they want and an *outstanding* way for Microsoft to find out where they should hold more events. Brilliant.

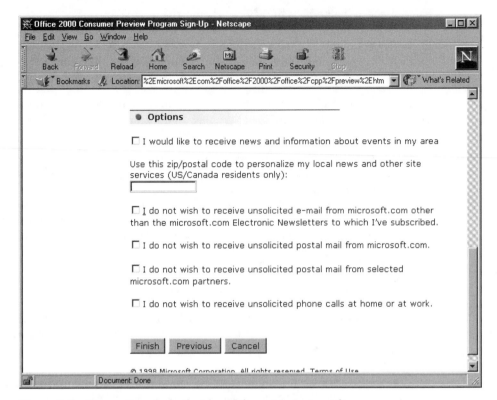

Figure 3.4 Microsoft works both sides of the opt-in/opt-out fence.

But then, Microsoft switches gears. The next questions were written opt-out style:

I do not wish to receive unsolicited email from microsoft.com other than the microsoft.com Electronic Newsletters to which I have subscribed.

Yes, we said we wanted to know about events in our area, but that's all. Please don't send a bunch of other stuff.

I do not wish to receive unsolicited postal mail from microsoft.com.

That email newsletter is fine, but don't cut down any trees on our behalf.

I do not wish to receive unsolicited postal mail from selected microsoft.com partners.

Whatever you do, don't hand out our address like candy.

I do not wish to receive unsolicited phone calls at home or at work.

What? Are you nuts? You think we enjoy getting up from the dinner table to talk to somebody trying to sell us the latest upgrade to PowerPoint?

We agree that offering not to market to somebody could be considered nice. But the combination of opt-in and opt-out here is a recipe for disaster. Yes, we wanted the information about events in our area and we clicked that box. We even typed in our email address. But that's all we wanted. So we scroll down to the Finish button without clicking on anything else and, the next thing we know, the phone is ringing. Wrong way to go.

Perhaps the lowest of the low are those who pretend they practice opt-in when they are merely spamming:

```
Date: 8/1/99 8:39:46 PM Pacific Daylight Time
From: xxx@hotmail.com
To: xxx@hotmail.com
Subject: Don't Get Ripped Off!!! There's only ONE Internet Spy and You
Software. (Mac or PC)

Due to popular demand, both PC and MAC Versions of "The Internet Spy &
You" are now available ONLY from Xxxxxx.
There are some dishonest people who have copied this advertisement in an
attempt to sell their own "cheap imitation" of the Internet Spy & You
program. Don't mistake this software for other $15 and $22 programs
being advertised on the net... you get what you pay for, and there's
only ONE "Internet Spy & You" program!!!
Please see disclaimers at the end of this mailing.

<><><><><><><><><><><><><><><><><><><><><
Welcome to another... ListBott "Opt-In" broadcast.
<><><><><><><><><><><><><><><><><><><><><

Dear Subscriber,
We have been FORCED TO LIMIT OUR DISTRIBUTION after August 14th!!! Don't
miss this very limited time opportunity...
```

"Please see disclaimers"? Equally as laughable. Notice that the following remove address is not the same as the reply address or even the same domain as the sender. Tacky and confusing.

```
This mailing is done by an independent marketing company. We apologize
if this message has reached you in error. Save the Planet, Save the
Trees! Advertise via Email. No wasted paper! Delete with one simple key-
stroke! Less refuse in our Dumps! if you wish to be removed from our
list, a simple "REMOVE" request sent to xxx@xxx.net will do it.
```

How can it possibly have reached you in error if it was an opt-in message?!

You Can't Borrow Permission from Others

I recently received an email message that puzzled me. It was from Fatbrain.com, a bookstore I had seen advertised frequently in print. I had never been to the Fatbrain.com Web site. I had never communicated with them at all to the best of my recollection. Yet here was the unsolicited message:

```
Date: Mon, 2 Aug 1999 22:00:46 -0400
From: fatbrain@emserve.com
To: jsterne@targeting.com
Subject: Get $15 off your next order at Fatbrain.com!
-----------------------------------------------------------------
NUOS's MIS Source (http://www.nuos.com) has made your email address
available to this organization whose products and services we think you
might find interesting.
If you do not wish to receive any future emails from Fatbrain.com please
email fatbrain.emserve.com with REMOVE in the subject line.
-----------------------------------------------------------------
Hi,
Fatbrain.com, the world's largest professional bookstore, has what smart
minds crave. We've got a great selection of resources on subjects like
Visual Basic, Linux, online investing and plasma physics. We've also got
great deals on our books, software and interactive training.
Here's one special deal. Now through August 13, you can take $15 off any
order totaling $30 or more (not including tax or shipping costs).
```

It then presented a URL to click in order to collect my $15 discount, included a couple of products on special, told me to hurry before the discount offer expired, and encouraged me to pass the message on to my friends, so they could get $15 off as well.

Being the curious type, I followed the link to the NuOS Corporation site (see Figure 3.5) to see who had given my name to Fatbrain.com.

I had never been to the NuOS Corporation Web site. I had never communicated with them at all to the best of my recollection. Yet here they were, willing to sell my name to Fatbrain.com.

My curiosity drove me to find out what they meant when they said I could "Find out about the ethical use of email marketing," so I clicked.

After admonishing one and all that "SPAM is annoying, wastes people's time, and is usually destructive to a company's reputation," they laid out their "points to remember":

Establish Contact First—Send a direct mail piece or make a telemarketing call first to establish contact.

Certainly an acceptable approach, although that telemarketing call is going to become less and less welcome over time.

Personalize Messages—Think of email as an electronic letter. Include formal addressing information in each message.

We're in agreement here.

Tell Prospects How You Know Them—Announce your email as a follow-up to a specific offer that prospects will recognize.

That's a good idea. We'll look at that more in depth in Chapter 6, "Writing an Email Masterpiece."

Maintain a No Email List—Always make it easy for people to be removed from your list.

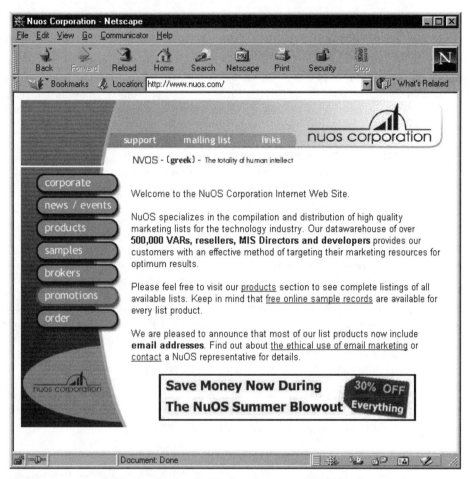

Figure 3.5 NuOS Corporation is a list broker that somehow thought I was happy to get unsolicited email from Fatbrain.com.

Hold it—that's not quite right. Yes, one should always make it easy for people to be removed from your list. But why on earth would you need to maintain a list of people who do not want to receive email?

This is an important distinction, and it's worth understanding the fine point. If you keep a list of people who have *asked* for email communications, then you can safely assume that anybody not on that list should *never* be sent a message. If you keep a No Email List, you are assuming anybody *not* on it is fair game. You would be wrong.

At the bottom of this page, they state, "NuOS Corporation is not responsible for the unethical use of email addresses by our customers. We strongly recommend the Direct Marketing Association's rules and guidelines for email marketing."

Ahhh, the problem begins to reveal itself. The Direct Marketing Association (www.the-dma.org) is the Grand Old Man of direct postal mail. Their annual conference is one of the largest gatherings of marketing people and there is good information to be found there. But, as each of us brings our history to the table when approaching the Internet, the DMA brings eight decades of postal mail philosophy with them, and it doesn't work on the Web.

The DMA encourages its members to "Responsibly Conquer a New Frontier with The DMA's Marketing Online Privacy Principles and Guidance" manual. The description of this manual (www.the-dma.org/busasst6/busasst-onmarkprivpr6a7.shtml) reveals their postal-oriented thinking.

ONLINE NOTICE AND OPT OUT

All marketers operating online sites, whether or not they collect personal information online from individuals, should make available to consumers their information practices in a prominent place.

Excellent. No trouble with that. Later on that page, the DMA recommends:

On-line email solicitations should be clearly identified as solicitations and should disclose the marketer's identity. Marketers using email should furnish consumers with whom they do not have an established business relationship with notice and a mechanism through which they can notify the marketer that they do not wish to receive future on-line solicitations. Marketers using email should furnish consumers with whom they have an established business relationship with notice and a mechanism through which they can request that the marketer suppress their email addresses from lists or databases rented, sold, or exchanged for online solicitation purposes.

Bzzzzzzt! Wrong answer, but thank you for playing. This suggests I have to go to every site that may have collected information about me over the years and tell them to stop sharing. Curiously, this statement is illustrated with a bright red mask you might wear to a masquerade party or to rob a bank.

Then they recommend spamming people to ask them if it's okay to spam them:

Ideally, marketers using email addresses and related information they have harvested should provide consumers with an opportunity to opt out prior to using the information for online solicitations. For example, a marketer could say, "We see that you frequent the [XYZ Corporation] site—we'd like to send you offers of [computer equipment]. If you don't want to receive these offers, just let us know."

This sort of approach works with postal mail and that's why the DMA thinks it should work here as well.

The results can resemble what happened to Tony Powell at www.generalwebsite .com, as he mentioned in a post to the ClickZForum:

```
I am always receiving what on first glance seem to be unsolicited
offers. But when I check to see from where these messages originate,
they are usually linked in some way (sometimes in the most tenuous of
ways) to something I did, indeed, sign up to receive.
So, my question: If I sign up for an opt-in service, am I giving my per-
mission to receive mailings from any company that subsequently signs on
to rent those lists? Technically, yes; in practice, of course not.
```

It also happened to Mark Gibbs.

Ethics and Acceptable Behavior

By Mark Gibbs

Network World, 07/26/99

"We are aware of your request not to receive email from Music Boulevard and respect it. However, because you are a valued customer, we wanted to take a moment to let you know that Music Boulevard and CDNow are now one company, with a brand-new store—CDNow."—Remarkably dumb pitch received by "Backspin" reader Matthew Steinhoff.

Certainly a dozen copies of a (previously described) bogus offer from an anonymous company addressed to a slew of random recipients is way beyond the pale, but what about the CDNow pitch received by Matthew Steinhoff? I think CDNow also crossed the line. Steinhoff had told Music Boulevard clearly (at least twice) that he didn't want to hear from it again. But not only did the company fail to remove him from its database, it handed him to CDNow. And CDNow could have handled the pitch with far more finesse than it did. Had CDNow said it had acquired Music Boulevard's records and wanted to assure him it was serious about respecting his privacy and would dispose of his data, I'm certain he would have been gratified, although he might have been annoyed that his wishes had been ignored.

But CDNow went over a boundary by not only showing that it had his data, but that it was also willing to use it to pitch him. And on top of that, it had the nerve to say it respected his wishes. Amazing! I wonder who was responsible for this breach of ethics? I would doubt it was an IS professional.

Now this is a situation in which many companies, yours included, may well find themselves. Over the next few months through acquisitions and mergers, you might well discover caches of old customer data and find that there are records flagged to show that the customers had opted out of some program. What should you, the IS professional, do?

Simple, make sure that the rest of the company understands that opt-out customers have really opted out. By getting involved you may be in danger of picking a fight with an 800-pound political gorilla, but you may also be saving your company's reputation and image.

When it comes to respecting privacy, IS professionals must educate the rest of the company about the ethics of the 'Net. If you don't, your companies will undoubtedly run full-tilt into trouble.

Global Opt-out Doesn't Cut It Either

The correct approach, according to the thought-leaders at places like SAFEeps (www.SAFEeps.com), is a worldwide opt-out database (see Figure 3.6).

SAFEeps [sm] is the service mark for the American Computer Group (ACG) email preference list system. SAFEeps [sm] allows consumers to opt out of receiving unsolicited commercial email on a global basis, while providing marketers with a means to determine which recipients might be interested in their mailings.

Figure 3.6 SAFEeps wants to be the single place for opting out of everything.

They're not alone. Others include No Junk Email (www.glr.com/nojunk.html) and NoThankYou.com (www.NoThankYou.com).

This approach would be wonderful if two things were true. First, everybody who gets an email address or a new/additional email address is automatically placed in the database. Second, everybody who thinks spamming is great would willingly honor the names in that database. It'll never happen.

The Association for Interactive Media (AIM; www.interactivehq.org), a subsidiary of the DMA, may hold the answer. They are a lobbying group for online commerce and are leading the charge for the DMA to create an opt-in email marketing policy.

AIM also has a subcommittee called the Council for Responsible Email (CRE), made up of industry leaders including MyPoints.com, Microsoft, AOL, yesmail.com, and so forth. This group focuses on helping the industry to define itself and set the benchmark for acceptable standards.

So rather than attack the DMA, let's just say they are working on a solution. That may be slow in coming, but they are sincerely trying to lead their membership.

The problem of privacy and ownership and permission is one of perception. Opt-in is explicit consent. It is not implied. It is not borrowed.

Implicit versus Explicit Permission

Wearing sales and marketing-colored glasses, the world is divided into suspects, prospects, and customers. If you're selling sporting equipment, everybody is a suspect. If you're selling shoes, everybody is a prospect. If you're selling a 30-frames-per-second digital video camera, you have to carefully pick your prospective customers.

If we go by the fax rules, then all of your customers and some of your prospects are fair game. You have a relationship with them. Once you convince your boss that just having their badges scanned at a trade show booth does not give you their consent to send them unsolicited email, it's time to explain about customers.

You *obviously* have a relationship with your customers. But is that enough? Nope. It's only implied. Your customers did not explicitly check the box and hit the Submit button. If a customer fills out the card that says, "Yes, I want more information," make sure there's a box she can check that says whether she wants it electronically or physically. If you don't specifically ask her if she wants it sent via email, you're making an assumption.

So how do you make doubly sure that people *really* want to get your e-messages? Ask them—twice.

Single and Double Opt-in

Full Sterne Ahead from Target Marketing is a single opt-in sign-up. You enter your email address, you click the button, and you get a notification that you are on the list. Once a month (or so) you'll get the next installment.

But other lists, such as discussion groups or advertising lists, may send you several messages every day—sometimes more. For them, only the double opt-in will do.

Take the case of yesmail.com. When you sign up with YesMail to receive information about the topic of your choice, you're allowing anybody with a message and a checkbook to send you email. The folks at yesmail.com want to be darned sure that you really want to get this sort of attention, so they send the sign-up verification notice:

```
From: subs@my.yesmail.com <subs@my.yesmail.com>
To:
Subject: yesmail Signup Verification -- RESPONSE REQUIRED : xxxxxxx : DO
NOT REMOVE THIS CODE

Date: Thu, 12 Aug 1999 00:26:46 -0500 *YOU MUST REPLY TO THIS MESSAGE*
to activate your free My.yesmail membership OR visit
http://my.yesmail.com/mymoptin.asp?subcode=xxxxxxx.
We have received your request to join My.yesmail through the yesmail web
site.
My.yesmail is an email information service designed to deliver informa-
tion only on those items of specific interest to you. Whether you wish to
```

```
gain a competitive advantage by staying on top of the latest industry
developments to hit the Net, or just want to find the best prices on air-
fares and hotels, the topics that you receive messages about are yours to
decide. You may modify or cancel your My.yesmail membership at any time.
Remember, if you submitted this subscription request, you *MUST* reply
to this message OR visit
http://my.yesmail.com/mymoptin.asp?subcode=xxxxxx
This will send a personal message to our verification system and *ACTI-
VATE* your subscription. We require this extra step in order to verify
your email address as well as to confirm that no one is trying to sub-
scribe you without your permission.
NOTE: This verification email address is only to be used once. Do *not*
use it to send questions, comments or other information to us. Send
questions or comments to info@my.yesmail.com.
If you have *NOT* requested this service, *DO NOT REPLY* to this mes-
sage. Instead -- and ONLY if you did NOT request this service - please
*FORWARD* this message to unsolicited@my.yesmail.com so that we may
track down the problem. Be sure to put the words "Unsolicited Subscrip-
tion" in the subject line of your message.
We do not send unsolicited email of any sort and do not wish to mail to
anyone except those who have specifically requested FREE subscriptions.
Thank you and enjoy My.yesmail.
yesmail
```

It may seem odd that they would send a message to confirm that no one is trying to subscribe you without your permission. Unfortunately, it happens often enough to be a concern. People with a chip on their shoulder have subscribed their enemies to dozens of lists, all generating dozens of messages a day. That leaves the poor recipient with the time-consuming task of unsubscribing from all of those lists.

If this happens to you, yesmail.com gives you two options: You can ignore the whole thing and it will die on the vine, or you can forward the message to them and they'll try to get to the bottom of it.

This double opt-in is the safest way of signing people up. It ensures they are who they say they are and that they were really serious about being on your list.

Pure Opt-in Is the Right Model

Opt-in is easy to identify. But then, so is the color white. Line up 30 blushing brides and you'll find they are bedecked with 30 shades of white satin and lace. *Pure* opt-in is much more straightforward. You ask for permission, you get it, you keep it to yourself, and you don't abuse the privilege.

Start by getting people to sign up.

Collecting Email Addresses

Get them to sign up in a very clear manner with no strings attached and with a clear regard for their privacy. In the new age of Internet marketing where the customer has control, integrity is going to play a larger and larger role.

Sony Music

Sony collects a lot of email addresses from people who are interested in music. Lots of others would be interested in getting their hands on the addresses Sony collects, so Sony assures visitors to their site that they are not in the business of selling names (see Figure 3.7).

From Sony, you get a string assurance. From other companies, you get a bonus—like a "what's on sale" notification from Sears.

Sears

Touted as a free, friendly service, the Sears email reminder (www.sears.com/email-rem) will be only too happy to tell you about the specials they have in their jewelry department just a few days before your anniversary. They'll be pleased to let you know about the sale on Craftsman tools for your husband.

You identify which holidays would be jollier with a little reminder from this $41 billion company. You tell them how far in advance you wish to be notified and even add a note to yourself. The result is a string around your finger that pops up just in time and carries a written message.

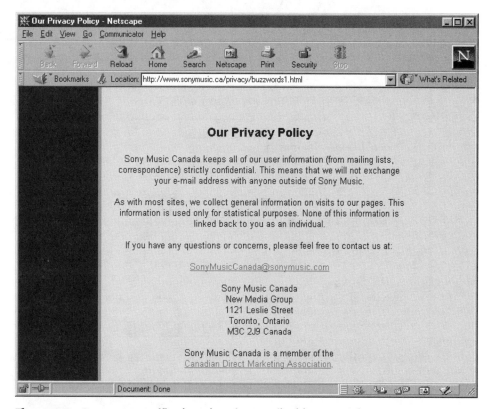

Figure 3.7 Sony gets specific about keeping email addresses under wraps.

And just before you hit the Submit button, they prove they are an opt-in shop by asking if you want information sent to you about Sears sales—and the default is "No" (see Figure 3.8).

MSI Consulting

Right between the two is MSI Consulting, a marketing consulting company (www.msiconsulting.com). They have several PowerPoint presentations on their Web site, which you can watch accompanied by an audio track or download to look at later.

They feel the value of these presentations is so high that they ask for your name and address as well. Fair enough. We're living in an information-as-coin-of-the-realm society and trading for equal value is the name of the game.

Then they invite you to enter your email address in exchange for more information, and you get to choose what interests you:

Corporate Brochure

Publications: VAR/Developer/Internet

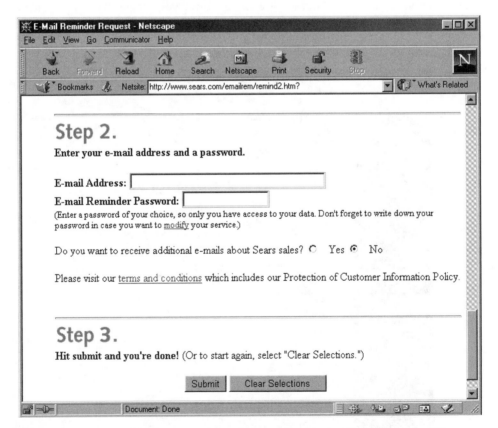

Figure 3.8 Sears makes the assumption that you do *not* want their advertising. Pure opt-in.

Publications: White Papers

Services: Market Entry Strategies

Services: Solution Strategies

Services: Route to Market

Services: Partnership Strategies

Services: Partner Programs

Services: Partner Management Systems

Virtual Seminars

This is a wonderful idea. Publish multiple newsletters and tailor them to each individual. We'll take a closer look at this approach in Chapter 7, "E-Newsletters, E-Promotions, and OPEmail."

But then MSI has one last choice in the list and it's an odd one:

No, I don't want any information.

We're left to wonder. If we didn't select any of the preceding topics and we didn't select the "don't send me anything" choice, what would we end up getting?

To get the facts and nothing but the facts, we turn to one Web site that's been doing email marketing since the beginning.

Amazon.com

Amazon was among the first to catch on to the power of email and use it as a tool for outright selling. They didn't start off trying to "add value" with newsletters, reminders, or downloads. They just wanted to sell you books, and they did it very well.

From *World Wide Web Marketing, Second Edition*

They came up with the idea of using email to notify you of new books you might be interested in. How did they know? At first, they asked. At the bottom of every book page, there's a list of the categories in which they classified that book. Which classification interests you the most? When you specify a category, or an author, or even a title, Amazon.com will send you email when a new book is published that meets your criterion. It's simple. It's neat. As a consumer I like it, and as a marketer I love it.

As a consumer, it saves me two hours and a hundred dollars every time I wander into a bookstore. As a reader, I try my best to keep track of my favorite authors. Another Jill Ellsworth or Kim Bayne? I want to know. A new Bruce Sterling? How soon can I get it?

But now a new day has dawned. There's a vendor who is willing to scour the shelves, keep track of my favorite authors and is willing to send me email telling me something I really want to know—for free! Amazon sends me an email, I click on the link, I read the

Continues

From *World Wide Web Marketing, Second Edition* *(Continued)*

review, I buy the book (or not). Amazon.com is simple, fast, elegant, and I always stay up to date on what's being published. From the seller's perspective, this is akin to the fish jumping into the barrel and handing you a loaded gun. "Sell me!" they plead. "Here's what I want to buy!" they shout. "I want to give you money!" they insist. Is this a seller's market or what?

There's also nothing like being able to accurately predict demand for your goods. When John Grisham puts out another legal-action-thriller, Amazon knows how many people want to hear about it and they know how many purchased his newest book last time. They know how many to buy in advance.

Seeing Shades of Gray in Black and White

Jupiter Communications (www.jup.com) wrote up a report at the end of 1998 called *Direct Email, Winning Long-Term Consumer Attention*. In it, they outline six categories ranging from opt-in to opt-out. They look like this:

1. Consumer requests and/or agrees to receive specific product information (Brand X, e.g., nail polish).

2. Consumer requests and/or agrees to receive related information from the same marketer/brand (Brand X, e.g., lipstick).

3. Consumer requests and/or agrees to receive related information from different marketer/brands (Brand Y and Z, e.g., beauty products).

4. Marketer rents names from either opt-in or opt-out lists by related product categories (e.g., broad health and beauty products).

5. Marketer mails to list with little relevance, but allows opt-out (e.g., get rich quick, vacation, diets).

6. Marketer obtains names through any means; minimal or no opt-out options (e.g., get rich quick, vacation, diets).

Jupiter labeled 1, 2, and 3 as opt-in; 4 and 5 as opt-out; and 6 as spam. They almost got it right. The real dividing line between acceptable and unacceptable practices by marketers falls right in the middle of number 4. If the rented list comes from an opt-in list—and if that list clearly states how it is to be rented—then all's well. If the marketer rents from an opt-out list, it's still spam.

Now that we've cleared up the fuzzy distinctions among opt-in, opt-out, and spam, there remains a question in the hearts of all true marketers: Where can you find a list of people who have opted in to a subject, beyond those who have opted in to yours in particular? How do you meet new prospects through email?

Rent the Right List

When you look in the SRDS book at the library (Standard Rate and Data Service, www.srds.com), you find a whole world of lists to rent for postal mail. There are lists of people who subscribe to *Arizona Highways* magazine and people who read *Goat Farmer* magazine. There are lists of people who attended self-esteem seminars in the last three months and lists of people who bought extended warranties on their dishwashers.

It seems like the world is at your feet. There are so many different lists, surely you can find one that is full of people interested in your offer. But there's a catch. Just because they were interested in goat farming does not mean they're going to be interested in hearing about your goat shampoo. That's why the response rates on direct mail are pegged at about 2 percent. The other 98 percent just aren't in a receptive mood or were the wrong targets altogether.

Online, however, your message is going to people who actively raised their hands and said, "Yes, I *want* to receive offers for products and services that relate to this subject" (see Figure 3.9). Because they explicitly requested information, they respond more frequently. And faster.

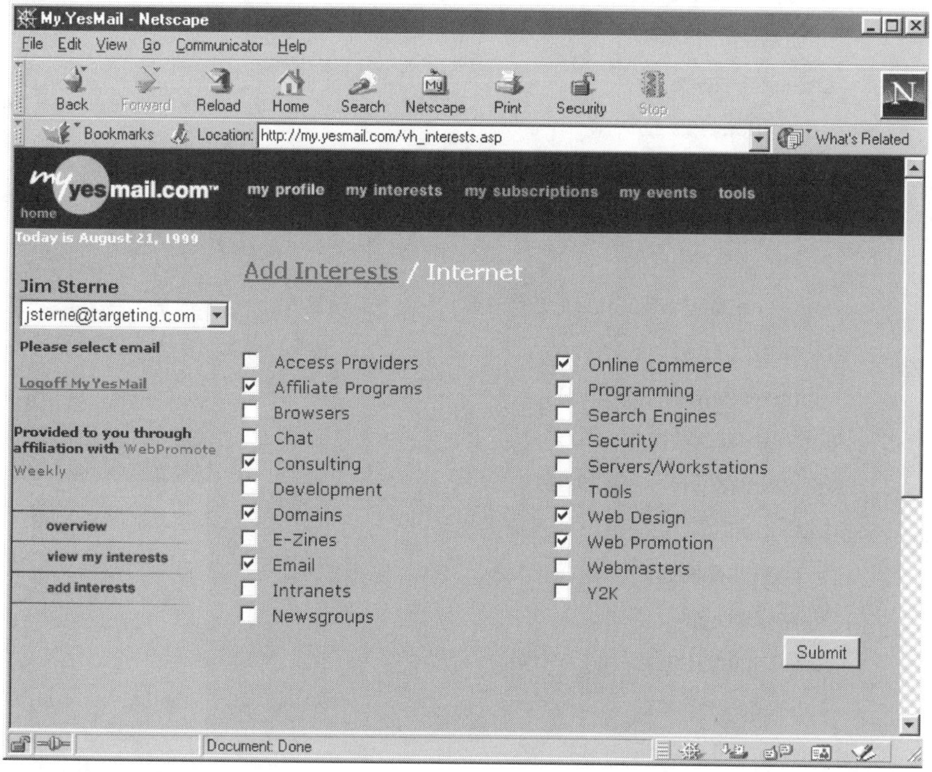

Figure 3.9   Choosing areas of interest is very easy for the subscriber at yesmail.com.

Your email announcement will be distributed to individuals all over the world who sign up to receive email messages about specific topics. They might be interested in business services, consulting, or specific fields like medicine or law. They might want to receive announcements relating to sports, entertainment, or computer technology. Without any effort and exhaustive research on your part, you have a targeted audience voluntarily requesting information on your business.

The response rates are high: from 5 to 15 percent and better. One Forrester report in March 1999 stated an average—an *average*—of 18 percent response. Why? These aren't just people who *might* be interested. They *are* interested. These aren't people who were interested at one point in time. They're interested *now*. As soon as their interest wanes, they get themselves off the list.

Finding the right list can be very easy. One example comes to mind immediately. As of August 1999, yesmail.com had a database that provided access to more than five million individuals delivering a response rate between 10 and 15 percent. Here's a partial listing:

YesMail Category Total List Names

Arts & Humanities 1,016,008

Automotive 192,305

Business 1,363,884

Careers 164,906

Computers 4,292,359

Cooking, Food & Wine 413,564

Education 1,312,045

Electronics 292,819

Entertainment & Games 1,175,314

Health 1,031,645

Home & Family 1,334,530

Internet 3,330,112

Investing & Finance 829,817

Kids 216,019

Music 1,139,391

News 438,663

Real Estate 31,894

Reference 315,237

Science & Technology 442,182

Shopping 2,912,474

Society & Culture 1,232,214

Sports & Recreation 2,511,744

Travel 390,690

The lists are divided into categories. They are diverse and they are narrowly targeted. The Automotive category, for example, is divided into 25 segments:

Alternative Fuel Vehicles

Antiques & Classics

Auto Parts

Auto Racing

Automotive News

Bus

Clubs

Dealers

Exotic Vehicles

Fuel

Insurance

Leasing

Limousines

Maintenance & Repair

Manufacturers

Motor Homes & Campers

Motorcycles

Museums

Other Auto Interests

Rentals

Reviews

Safety

Sport Utility Vehicles

Trucks, RV's & Tractors

Used Vehicles

The Business category includes:

Advertising

Business Schools

Communications

Consulting

Conventions and Conferences

Data, Statistics & Standards

Electronic Commerce

Engineering

Entrepreneur

Ethics and Responsibility

Exports/Imports

Human Resources, Benefits & Incentives

Insurance

International Business

Law

Management Science

Marketing

News & Guides

Opportunities & Franchising

Organizations

Printing

Regulation & Government

Research & Development

Sales

Shipping & Distribution

Small Office, Home Office

Supplies

Choose your audience, create your message, and hand it over to yesmail.com. They send the message off, ensuring the sanctity of each address.

It's about Ethics as Well as Profits

The American Marketing Association (AMA) Code of Ethics for Marketing on the Internet is posted on their Web site (www.ama.org/about/ama/ethcode.asp) and it hits the bull's-eye (see Figure 3.10).

The AMA doesn't try to finagle a way to send people something they might want if only they knew about it. The AMA stands for respect and privacy.

Under a heading labeled *Privacy*, the AMA makes it pretty clear:

Information collected from customers should be confidential and used only for expressed purposes. All data, especially confidential customer data, should be safeguarded against

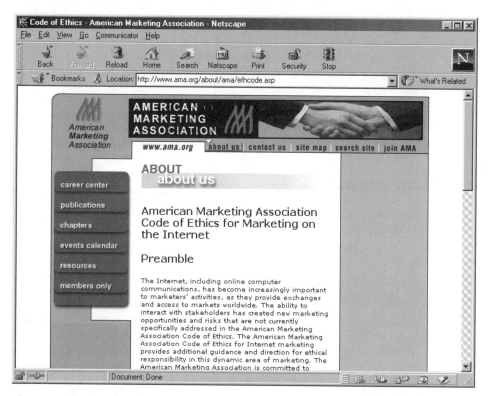

Figure 3.10   The American Marketing Association takes a pure opt-in approach.

unauthorized access. The expressed wishes of others should be respected with regard to the receipt of unsolicited email messages.

Note the term *expressed* and not *implied, assumed, indicated, presumed,* or *postulated.*

Opt-in May Alter Offline Marketing

The opt-in model is a strong one. It obviously benefits the company doing the marketing by offering up only those people who want to hear your message. But it benefits the customer as well.

We are assaulted with anywhere from 3000 to 6000 commercial messages a day. The opt-in approach might just be the formula of choice for millions of us who are growing tired of the clutter and becoming more and more able to tune it out. You never want to see another ad for tires again in your life. Until, that is, you're in the market for new whitewalls for your chariot. Then you want to know.

The next Internet start-up on the horizon? The Web site that offers to do with postal mail what yesmail.com does with email. People who want brochures on trekking through Nepal can sign up. The split second they come back from their trip, they can unsubscribe. This could catch on.

In the meantime, you're facing a new marketing medium and some pretty high expectations. Figuring out how to make the most of email marketing is what this book is all about. And, as with any marketing program, the first step is devising a game plan that will deliver the best response for the least investment. We get to the heart of the matter in the next chapter, "Crafting an Email Campaign."

Crafting an Email Campaign

Kristen Zhivago, editor of the (paper) *Marketing Technology* newsletter (www .marketing-technology.com), ran an email campaign to launch one of her very successful seminars. She found one drawback: "The only problem with Web marketing is that it's addicting. The marketer in me can't resist trying yet another approach. You know so quickly if it has worked or not, and you can then use that knowledge to improve your campaign. It's a fantastically steep and quick learning curve."

It does happen quickly. Responses start coming back immediately because more and more people are online all through the day. They see an email show up and they read it right then. Some who respond do so instantly. The ability to create an instant reaction is exhilarating. It can also be very cost efficient.

One European industrial company decided to try opt-in email to offer a print catalog to prospects in specific geographic areas throughout the European Union. The response rate was 10 percent higher than it had been for their past direct mail efforts. They calculated that they saved over $30,000 in expenses which they would have incurred using traditional direct mail, and they would not have achieved such a high response rate. As a result, they could use the money they saved to do additional marketing to their target audience online.

But the exhilaration and the savings don't happen by magic. The only way your email efforts are going to succeed is through careful planning. People aren't getting 15 percent response rates by simply emailing information to gobs of addresses and then reaping the rewards. Sending the right message to the right person at the right time is still the goal. The steps for creating a high-return marketing program may look the same, but you don't want to fall prey to some of the same old assumptions you're accustomed to working with.

So we start with the familiar steps, which begin at the highest level:

1. *Develop a strategy.* What is the purpose of your campaign?
2. *Define your objectives.* What are you trying to accomplish?
3. *Create the plan.* How are you going to achieve your goals?
4. *Target your message.* Whom are you going after?
5. *Create the offer.* What do you want to tell them?
6. *Determine frequency.* How often are you going to communicate?
7. *Test your assumptions.* How does the response change if you tweak a few things?
8. *Measure the results.* How well did you do?

Because the medium is new, you'll need a fresh pair of eyes when you create your first email marketing program.

Developing a Campaign Strategy

Strategy. Goals. Tactics. They often get pushed together due to lack of time, energy, or money, which is really a shame. Starting out at the highest level ensures that everybody pulls together in the same direction.

If you want to approach the whole strategy portion of your campaign in a formal manner, there's always the SWOT analysis. This type of evaluation lets you focus your attention on the most important strengths, weaknesses, opportunities, and threats you face at the moment:

Strengths. What are your company's and product's advantages? What do you do well? What do you have that your competitors don't? What is it about your relationship with your customers that you can use to your advantage?

Weaknesses. Where is there room for improvement? Where does your company trip up? How would the marketplace describe your weaknesses? What does the competition have that you don't?

Opportunities. What's happening out there that you can take advantage of? What new, useful technologies are coming? What changes in buying or usage habits can you exploit?

Threats. What outside events or competitors are waiting to hit you when you're not looking? What potentially harmful regulations are grinding through the government?

Put all these together and they spell out where you are superior and where you need to do some work. You'll be able to quickly identify the areas that are going to provide the greatest return on investment, and you may even uncover some potentially life-threatening situations that need immediate attention.

If the overall strategy is to cut costs, you're going to have different objectives than if the strategy is to beat out a competitor. And those objectives are going to define different plans of attack. So start high. Spend a few minutes thinking about the overarching message you hear from your CEO. What does the annual report say about the company's direction this year? This is not a waste of time or a futile effort—this is the way to secure funding and management support.

If you work for Hewlett-Packard, it doesn't take long to find one of the key points in former chairman Lew Platt's 1998 "To Our Shareholders" letter (www.hp.com/financials/98annrep/letter/letter.html). See Figure 4.1.

Down near the bottom, amid all the text, there's one of only two sentences deemed worthy enough to make into a graphic so it really stands out. It says, "We are working hard to offer customers in all our businesses the speed, convenience and flexibility that electronic commerce offers."

Any marketing manager worth his or her salt at HP is going to be darned sure to create a strategy that includes speed, convenience, and flexibility. Other phrases from that document should find their way into a program strategy. They should proudly proclaim, "We will remain aggressive in building a powerful online presence," and

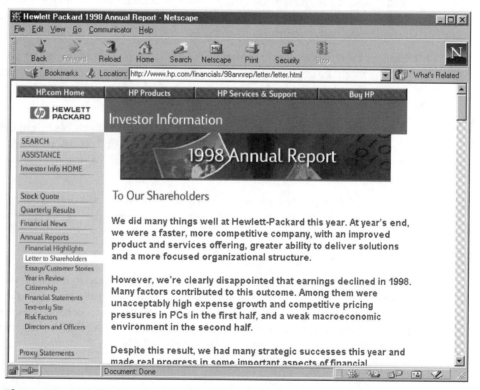

Figure 4.1 HP's "To Our Shareholders" letter holds keys to HP marketers' strategies for the year.

recognize "the need for focus, better execution and improved responsiveness in the fast-moving markets in which we compete."

Knowing what the boss's boss's boss is thinking never hurt anybody. But these phrases should also act as a guiding light. If your email marketing strategy is not closely aligned with your corporate mission, you should spend more than a single lunch hour making sure you're meeting more than tactical goals.

According to Forrester's *Opt-In Email* report (Forrester Research, March 1999), 66 percent of those asked were using email for promotions and discounts. Newsletters were cited by 48 percent, product releases by 34 percent, advertising and marketing by 28 percent, alerts and reminders by 24 percent, and market research by 8 percent. How *you* use this new medium depends on the goals that you set for yourself, which should be dictated by your overall strategy.

Defining Your Objectives

If your business strategy is to grow market share, then one of your objectives might be to increase sales by 20 percent by doubling the number of leads that come in every month. Another might be to lower the turnaround time from inquiry to fulfillment from four days to one day. Another might be to strengthen your branding and positioning through advertising.

If your goal is to build stronger relationships with your current customers, your objectives might be improved frequency of communication, deeper segmentation of your customer database, and broader diversity in the information you send to selected groups.

If your goal is to create new product line extensions, your objectives might be to survey your current customers for product ideas, create a public relations/media buzz, partner with new associates in the market, and build a critical-mass database of new prospects.

If your goal is to institute a proactive policy that will unify corporate departments by empowering individual units to enact their own policies, then you've spent too much time at www.dilbert.com.

Just what the heck are you trying to accomplish?

Be sure your objectives are reasonable and achievable, but see to it that they are not too easily won. A person's reach should exceed his or her grasp and all that. In a postal direct marketing campaign, a 2 percent response rate is considered good and a 1 percent response rate is considered acceptable. Opt-in email lists, by contrast, tend to generate higher response rates, as high as 5 to 15 percent.

Your goals should be easy to understand and easy to measure.

Your objectives, based on your strategy, depend on which stage of the customer relationship continuum you're focused on at the moment. We can divide that continuum as follows:

Research

Awareness

Prospecting

Qualification

Acquisition

Customer management

Up-selling and cross-selling

Retention

Once you have figured out the purpose of your email campaign and have identified understandable and achievable goals, it's time to do what you were going to do in the first place: Determine just what it will take to achieve those goals. The difference is that you now have a direction that's in keeping with the rest of the company, a clear set of objectives so you'll be able to tell if your plan works, and a much better chance of getting management buy-in when you go asking for funding.

In order to get funding, you'll need to get a handle on the steps you'll need to take to make this all come true. In other words, a plan.

A Few Words about Words

Here's a quick review of some of the terms used in this chapter:

Customer relationship stage. See the customer relationship continuum list in the preceding section.

Sales cycle. The steps necessary to find, qualify, and close a sale.

Sales cycle phase. The specific step a prospect is in at a given point in time.

Campaign. A planned set of communications with prospects and customers with a specific purpose.

Offer. A specific overture sent to elicit a specific response (such as 10 percent off, or buy one and get one free).

Research

Research is where all good marketers begin. Instead of building the product and then finding the buyers, you want to go out into the marketplace and find out what people might want to buy. Ask a lot of questions, read a lot of reports, crunch a lot of numbers, and try to determine the perfect product that will be snapped up faster than Cabbage-Patch dolls, Power Rangers, Furbies, or Beanie Babies.

The research phases give you the chance to reach into the minds of your would-be customers. You get to ask them as many questions as you can think of, tempered by the number of questions they are willing to answer. Starting an email questionnaire with the instruction, "Please answer the following 427 questions. It should only take four and a half hours," would be suboptimal.

But using email for marketing research is significantly cost efficient. Just be sure to apply the general rules of email marketing and get their permission first. Chapter 10, "A Look toward the Future," goes into more detail about using email as an electronic focus group. For now, we'll just concentrate on the art of being a good interlocutor.

Asking Good Questions

Quantitative questions are easier for people to answer and you may get more of them to answer more questions. Anybody who can type an X can answer quantitative questions without worrying about spelling or grammar. The answers are also easier to tabulate and analyze.

One the other hand, if you don't provide enough answers to choose from, you accidentally set artificial limits. If the only choices about buying toner cartridges are "once a month," "twice a month," and "three times a month," those who buy toner cartridges once every two months will give you misleading answers.

Digging Deep

Rolling out a sequence of research questions can give you the power to delve deeply into attitudes and beliefs. The first set of questions separates the men from the boys. If the first set comes back with answers from some individuals that are way off the mark (intentionally silly, obviously misunderstood, or so far out of the norm as to upset the statistical applecart), it makes sense to reply instantly with a thank-you note.

The other respondents may get different sets of follow-up questions, depending on their answers. If they answered yes to question number four, you may want to know a little more. If they answered yes to number four, but no to number five, you want to ask your questions a bit differently. Doing this online with large quantities of responses cries out for automation.

Managing the Response

If hundreds of answers come in, you want your computer to do the work of tabulating those answers. Since the replies come in via email, the format is very straightforward and not too difficult to programmatically parse and reckon. If you don't have a staff of programmers at the ready, you might consider a ready-made survey tool.

The Survey System from Creative Research Systems (www.surveysystem.com) is one such tool (see Figure 4.2).

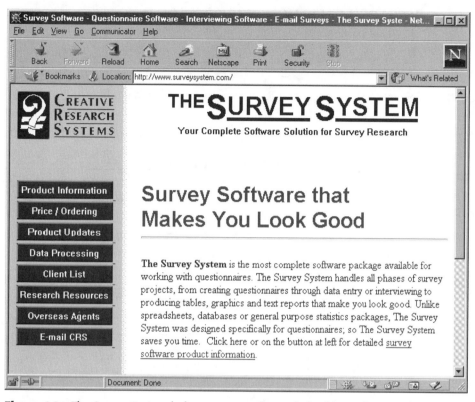

Figure 4.2 The Survey System helps automate the analysis of incoming email questionnaire responses.

In their own words:

> The Survey System's Email Module lets you send out blank questionnaires and receive completed questionnaires via email. You can attach files to email questionnaires to get people's reactions to graphic images, sound files or documents.
>
> Using the Survey System as your Internet, Web or intranet email survey software saves you time. You enter instructions only once and use them for your email questionnaire and to create tables, text reports and graphics that make you look good.
>
> The Email Module prevents multiple responses from the same person and rejects forwarded or passed-along questionnaires. It also checks each returned questionnaire to see that it matches the survey instructions (e.g., it will not allow a person to give 2 responses to a question allowing only one response). You can edit or discard faulty questionnaires. You can identify which responses come from which person or ensure anonymity as needed.

For more on designing questionnaires and running surveys, see these Web sites:

DSS Research (www.dssresearch.com/library/general/quesdesi.htm)

Griggs-Anderson Research (www.gar.com/primer/question.htm)

Analytic Technologies, Inc. (www.analytictech.com/mb313/principl.htm)

RESEARCH CAMPAIGN WORKSHEET

Campaign identification: _____

This research is being conducted to support (project name): _____

_____

The main purpose of this research is to determine: _____

_____

_____

Other research that's covered this subject: _____

_____

_____

Other individuals who can shed light on this subject: _____

_____

_____

The people asked to answer these questions will be chosen based on the following:

_____

_____

The following demographic and psychographic questions will be asked of each
individual: _____

_____

_____

_____

_____

The questions will be:

☐ Yes/no

☐ Multiple choice

☐ Likert scale (Strongly agree, Agree, Neither agree nor disagree, Disagree, Strongly disagree)

☐ Semantic differential (very interested /_/_/_/ not interested)

☐ Scale of

    ☐ 1 to 5

    ☐ 1 to 10

    ☐ 1 to 100

☐ Rank order (number the choices from best to worst)

☐ Essay (anecdotal)

☐ Word association (the first word that comes to mind)

☐ Sentence completion ("If I bought this product I could . . .")

There will be at least _____and no more than _____total questions.

The questions will be:

☐ Sent out all at once

☐ Sent out in batches of _____

Each respondent will receive no more than _____email questionnaires

Each questionnaire will take no more than _____minutes to complete

The answers will be tallied/analyzed by:_____

_____

_____

The budget for this campaign is: _____

_____

This questionnaire will reach no fewer than _____ and no more than _____ people

The budget for this research campaign is: _____

This series will commence on (date) _____ and end on (date) _____

Questionnaires will be sent in order to arrive on (day of the week) _____ at (time of day) _____

The format will be:

☐ Straight ASCII text

☐ HTML

☐ Both

The copy for these questionnaires is:

☐ In development

☐ Awaiting approval

☐ Approved

The support plan is:

☐ In development

☐ Awaiting approval by _____

☐ Approved by _____

The testing plan is:

☐ In development

☐ Awaiting approval by _____

☐ Approved by _____

The metrics of success
used in this campaign will be:

Success will be
achieved at (quantity):

_____   _____

_____   _____

_____   _____

_____   _____

_____   _____

Awareness

When launching a Web site, announcing a merger, or rolling out a new product, your means of communication and the tone of your message are going to be different than at other stages in the relationship continuum. You're going to be a little more aggressive and a little more formal. In this stage, your aim is to let people know you're there. You're trying to get people who have never heard of you to pay attention. This is serious advertising territory.

The notion of advertising usually includes putting your message in the middle of somebody else's medium. Your 30-second commercial goes in their half-hour TV program. Your full-page spread goes in their magazine. Your banner goes on their Web site.

This is a big subject and you might want to delve into it in detail in Jim Sterne's *What Makes People Click: Advertising on the Web* (Macmillan, 1997), but if you just want to focus on email marketing, you need only wait until the section in Chapter 7 of this book called, *Advertising in Other People's Email.* But when it comes to raising awareness using your own email marketing messages, you've come to the right place.

Your awareness campaign might be the initial moment of introduction. You step up to a stranger and say, "Hello. I'm in your face because I rented a mailing list and I have something wonderful to tell you." Your awareness campaign may be your way of telling people you already know that you have something brand new to show them. Either way, it's an overture, a beginning, a commencement.

Why?

The first step is figuring out what is being announced and what you'd like people reading the announcement to do about it. Is it the acquisition of another company? Are you announcing the release of a new version? The hiring of a new CEO? The launch of a new feature on your Web site that you hope to spin off into a skyrocketing IPO.com company?

What, then, do you want them to do about it when they receive it? You might simply be passing along information. You want them to read the message, be aware of the contents, and go on about their business. But maybe there's more to it than that.

Maybe the announcement is simply the mule to carry a response-invoking call to action. Perhaps you want them to come to your Web site for more information and, oh by the way, sign your petition to have the wetlands east of town declared a protected wilderness area. Perhaps you want to prompt them to download your latest screen saver. Whatever you want them to do, you'd better have it clearly identified well in advance. Otherwise, the list can't be properly selected and the message cannot be well written.

Who?

Pick a target. Identify who is to be on the receiving end of your email brilliance and make sure you keep them firmly in mind through the entire development process. Knowing who your target is will determine the style and tone of your message, the selection of the list, the manner in which you provide response support, and more.

Do your level best to know that recipient inside and out and you'll be able to decide:

- How long your message can be
- How many messages you can send
- Whether it should be straight text or dressed up like a Web page in HTML
- Whether you send different messages to different recipients
- What time of day it should arrive on their desktop

What?

In a world that demands integrated marketing, this email message you're sending out has to be one leg of an overall marketing plan. If so, what other media are going to be used to get the message out to the public? How is the message going to be coordinated across the different media?

When?

Perhaps the most important part will be the coordination of the schedule. It takes time to get the brochure printed, the trade show booth constructed, the press release written, the press conference speech written, and the PowerPoint presentations developed. When that email hits the Internet, everybody will be focused on you during your 15 milliseconds of fame. If the message goes out one day before the Web page is fully stocked with follow-up details, you have called the world to dinner and have nothing to feed them. They will be unlikely to accept another invitation.

AWARENESS CAMPAIGN WORKSHEET

Campaign identification:_____

This campaign is being conducted to announce (product/event/etc. name):_____

_____

The purpose of this announcement is to get people to

☐ Remember _____

☐ Read _____

☐ Sign up for _____

☐ Try_____

☐ Buy _____

☐ Recommend _____

☐ Other _____

Other media being used to make this announcement:

_____

The primary target for this announcement will be people who:

_____

The secondary target for this announcement will be people who:

_____

This announcement will reach no fewer than _____and no more than _____people

There will be at least _____and no more than _____total messages in this
series

The budget for this campaign is: _____

This series will commence on (date) _____and end on (date) _____

Messages will be sent in order to arrive on (day of the week) _____ at (time of day) _____

Each announcement will be no more than _____ lines in length

The format will be:

☐ Straight ASCII text

☐ HTML

☐ Both

Distinct messages will be written for the following targets:

☐ _____

☐ _____

☐ _____

☐ _____

The copy for these messages is:

☐ In development

☐ Awaiting approval

☐ Approved

The messages will include links to:

☐ Our homepage

☐ A bridge page _____

☐ Another Web site _____

☐ Other _____

The response plan is:

☐ In development

☐ Awaiting approval by _____

☐ Approved by _____

The testing plan is:

☐ In development

☐ Awaiting approval by _____

☐ Approved by _____

The metrics of success used in this campaign will be:	**Success will be achieved at (quantity):**
_____	_____
_____	_____
_____	_____
_____	_____
_____	_____
_____	_____

Prospecting

Advertising is the act of raising awareness and making people feel comfortable with your brand name—it's the art of drawing people into your sphere of influence. Think of it as laying a trap and waiting for the game to come to you. Prospecting, on the other hand, is much more like hunting.

If you've ever been in an outside sales position, you know prospecting means knocking on doors and making phone calls. Lots of doors and lots of calls. You make some assumptions about who might be interested in your offer and you go out and see if you can find them in their natural habitat.

When using email for prospecting, you're sending out a message in hopes of sucking people into the top of the sales funnel: That's the one with suspects hovering over it, prospects in the wide area at the top, and customers dropping out the bottom neck.

Lester Wunderman started off *Being Direct* (Adams Media, 1998) with "Nineteen Things." Number10 is: "Suspects are not Prospects."

> "Prospects" are consumers who are able, ready, and willing to buy; "suspects" are merely eligible to do so. Communicating with prospects reduces the cost of sales; communicating with suspects raises the cost of advertising.

As with other campaigns, you want to focus on just what you're trying to accomplish. Whom are you trying to reach? What do you want the recipients to do when they get your message? How are you going to entice them? How will you track your success? How much are you willing to spend?

As with the research and awareness stages, this is an ideal time to look to an outside source for email addresses of people likely to be interested in your communication. That's a subject worthy of more detailed discussion in Chapter 5, "Setting Your Sights: Targeting Your Message."

PROSPECTING CAMPAIGN WORKSHEET

Campaign identification: _____

The purpose of this campaign is to get prospective customers to (check all that apply):

☐ Ask for more information

☐ Call for an appointment

☐ Sign up for a seminar

☐ Sign up for a trial

☐ Enter the next phase of the sales cycle

☐ Buy_____immediately

☐ Other _____

The specific offers being made in this campaign include:

_____

_____

Other media being used to make these offers:

_____

The primary target for these offers will be people who:

_____

The secondary target for these offers will be people who:

_____

This campaign will reach no fewer than _____and no more than _____people

There will be at least _____and no more than _____total messages in this campaign

The budget for this campaign is: _____

This series will commence on (date) _____and end on (date) _____

Messages will be sent in order to arrive on (day of the week) _____at (time of day) _____

Each offer will be no more than _____lines in length

The format will be

☐ Straight ASCII text

☐ HTML

☐ Both

Distinct offers will be created for the following audience segments:

a) _____

b) _____

c) _____

d) _____

Specific offers:

a) _____

Bridge page link: _____

b) _____

    Bridge page link:_____

c) _____

    Bridge page link:_____

d) _____

    Bridge page link:_____

The copy for these messages is:

    ☐ In development

    ☐ Awaiting approval

    ☐ Approved

The messages will include links to:

    ☐ Our homepage

    ☐ A bridge page

    ☐ Another Web site _____

    ☐ Other _____

The response plan is:

    ☐ In development

    ☐ Awaiting approval by _____

    ☐ Approved by _____

The testing plan is:

    ☐ In development

    ☐ Awaiting approval by _____

☐ Approved by _____

**The metrics of success
used in this campaign will be:**

_____

_____

_____

_____

_____

**Campaign will be deemed
successful at (quantity):**

_____

_____

_____

_____

_____

Qualification

Prospecting is the very top of the funnel that leads to the sale. This is where suspects turn to prospective customers. Once that's accomplished, it's time to separate the wheat from the chaff. Who's really going to buy? What steps are necessary to qualify and then close a prospect?

The qualification process varies widely depending on the type of product sold and the total cost of the deal. To qualify as a buyer of chewing gum, you need to have some loose change in your pocket. To qualify as a buyer of a home, you have to have a solid credit rating and enough cash for the down payment. To qualify as the buyer of a complex satellite networking system, you have to have sufficient need and sufficient internal agreement to make it worth the salesperson's time.

Without the right amount and type of need, the salesperson is just spinning her wheels. A prospect might be interested, but not qualified. So a series of steps is necessary to walk the prospect through the sales cycle. Are they willing to commit to visiting another installation? Are they willing to gather their senior-level executives together for a presentation? Are they willing to reveal their current situation, warts and all, so the sales rep can generate the proper proposal? Do they have the prerequisite technical equipment and capabilities?

All qualification steps happen in their own time and are unique to each industry, each product, and each prospect. The qualification stage of the customer relationship continuum has its own phases. Over time, you can get a general sense of the qualification process and create an outline of the phases each prospect must step through to reach the purchase.

The phases of your sales cycle and just how you use email to move prospects from one phase to another will vary depending on what you're selling. The value of an email campaign is that it lets you schedule the next step for each prospect.

What separates this stage of the relationship continuum from the previous stages is that you now know whom you are dealing with. Chapter 5, "Setting Your Sights: Targeting Your Message," spends some time on this issue. But as you review the following form and determine how you might alter it to meet your specific needs, be cognizant of the need to have previously recorded some attributes about the people you are hoping to move closer to a purchase. *That* particular issue will be addressed in detail in Chapter 8, "Testing Your Talent, Reckoning Your Response, and Managing Your Email."

And as for the offers you create for each of these different prospects, more time will be spent on that in Chapter 6, "Writing an Email Masterpiece."

QUALIFICATION CAMPAIGN WORKSHEET

Campaign identification: _____

The purpose of this campaign is to move prospective customers from phase (X) to phase (Y):

☐ Visited Web site

☐ Talked to sales rep.

☐ Identified competition

☐ Scheduled on-site meeting

☐ Asked for quote

☐ Asked for detailed proposal

☐ Signed up for trial

☐ Identified selection committee

☐ Contract signed

☐ Product/service in use

☐ Other _____

☐ Other _____

The specific offers being made in this campaign include:

_____

_____

_____

_____

Other media being used to make these offers:

_____

The primary target for these offers will be people who:

_____

The secondary target for these offers will be people who:

_____

This campaign will reach no fewer than _____and no more than _____people

There will be at least _____and no more than _____total messages in this campaign

The budget for this campaign is: _____

This series will commence on (date) _____and end on (date) _____

Messages will be sent in order to arrive on (day of the week) _____at (time of day) _____

Each offer will be no more than _____lines in length

The format will be:

☐ Straight ASCII text

☐ HTML

☐ Both

Distinct offers will be created for the following audience segments:

a) _____

b) _____

c) _____

d) _____

Specific offers:

a) _____

Bridge page link:_____

b) _____

Bridge page link:_____

c) _____

Bridge page link:_____

d) _____

Bridge page link:_____

The copy for these messages is:

☐ In development

☐ Awaiting approval

☐ Approved

The messages will include links to:

☐ Our homepage

☐ A bridge page (see offers above)

☐ Another Web site _____

☐ Other _____

The response plan is:

☐ In development

☐ Awaiting approval by _____

☐ Approved by _____

The testing plan is:

☐ In development

☐ Awaiting approval by _____

☐ Approved by _____

The metrics of success used in this campaign will be:	**Campaign will be deemed successful at (quantity):**
_____	_____
_____	_____
_____	_____
_____	_____
_____	_____

Acquisition

Also known as closing the sale, *acquisition* is getting them to sign on the dotted line. Getting them to say yes. Getting them to fork over their hard-earned cash.

This can be as simple as a Web form where they enter their credit card number or as hard as 12 signatures on a 250-page contract. It may require a single banner ad to convince them to make the purchase or an 18-month sales cycle of meetings, presentations, visits to other customers' sites, and golf outings.

The Complex Close

With a very complex sale, this should be a very personal email. An individual sales representative will send a hand-crafted email to the individual on the buying side that comes right out and asks for the sale. While this is no time for a mass-marketing, database-driven, fully automated barrage of messages, there are still some ways you can help the salespeople with this task.

When selling elaborate products, salespeople depend on the marketing department to come up with positioning statements, competitive analyses, branding promotions, and more. They can also look to the folks at corporate headquarters for templates to be used as introductory letters, PowerPoint presentations for use during sales calls, and a whole bucket of boilerplate paragraphs that can be sprinkled throughout a closing message.

The closing message needs to be specific to the prospect, to be sure. But there are a limited number of benefits your product offers and each one of these benefits deserves its own paragraph. The salesperson can then grab the three most critical paragraphs and drop them in place.

```
To: John_Prospect@buyer.com
From: Julie Salesrep@delavangt.com
Re: Now's the time

Hi John:

It was good seeing you last week and working out the final details
of our contract. I understand you have it on Mr. Big's desk at the
moment and I wanted to bring two important issues to your (and his)
attention.

First, because your standards are so very high for this project, I
wanted to remind you that Delavan's aerospace background gives
Delavan a distinct edge in fuel nozzle design, testing, research,
and development.

Second, you mentioned your company's need for high-quality, ISO 9000
parts delivered fast and reliably. Delavan Gas Turbine has been trimming
costs and lead times with cross-functional teams long before the term
"concurrent engineering" was ever coined.

We can get that gas turbine installed and operational in time for your
next development phase if we move on this soon.

Our production backlog is growing and I'd like to encourage you to fax
the completed order page to me before the end of the week. That way I
can be sure to get it into our schedule without a hitch.
Everybody on the Delavan team is looking forward to working with you
closely on this project.

It's our goal to make you look good.
```

It's not very hard to imagine that most of the preceding email message came from pieces of previously produced prose. But it's not that easy for Mr. John Prospect. He really did discuss these issues with Julie and he really does feel strongly about them. They actually do provide a bit more motivation to saunter into Mr. Big's office and ask if the completed order has been signed.

The point is that even with the most personal email, automation and a little hard work in advance can make it easier for salespeople to turn prospects into customers.

The Simple Close

On the opposite side of the sales landscape, you might be selling Birds of North America version 2.5, a birding CD-ROM with pictures, maps, sounds, videos, quizzes, and screen savers, for $70. There's not much in the way of a sales cycle here if you have the right list (see Chapter 5, "Setting Your Sights: Targeting Your Message") and the right offer (see Chapter 6, "Writing an Email Masterpiece").

Just a few sentences can entice the avid birder to move from suspect to buyer in the blink of an eye.

```
To: Birders of America and Canada
From: Thayer Birding Software

Birds of North America is an easy-to-use CD that gives you instant
access to all 925 birds and their songs, videos, range maps, summer and
winter abundance maps, identification tips, habitat description and
more! The taxonomy follows the latest AOU 7th edition checklist.

250 Quizzes test your identification skills. Use the Identify feature to
find a bird -- even if you do not know its name. Birds of North America
also lets you compare photos, range maps, abundance maps and even songs
for two birds...at the same time.

The Avian Jukebox lets you select any group of birds and listen to their
songs. The Birder's Handbook by Ehrlick, Dobkin and Wheye is included in
this CD-ROM in electronic format.

To get all the details about the Birds of North America CD head over to:
http://www.birding.com/bna.htm

Or you can order your copy right now by calling Thayer Birding Software
at 800-865-2473.
```

But let's say you want to make it a two-step process. Rather than just selling them the one product you have on the shelf, you want to try to move them up to something really special. Something with a little more panache. Something with a little more profit.

Up-Selling and Cross-Selling

As you learn more about your customer during the sales cycle, you can start to make suggestions. They're interested in a Ford Explorer? How about the XLT model? Oh, they are already interested in the XLT? Wonderful, then it's time to suggest the Eddie Bauer Edition.

They already seem to have that acquisitive gleam in their eye. They've already made the emotional decision to purchase. Now it's simply time to identify the proper model.

Once they decide on the proper model, it's time to roll out the options. Towing package? Six-CD changer? Running boards? Would you like fries with that? It may be a common punch line, but that last one is a major moneymaker for the fast-food industry.

If you find yourself dealing with buyers who have a choice, there's nothing like a short little email to encourage them to make the better choice. As with all marketing, you don't want to be too aggressive about it. But with email you need to pay a little closer attention.

Email can be a bit aggressive all by itself. A phone call in the middle of dinner, even if it's your mother, is an annoyance. An email reminder to buy something more expensive than the buyer had in mind, even if it's from a trusted source who has their consent, may be a bit pushy.

If you're going to up-sell, do it delicately. If you're selling sports cars, emphasize the extra horsepower of the bigger model. If you're selling room-to-room intercom baby monitors, play up the sensitivity of the more costly choice. If you're trying to get them into an upgraded business suit, accentuate the comfort and the status.

Each product you sell has multiple benefits that may be of varying interest to multiple prospects. Hitting the right combination at the right time turns them into customers. Keep the conversation going and your customers will buy up your product line. At each step of the way, make sure you're there to help them get the most out of the previous purchase. That's the best way to prepare them for the next one.

Customer Management

Right after the sale comes the honeymoon. What does it take to build, ship, install, integrate, and start using your product? Will customers need to cut holes in their walls in order to get it through the door? Will they need to add more memory to their server to install your software? Will they need to upgrade their fuse box to plug in your freezer? What's the difference between light-use customers and heavy-use customers? Will they need you to hold their hand as they traverse the treacherous terrain of buyer's remorse? What does it take to get them from happy buyer to happy user of your products?

This area blends customer service with marketing, but it's all part of customer relationship management. You still have to make sure they're glad they bought it, and you still have to convince them that the entire sequence of installation and training steps is important and necessary to their well-being.

You still have to sell, so you still have to make offers. Entice them to train their new staff. Coax them to bring their car in for its first maintenance service. Remind them that you have the best supply of toner for their new printer. Show them how they can make bigger pancakes by using a little more of your flour.

Because you are reaching out to customers, you have the advantage of knowing everything about how long they've had your product, how much training they've had, and which offer should be the next in line for their attention.

Retention

What happens when a repeat customer stops buying? You've sold the printer and they've stopped coming back for the toner. You've sold the razor and they've stopped calling you for the blades? They bought the Explorer but you've never seen them for maintenance service. You need to reignite these customers.

It's time to reacquaint them with your value proposition. Time to get them fired up and back on board as a happy, recurring customer. It's time for special offers and loyalty programs.

Don Peppers and Martha Rogers (www.1to1.com) like to ponder why companies are so willing to lower prices and cut great deals to bring on new customers when it's the current customers who are the most valuable. If a new customer can get 50 percent off the first purchase, the message sent is that current, happy, loyal customers aren't worth bothering with. That's why the long distance phone industry has spinners— people who change their service every couple of months to take advantage of the "new customer" discounts and freebies. You need to reward your current customer for being loyal.

American Airlines kicked it into high gear in May of 1981 when they launched their Frequent Fliers program. Before that, the world of incentives/affinities/loyalty programs was limited to Green Stamps and Blue Chip Stamps.

According to FrequentFlier.com, the programs boast over 100 million members. The large U.S. FFPs (American's AAdvantage, United's Mileage Plus, Delta's SkyMiles) have more than 20 million members each.

"Members receive 10 million awards per year. What makes loyalty programs attractive (from the consumer standpoint) and effective (from the airline standpoint) is the reward side of the equation. And for most FFP members, the reward is a free ticket. The most popular among members of U.S. FFPs: tickets to Hawaii and London," says FrequentFlier.com.

Strategies for Keeping Customers

You have an insurance policy against a fire burning up your IT department or a flood taking out your warehouse. But what are you doing to protect your most valuable asset, your customers?

Inside 1 to 1

Don Peppers and Martha Rogers
May 1997

www.1to1.com

There are at least four separate strategies an enterprise can use to improve customer retention, and each is effective in its own way, depending on the nature of the customer base and the enterprise's capabilities. In order of their increasing effectiveness, they are:

Continues

Inside 1 to 1 (Continued)

1. Customer recognition
2. Loyalty purchasing
3. Product quality and customer satisfaction
4. Customization and collaboration

1. CUSTOMER RECOGNITION

Recognize MVCs ("Most Valuable Customers") with some sort of special treatment. This approach can be especially effective in a high-end, personal service business. Inter-Continental hotels and resorts produce personalized luggage tags for their most valuable customers—baggage tags that discreetly but immediately identify a guest as a Six Continents Club member. When a bell hop sees such an emblem, he knows that the baggage owner is an MVC, and he pays immediate, special attention to this customer.

The elements of a customer recognition program should be both personal and practical. If a customer is valuable enough to be an MVC, then he is almost certainly valuable enough to warrant some level of actual human contact, or at least a zero-defects, customized letter.

There is a business practice we call "best-interests" marketing which should be an element of any customer recognition program. It involves putting a customer's own best interests at the forefront of whatever policy or marketing program is being executed. For example, phone companies and banks should review the accounts of MVCs and recommend the best plan for each customer. While best-interests is a business practice that makes sense when dealing with any customer, it requires a level of personal care and attention (as opposed to a standardized, one-size-fits-all program) that is often impractical to apply to levels much below that of an MVC.

2. LOYALTY PURCHASING

This is what frequent flyer programs are all about. Because they have escalating awards rates with mileage earned, frequent flyer plans are good examples of how to gain greater customer loyalty as individual customer volume increases.

Buying customer loyalty is the first instinct at most large firms when they are faced with significant customer attrition. But as a tactic it has limited long-term utility. It is easily matched by the competition, and it often smells to customers like just another cheap marketing promotion. In the long run, purchasing a customer's loyalty is not much different from reducing the price to attract new customers.

Even frequent flyer programs, with their escalating rewards structures and a highly attractive "currency" (mileage), provide only a short-term retention advantage in the face of predatory customer acquisition efforts. American Airlines can steal United's best customers by (a) identifying them individually, either through a marketing promotion or by partnering with another travel firm, and then (b) selectively "upping the ante" of privileges, mileage bonuses or upgrades—but just for these particular MVCs. United's only defense against such loyalty "share stealing" would be to raise the ante itself, and the struggle once again would descend to the level of price cutting and margin squeezing.

3. PRODUCT QUALITY AND CUSTOMER SATISFACTION

There is no substitute for quality. No customer will return for more of a bad product, so having product quality at least on par with the competition is essential for a 1to1 enterprise. Keep in mind, however that customer satisfaction by itself is usually not sufficient to generate loyalty.

Many firms measure their customer satisfaction index (CSI) by surveying customers and asking them to rate the product to indicate whether they are "very satisfied" or "very dissatisfied." Some companies go so far as to incorporate CSI into the overall management of the business, constantly comparing one division to another, this year to last, and so forth. Among firms that do rely on CSI measurements, there is a widely held belief that the only kind of customer satisfaction that really counts is the "top box"—the highest possible satisfaction rating. Studies have shown that it is not enough to achieve satisfaction ratings that are merely good (satisfactory satisfaction?). Only stellar performance seems to have any measurable benefit in terms of customer loyalty at all.

4. CUSTOMIZATION AND COLLABORATION

By far the most effective strategy for keeping customers is for a firm to customize its service to each individual customer's needs, allowing the customer to "teach" the firm how he likes to be served, and then giving the service or product back to him according to those specifications. In this way, the more the customer teaches the firm, the more difficult it will be for him to obtain an equivalent level of service from another firm—because he would first have to re-teach the competitor what he has already gone to the trouble of teaching the original firm. This is the nature of a "Learning Relationship" with a customer, a relationship that gets smarter and smarter with every interaction.

Reliable, dependable customer retention occurs only when a customer is committed to the enterprise, relative to its competitors. The best way to ensure this commitment is to collaboratively link individual customer feedback to the customization of products and services. If you can convince a customer to spend some time or energy teaching your firm how to cater better to his or her individual tastes, then you can keep this customer loyal for a longer period, out of the customer's own self-interest. The more time and energy the customer expends in teaching the enterprise how to customize to his own tastes, the more trouble it will be for the customer to obtain the same level of customized service from a competitor.

Learning Relationships are based on the deceptively simple idea that when a customer spends time teaching your firm, the customer himself develops a stake in the benefits of this learning. Getting an individual customer to teach the firm about his own particular needs is a completely foreign idea for any business not accustomed to thinking of its customers as individually interactive.

Any firm seriously interested in improving customer loyalty should be on the lookout for products and services that can be tailored to individual tastes and needs, and then it should use these products to lock customers into Learning Relationships.

You don't necessarily have to implement a buy-ten-get-one-free program of your own to keep customers coming back. Sometimes it's simply a matter of reminding them you're still thinking of them. Offering a newsletter (see Chapter 9, "Stories from the Front Line") can be a very effective way to keep your name on the tips of customers' tongues.

No matter what you're sending out, whether it's a newsletter, a great discount offer, a pat on the back, or a reminder that you think about your customers all day and dream of them all night, there's a tricky question of how often you should get in touch.

Frequency and Timing

Let's see the hands of everybody out there who never received an AOL diskette or CD in the mail. . . . We thought so. Direct mail through the postal system is regulated by cost. If, like America Online, you could afford to send out a billion diskettes and CDs, you would, but paper, ink, and postage tend to limit the number of times we get in touch with prospects and customers.

Email isn't like that. You still pay for good ideas. You still pay for good words. You still pay for good follow-through, and you pay for good email addresses. But not for materials and delivery. With the monetary restriction removed, you can perpetually pummel prospects with propositions. So why not send something every hour? Because there is a point at which they'll stop responding.

How Much Will They Stand For?

Once is happenstance, twice is circumstance, three times is enemy action.
Goldfinger, Ian Fleming

Are three enough? Are six too many?
Laxative commercial regarding the vagaries of the prune

How often should you get in touch with your customers? How often are they going to be pleased to hear about your offer to sell their home, fix their car, or straighten their teeth? A lot of your decision will depend on the target audience and their buying cycle.

Are Three Enough?

Jupiter Communications' 1998 report on direct email marketing pointed out that the rise in the amount of email people receive will cause email burnout. Commercial e-solicitations will have to compete against notes from friends and family. In a survey they conducted, email users told Jupiter that access to email anywhere and anytime was their most avid desire, with spam filters as a very close second.

One-third of the respondents to the Jupiter survey said they don't read email that comes from senders they don't recognize. The lesson? Make sure you keep your name in front of your prospects and customers frequently enough to keep your name on their minds.

Conventional wisdom in advertising, sage advice in direct mail, and statistical calculations in Web site banner advertising show that three impressions are optimal for generating the most response out of a campaign. Only two impressions leaves money on the table, and the fourth and fifth tend to be recognized only as something that can be safely ignored.

In *Successful Direct Marketing Methods* (NTC Business Books, 1996), Bob Stone lists 25 "Timeless Truths About Direct Mail." One of these is, "A follow-up to the same list within 30 days will pull 40–50% of the first mailing." When mailing paper, the postman should always ring twice. Through email, it depends entirely on the type of relationship you have.

The goal is to get them to think of you often enough, so that when it's actually time to make a purchase decision, your product comes easily to mind as one of the contenders. If you only send us one message every six months, we may make a buying decision in the fifth month and not remember to include you in the running. But much worse than that is the relatively short half-life of permission.

Memory fades. People forget. What caught their attention two months ago simply doesn't matter to them anymore. If you don't remind them that they were interested, they may well forget that they even signed up. It's very common these days to get hate mail from people who registered for your valuable insights and then promptly forgot.

Nick Usborne is a direct response copywriter and chief forking officer of forkinthe-head.com. He spelled it out pretty well in his July 26, 1999, article in the daily ClickZ newsletter (www.clickz.com) called "Permission Fades":

> Permission marketing is all the rage right now. In fact, it's so cool almost everyone is practicing it. Trouble is, a lot of people appear to have forgotten how permission works. Or at least, how it works at its best. Here is an attitude that appears to be prevailing out there right now . . .
>
> "Hey, we got Nick's permission once, so now we can email him as much as we like."
>
> I don't think so. In real life, permission granted isn't a contract; it's a state of mind. The customer's state of mind.
>
> Let me put that another way.
>
> The moment your customer no longer feels as if you have permission, you no longer have permission. Whether you like it or not. The trouble is, in most cases, you'll never get to know when your customer is approaching or has crossed that line. As a result, permission granted can turn into, "How the heck can I get off this dumb list?" before you know it.
>
> And long before that moment, the likelihood of your customer responding to any offers will fall to almost zero. That gradual erosion of permission sends your conversion rates down the tube in a hurry. As an example, I signed up for one of the major points/reward programs a while back. I was curious to see how it worked.
>
> Here's my experience, as a real life customer:
>
> 1. I went to their site, looked around and signed up.
>
> Key point: Now, about two months later, I have absolutely no recollection of their site. I don't remember what it looked like. More significantly, I don't remember what I did there. Did I just sign up? Or did I opt-in to receive information on particular areas of interest to me? I have no idea. Just can't remember.

This is pretty important, because if I can't remember what permission I granted, they essentially no longer have my permission. They may think they have. But in terms of my actual participation in the program, they don't.

2. I waited with anticipation for my first offers.

Sure. When permission granted is fresh, it's exciting. In fact, as I recall, I was kind of annoyed that it took them a couple of days to get back with their first offer.

3. I continued to be interested for about a month.

These guys send me an email exactly once every two weeks. To begin with, that felt fine. Not too many, not too few. But now? Now I just want to get off the list. Why? Because they let my permission erode, lapse and collapse.

4. Now I just want them to go away.

Trouble is, they don't want me to go. Can I get off the list with one click on the emails they send me? Nope. Do they tell me at the end of their mailings how I can say goodbye? Nope.

They got me. They want to keep me. And they are going to make it hard for me to leave.

Is this smart? Nope. Because now they are spamming me.

Permission withdrawn means that your future emails are spam. You can argue that technically I'm wrong. But who cares what you think? It only matters what the customer thinks. And if the customer feels they're being emailed stuff they no longer want, you're spamming them. So what's the answer?

Think about it this way.

If you go on a date and get permission to come by his or her home the next evening, have you just received permission to go to that person's home every evening for the next five years? No, you haven't.

If you want permission granted to translate into long-term sales and a growing ROI, you need to keep that permission fresh and renewed. Those points/reward people should give me the opportunity to renew, refresh or even withdraw my permission on an ongoing basis.

In a permission-based online relationship, the customer's perception is your reality— whether you like it or not. So treat that permission with care. Look after it. Respect it. Renew it. Continue to earn it. Or the whole concept of permission marketing could quickly descend into another sneaky way to spam people.

Be sure to keep the relationship alive by not letting them forget who you are. On the other hand, even the most anticipated, thought-provoking, valuable communication can become unwelcome when overdone.

Are Six Too Many?

A Word A Day (www.wordsmith.org/awad/index.html) is a wonderful daily blurb that offers just enough value to have attracted over 200,000 linguaphiles in more than 167 countries. A special word, its definition, and a short aphorism take but the work of a moment to read, enjoy, and delete. Started by Anu Garg, an Internet engineer at AT&T Labs, AWAD, as it's affectionately called, is a joy. It's simple. It's noncommercial. It's brief. But Five Words A Day? *Ten* Words A Day? Too much. A Word A Day without the aphorisms? It wouldn't be the same—it wouldn't be enough.

The only other daily emails that survive are brief (www.joke-of-the-day.com) and timely (weather reports, traffic conditions). The content changes on a daily basis. The likelihood that your company will come up with a daily message that people will sign up for in droves is limited. If you come up with a good one, spin it off as a dot-com company and file for an IPO immediately.

ResultsLab (www.resultslab.com) says the key to being able to mail frequently, and have it appreciated instead of resented, is to make sure that each mailing is a gift of learning, news, or valuable links (see Figure 4.3). Make sure your mailings are never sales-y; and never look like spam; never employ pressure, manipulation, or evasion. These destroy trust and loyalty.

The best suggestion? Ask your customers and then test. Try it and see if it works. You were hoping for more advice than that? Just wait until Chapter 8, "Testing Your Talent, Reckoning Your Response, Managing Your Email."

Finally, try to do everything in your power to ensure recipients don't end up with multiple copies of your message. This will hurt your brand quickly. It makes you look

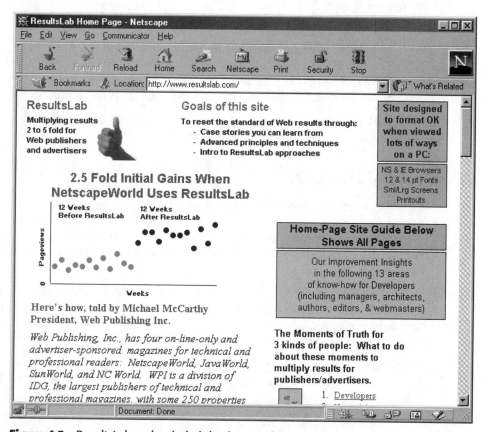

Figure 4.3 ResultsLab makes it their business to increase response to banner ads, internal site links, and, for the last several years, direct email.

like a spammer indiscriminately sending off messages without paying the least amount of attention to where they go. In an article in *Webmerchant* magazine (www.webmerchant.com; Summer 1999), Regina Brady, vice president of interactive services for Acxiom/DirectMedia, said, "The worst thing in the world is for the same potential or existing customer to receive multiple mailings from you at once. Merge-purge to maintain your list."

Plan a Series

You don't need to fire all of your guns at once. You might want to put together a series of messages that go out over time. Remember the old Burma Shave signs. They were short, sweet, and to the point; they offered light humor; and they were placed about three seconds apart. That's not recommended for email.

Send us email

Too close together

And we will cut this

Email tether

(and unsubscribe)

"Each mailing can have a different theme," according to Ron Richards. "For publishers mailing four times a month, a schedule should be set up. For example, the first email each month introduces the new issue, the next a special topic, the next the new mid-month topics, and the last can describe some special event or product feature."

Like Goldilocks, you've discovered the importance of not too few, and not too many, but just enough. The next question is, when?

When's Good for You?

In that same Summer 1999 *Webmerchant* article, Acxiom's Brady said, "If you're marketing to consumers, you can get away with mailing toward the end of the week because many will check their email on the weekends. On the other hand, if you're a business to business marketer, you should have your email in there first thing Monday morning."

Let's see the hands of all those out there who are a little bit overwhelmed by the amount of email you face at the office on Monday morning? Just as we thought. Monday morning may actually be the worst day for email because the old e-in-box is clogged with spam. Here's a different approach, discovered quite by accident.

Jim Sterne's *Full Sterne Ahead* newsletter goes out periodically, although not with regularity. After it was sent out one Friday afternoon, Chris Carter at Nuforia wrote back:

```
I was just reading your newsletter, and found myself asking "why?".
Wait! Before you think of this as a slam (it's not)... I'm flooded with
info (duh). So, I was trying to figure out why I was reading this par-
```

ticular one... Not just because of your compelling content (sorry), but rather it was the timing. Friday afternoon. I'm sitting here in my office, worn down by the week, and putting off any of the less savory and/or taxing items left on my To-Do List. Then, voila, there is _Full_Sterne_Ahead_. I know that the rule is that press releases should *never* go out on Friday if at all avoidable, so I naturally assumed that this would apply to newsletters as well. I have changed my mind... You hit me when I was most vulnerable, and therefore receptive, to giving you my attention.

When's best?

Run a test.

To Each His Own

If you are a Web marketing connoisseur, you automatically consider a truth we hold to be self-evident on the Web: Let the customer control his or her own destiny.

The whole idea of one-to-one marketing is remembering details about each customer. Put them in control of the relationship. Let them decide which topics they're interested in. Let them choose how often they want to get an update. Let them choose when your email shows up.

And then work like hell to ensure their wishes are respected.

Flow Control

The larger your company, the bigger the problem. Lots of different divisions sending lots of different messages to lots of different recipients? Fine. But what happens when the lists everybody is using are not so different? What happens is that your very favorite people on the planet—your customers—end up with lots of messages from one company.

To you, your company is made up of divisions and departments and business units and they all run in different directions after different marketplaces with different goals, different budgets, and different management styles. To your customer, your company looks like your company. That's it. One monolithic black box from which all of these emails flow.

Jupiter Communications recommends a gatekeeper to manage the outpouring of email in order to protect each individual in your collective databases. The master of merge/purge would be the final owner of the Send button. If the sales team has a great idea for up-selling current customers, your promotions people are running new contests, the public relations folks put out a new press release, and customer service wants everybody to know about their new online knowledge base—all multiplied by several product lines—even opt-in email becomes annoying.

Somebody needs to ride herd on the torrent of electronic transmissions to protect the customers on the one hand, and the company's brand on the other.

Ready, Aim . . .

You have now identified the customer relationship continuum stage you're addressing. You know which stage of the sales cycle your audience is in at the moment. You've worked out the details of when your e-terms of endearment will be unleashed upon the happy beneficiary. Now it's time to focus the scope of your email cannon on the audience themselves.

CHAPTER 5

Setting Your Sights:
Targeting Your Message

You've got the best hardwood bow money can buy. You found the top-of-the-line nylon and wax to create the string. You've turned perfectly straight arrows on your own lathe and you hand-fletched (attached feathers to) each one. You're ready. Now then, where's the target?

Permission marketers need to determine the characteristics of prospects who would be most able, willing, and ready to buy. In some industries, the best client targets are those who bought most recently, who buy most frequently, and who spend the most. Good prospects can also be identified by age, gender, income, education, geographic location, and so forth.

Occasions can also be a good segmentation denominator. Newlywed couples will be looking for housing, furniture, appliances, bank loans, and so on; college freshmen will be on the lookout for credit cards and computers; new mothers will be in the market for baby clothes and toys. Consumer interests are also easy to identify. Computer buffs, gourmet cooks, outdoor sports enthusiasts, gardeners, thespians, philatelists, and fletchers are all ripe for targeting.

Once the target market is identified, it's time to find an opt-in list for that target. Where do you find lists of people who might be interested in your words of e-wisdom? There are only three ways to find those names: Rent them from a primary opt-in list owner, rent them from an opt-in list management company, or start collecting them yourself.

Renting a List

A rented list is a living list and a purchased list is dead. A purchased list is static. If somebody offers to sell you a list of email addresses, smile, thank them, and then quietly move away from them as quickly as possible. You don't buy lists from magazines, you rent them. That's what you should do with opt-in email lists.

A living, rented list has people subscribing and unsubscribing all the time. Two seconds before you send out your message, more people decided they needed to know or decided they had enough. That means you always get the most qualified people.

The first place most people think to look for a list is the same place they look for postal direct mail lists: You go to the people who are directly collecting names and permission. How do you find them? The same way you find magazine lists. You go to a broker.

Going for Broker

List brokers are companies that keep track of who has lists to rent. They've been at it for quite a while and they serve two purposes. First, they help you find a list worth your attention. Second, they help people who have lists to rent find people to rent them.

If you have any type of list at all, there may be a market for it. Obviously, you have a list of customers. Do you want just anybody to mail anything to your customers? No. You want to make sure (1) the stuff they receive is actually of interest to them, and (2) your competitors don't get anywhere near them. The list broker manages your list for you and takes a commission.

You also have lists you never knew were important. People who came to a free seminar on self-improvement. People who asked for more information on saving for retirement. People who asked for a list of bed-and-breakfasts in the Northeast. All of these might be of use to somebody with a brochure to mail.

They might also be of use to somebody with an email to send. That's where we start approaching that fine line.

Worldata Information Marketing Services (www.worldata.com) brokers lists to the business-to-business, consumer, high-technology, financial, and publishing markets. They have over 100 sales, marketing, and technical people all working at matching up the right list to the right renter, and they offer a handful of opt-in email lists (see Figure 5.1).

But approach these lists with caution.

"Email Addresses of Individuals Who Have Requested Free Trial Subscriptions to Technology Publications" might sound useful if you're selling analog-to-digital converters, but it's worth digging a little deeper to find out more about this list.

They describe this list this way:

Tech Magazines.com (www.techmags.com) is a new Internet site that allows users to apply for free trial subscriptions to many popular computer related publications. The online site also provides complete descriptions of each magazine so that users can deter-

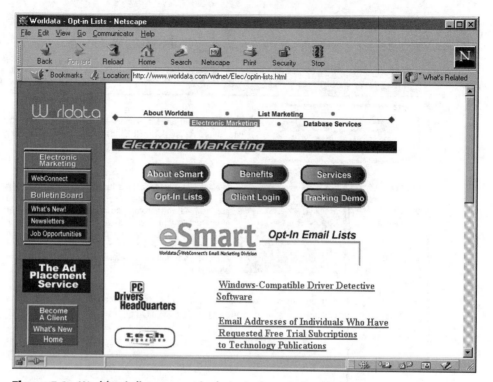

Figure 5.1 Worldata's lists are opt-in, but are they on the mark?

mine which magazines are of interest to them. The free trial magazine index includes magazines on a variety of professional computer subjects, including data warehousing, disaster recovery, software development, Ecommerce, web development, networking, telecommunications, system administration, UNIX, Windows and Windows NT development, programming, call center/help desks, C++ and more.

The Tech Magazines.com Email List includes the Email addresses of individuals who have accessed the Tech Magazines.com site and requested free trial subscriptions to technology publications. They are professionals at businesses and home who are interested in technology. They include technology professionals, MIS professionals, developers, and IT resellers. All these individuals have opted to receive targeted information.

Sounds great. And Tech Magazines.com looks very useful to the subscriber (see Figure 5.2).

Unfortunately, it's not as up-front as it might be about what the subscriber might get besides magazines. The term *up-front* is used very purposefully here. Tech Magazines.com has a "Terms and Conditions" page that clearly spells out what you get.

The information we collect is used to notify consumers about updates to our Web site, shared with other reputable organizations to help them contact consumers for marketing purposes and used by us to contact consumers for marketing purposes.

If you do not want to receive email from us in the future, please let us know by sending email to us at the above address and telling us that you do not want to receive email from our company.

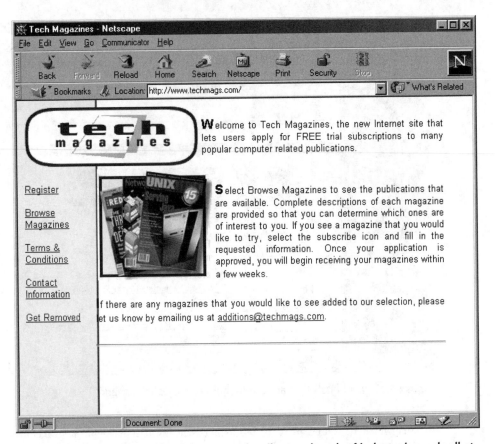

Figure 5.2 Tech Magazines.com lets you subscribe to a bunch of industry journals all at once.

From time to time, we make the email addresses of those who access our site available to other reputable organizations whose products or services we think you might find interesting. If you do not want us to share your email address with other companies or organizations, please let us know by sending email to us at the above address and telling us that you do not want us to share your email address with other companies.

From time to time, we make our customer email list available to other reputable organizations whose products or services we think you might find interesting. If you do not want us to share your email address with other companies or organizations, please let us know by sending email to us at the above address.

The subscription form does not have a direct link to these terms and conditions and the terms themselves point out they are using an opt-out method of list management. As a result, these folks may not be the most receptive to an email about analog-to-digital converters.

For the widest variety of lists, turn to the same source you've used for postal lists: SRDS.

The SRDS Direct Marketing List Source (www.srds.com) launched index and search functions that highlight email lists in June of 1999. At that point, they had identified over 200 different lists that included email addresses. In their press release, they pointed out, "The SRDS market classifications that have email lists vary widely, and contain some surprising niche markets. Business email lists range from the obvious (computers, business firms and executives) to the unusual (mushroom growers, hairdressers, and painters/decorators). When targeting consumers, subscribers might expect to reach those with home computers, but they can also reach sports fans, philanthropic contributors, and even mobile home owners."

The SRDS subscriber hunts down those lists online (see Figures 5.3 through 5.5).

Reading the listing for *The Industry Standard,* we learn that it's owned and managed by IDG Communications in Framingham, Massachusetts; it caters to senior-level executives, known as *Internet business strategists,* who are responsible for driving the new multi-billion-dollar Internet economy; and its audience is 78 percent male, 15 percent female.

SDRS lets you know right up front that *Industry Standard* subscribers "gave direct permission through an opt-out question to receive third party emails." This is the most honorable example of subscription information you're likely to find. It *is* opt-out, but only the most scrupulous Web managers would call it so.

The sign-up page at www.thestandard.com offers nine different choices for the type of content that might interest you. Then they ask the all-important question: Would

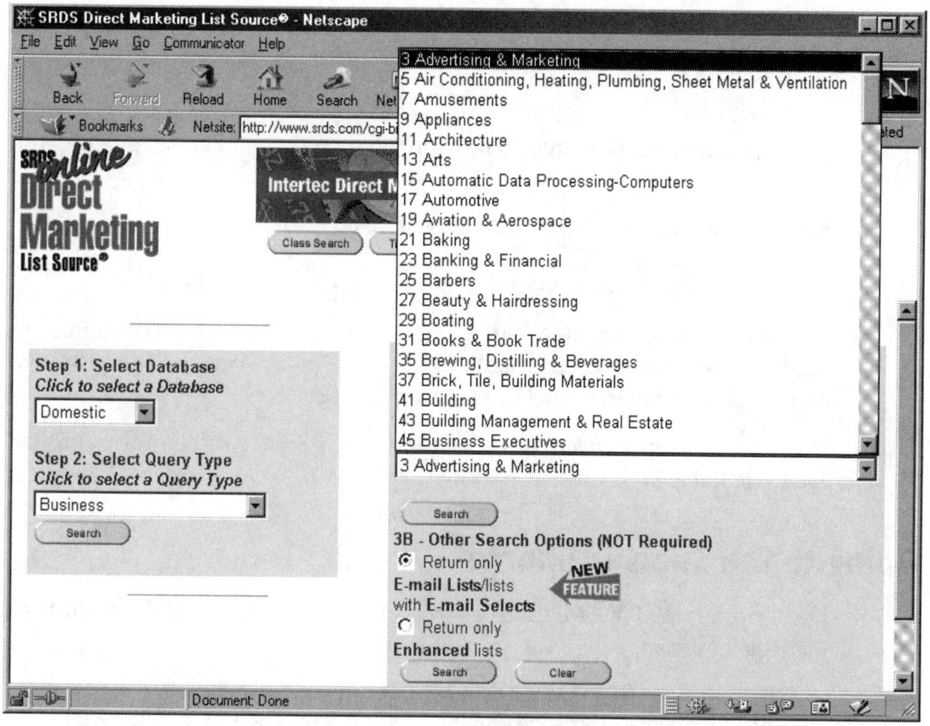

Figure 5.3   A simple interface lets SRDS users choose from over 200 categories of lists.

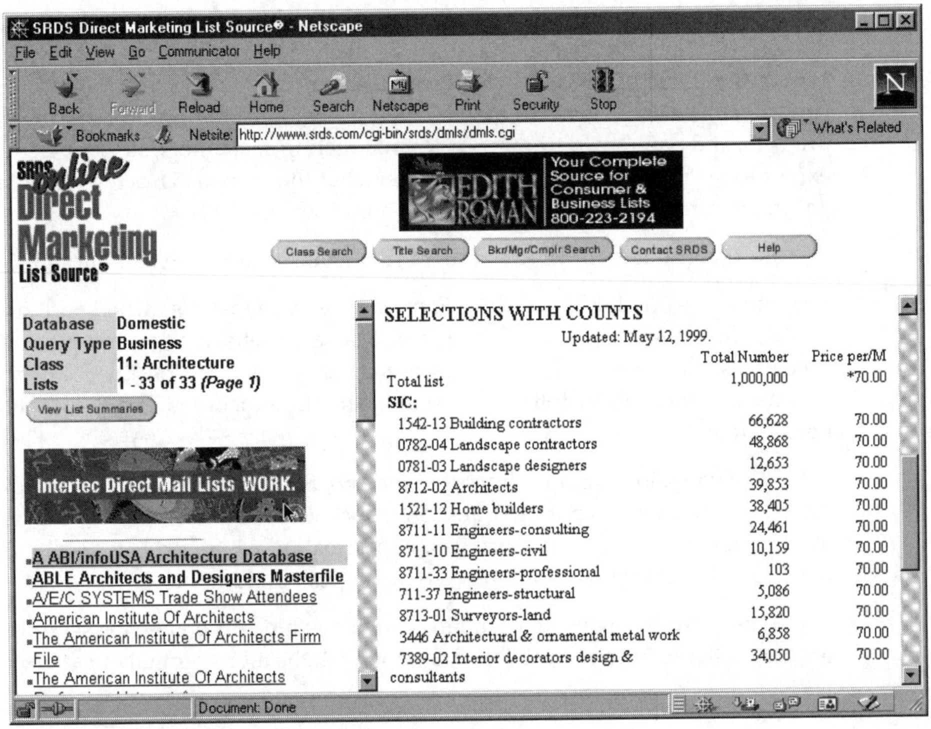

Figure 5.4 Each list contains a further breakdown of who's in the list and what it'll cost to reach them.

you like to receive more information on what you've explicitly signed up for? (See Figure 5.6.)

Had the magazine set the default to No (X), instead of Yes (B) . . .

```
<input TYPE="radio" NAME="EmaPerm" VALUE="B" CHECKED>
```

. . . it would have been an opt-in list. The vast majority of email collectors and renters might not have been so conscientious and would have called it opt-in anyway. Hats off to this publication for being as accurate as possible.

Once *The Industry Standard* has been located, it's time to call on the publisher directly. That would be IDG.

Going to the Specific Source

Head over to the IDG Web site (www.idglist.com) and you can learn quite a bit about the lists they manage.

THE INDUSTRY STANDARD Email List can be selected in the following ways: For more information contact Christine Cahill at christine_cahill@idg.com or click here.

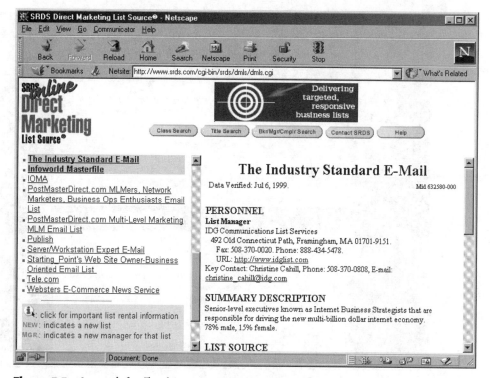

Figure 5.5 A search for "business executives" can lead to the subscribers of *The Industry Standard* magazine.

JOB TITLE—$10.00/M

CEO/President/Chairman/Owner/Partner/Board Member

COO/EVP/SVP/GM

VP Business Development/Strategic Development

CFO/VP Finance/Treasurer

VP Sales/VP Marketing/Chief Marketing Officer

VP New Media/VP Interactive/VP New Technologies/Chief Interactive
   Officer

VP IS/CIO/VP Telecommunications

VP R&D/CTO/CS

VP Other

IS/IT Director

Director Other

Analyst/Consultant

Department Manager/Project Manager

Webmaster

Other

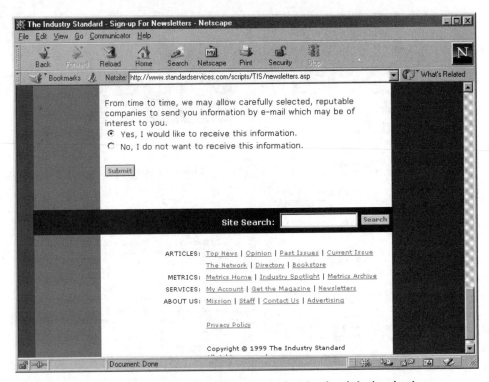

Figure 5.6 *The Industry Standard* could be opt-in, but for the default selection.

PRIMARY BUSINESS—$10.00/M

General Industries

Finance/Banking/Insurance/Real Estate/Venture Capital

Legal/Recruitment

Entertainment/Broadcast/Cable

Publishing/Media

Manufacturing (non-computer/telecom)

Retail

Utilities/Transportation/Travel/Hospitality

Aerospace/Engineering/Construction

Health/Medical

Advertising/Public Relations/Marketing

Consulting

Government/Education

Business Services

Technology

Computer Manufacturer

Software and Services

New Media/Internet/Multimedia

Telecom/ISP/Communication Services

Commercial/Internet Online Service

Technology/VARs/System Integrators/Reseller

Computer/Internet Consulting

Web Developer/Web Design/Interactive Marketing

Other

UTILIZATION OF THE INTERNET—$20.00/M

Direct Sales/E-Commerce

Customer Support/Retention/Loyalty

Vendor/Supplier Relations/Extranet

Internal Employee Relations and Support/Intranet

Publishing/Content/Media

Advertising/Marketing/Lead Generation

Telephony/Video Communications

Archiving/Catalog/Library

Other

INTERNET DEVELOPMENT SPENDING—$20.00/M

$100 Million or more

$50 Million to $99,999,999

$20 Million to $49,999,999

$10 Million to $19,999,999

$5 Million to $9,999,999

$1 Million to $4,999,999

$500,000 to $999,999

$250,000 to $499,999

$25,000 to $249,999

Less than $25,000

If it suits your needs, you can send a message to all VPs of business development and strategic development in the retail industry who use the Internet for direct sales and spend between $5 million and $10 million on Internet development.

With almost 40,000 subscriber email addresses, ID charges $300 per thousand base price ($300 CPM) and $125 per thousand transmit price. The minimum order is 4000 names or $1700. You'll pay another $10 per thousand to choose by job title, $20 for the Internet development spending category, and so forth.

Deb Goldstein, president of IDG List Services, kicked off the email rental business for IDG in the summer of 1998 with email questionnaires to subscribers of Java World and Sunworld Online, asking if they would like to receive third-party email. About 20 percent declined. Right on the border between opt-in and opt-out.

As is true with printed magazines, email lists are collected by electronic publications of narrower and narrower interests. If you want to center soy eaters in your e-crosshairs, you can find a place to do it at www.soyfoods.com.

The U.S. Soyfoods Directory (www.soyfoods.com) publishes *Soyfoods USA,* a free email newsletter about tofu, tempeh, meat alternatives, and other soyfoods, which includes new recipes every month (see Figure 5.7). This email newsletter is "designed to inform media sources, dietitians, and consumers about the latest soyfoods information."

When you subscribe, you are notified:

It is our policy NOT to sell or distribute names and addresses of subscribers to SOY-FOODS USA unless you indicate otherwise. Occasionally, soyfoods manufacturers wish to "rent" our email list for the purpose of announcing new products, promotions and discount coupons. The list is regulated to prevent abuse, and we will rent it only for those purposes we deem appropriate for Soyfoods USA subscribers. Please indicate whether or not you wish to receive this information by email (you can always unsubscribe later if you wish).

So these people are willing to receive commercial email generally connected to the world of soybeans as a way of paying for the newsletter. Just as we're all willing to put up with TV commercials as a way of paying for the programming that beams into

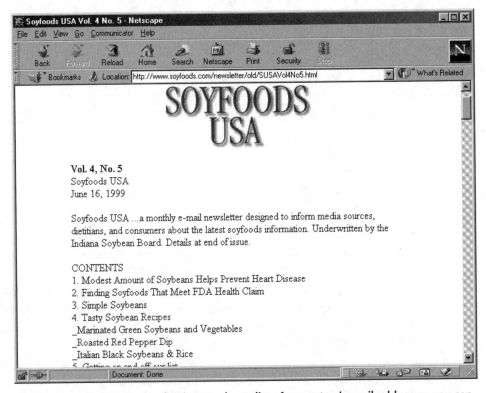

Figure 5.7 The U.S. Soyfoods Directory has a list of soy eaters' email addresses you can rent.

our homes. But there is a type of list that provides a more robust audience. An audience more likely to respond. An audience that has an active interest in a *specific* area and who *explicitly signed up to receive email about it.* Pure opt-in/permission lists.

Renting from a Permission (Opt-in) Service

Yesmail.com is an opt-in email network. It manages its own list of people who sign up at the site, and it allows other list holders to add their recipients to the database, giving network partners access to a wider audience, and giving network partner audiences access to a wider variety of targeted information.

From the recipient's perspective, it's all very simple as described at www.yesmail.com:

> With your My.YesMail account you'll get exactly the offers and information you want, only when you want them. It's your remote control to tap into the YesMail Network. An Internet community where you, the member, are in control over the information you receive and it's FREE! Just take a look at the tools you'll get:
>
> **MY.INTERESTS**
> Instead of surfing the Internet looking for information, it's brought directly to you. Select from over 1,000 categories of information that interest you or recommend a new one. Your My.Interests profile lets you quickly and easily tell us what you want to hear about and more importantly—what you don't.
>
> **MY.SUBSCRIPTIONS**
> Unsure what lists and sites you've subscribed to while surfing the Net? Well now you can use My.Subscriptions to keep track of all the email lists and electronic newsletters you've asked for. Choose which ones you want and let YesMail software handle subscriptions and cancellations—through your My.YesMail account.
>
> **MY.EVENTS**
> Sometimes you may forget what you want, or more importantly when you want it! Birthdays, anniversaries, holidays, business meetings, or any other event that you need to remember can be set up in your My.Events profile. We'll send you a reminder along with some suggestions of just what you might want to get for that all important event via email prior to the big day.

From the marketer's perspective it gets a touch more sophisticated.

Selecting a YesMail Audience

With over 7 million people across 1000 interests, you choose exactly whom you want each message to reach and when. You select an audience by searching for a category/characteristic and mix or match them to shape the audience you want. Instead of just selecting several hundred thousand computer enthusiasts or professionals, you can drill down into computer peripherals. Instead of selecting 100,000 people interested in computer peripherals, you can narrow your criteria to the 60,000 or so who specifically identified printers as their main area of interest.

Yesmail.com personnel help create your target audience by using an automated thesaurus to recommend related categories/characteristics on search results. Each selected market segment goes together like a recipe. More than just interests, some records have geographic data, personal demographics (gender, age, education, marital status, income level), and business demographics (job title, department, organization people size, organization revenue size, industry) to help narrow the field. The right mix makes for the best results and each mix gets a specific title, so you can identify multiple audiences for multiple messages and reach out to them in the future without having to rewrite the recipe.

Audiences can be made up of unions of these categories (everybody interested in printers, plus everybody interested in graphics software) as well as intersections (everybody interested in scanners on the West Coast). You can also spread a target audience size over selected categories by flat or weighted percentages.

At each step, the YesMail system keeps track of how many you've identified and how much it'll cost to send out a message to them. That makes it very easy to create a campaign with an eagle eye on your budget.

You can set up a whole string of messages to go out to specific audiences, at specific times, and in response to specific links they've clicked on in your message.

Choosing the Right List Vendor

Now that you know how it works, it's time to pick the best vendor for the job.

The big question to separate the players from the wannabes is how many lists they have and how many names overall. Granted, if it's only one list that happens to be made up of just the sort of people you want, then it's worth talking to them. But, chances are, you're in the market for a large number of people for a serious cross-reference selection.

How did they come by those names? Were they pure opt-in? If you ever hear the word *harvested,* it's time to put down the phone and hope they don't have Caller ID on their phones. Harvesters send spiders out to collect email addresses off of Web sites and from newsgroups and lists. Spiders are programs that roam the Internet looking for email addresses and reporting back to their keepers. They'll grab webmaster@company.com and staff@company.com and every other email address listed for all to see.

To make sure you understand how different vendors create different lists, ask them for the specific language used to get people to sign up. That makes it much easier to compare apples to apples.

Next, check for the qualification quality of the people on the list. Anybody will sign up for a chance to win a million dollars. Did these people identify their interests? Did they fill out a questionnaire? Did they leave their names and addresses, and say yes to receiving vendor email in exchange for an esoteric white paper indicating a strong interest in your special area?

Ask your prospective vendors what happens when they send out commercial messages. What percentage of the addresses in their database bounce? What percentage unsubscribe? What's been the typical response rate for email sent to these lists?

Price will be an important guide. Don't forget to get all of the numbers. IDG, the magazine publisher, has a base price of $300 per thousand for some lists, but they have another $150 per thousand transmit charge as well.

What's the vendor policy when it comes to running tests? You'd like to test your format by having them send one to you. Can they accommodate you? You'd like to run small tests to see what the response is going to be. Do they make it easy? Do they charge extra for that?

How long does it take them to get your message out to the masses from the time you get it to them? Some shops can turn a message around in a day; some take several days. Some will quote you a time in hours.

What are the vendor policies and requirements regarding the To: field and the From: field? Does it have to be from them? Does it have to be from you? What does the header information look like? Do they insist on three paragraphs on how to unsubscribe? Or do they handle it with more aplomb? What about at the end of your message? What additional language will they tack onto the bottom?

Finally, ask them for references. Sure, they'll give you the names of their best customers. Who wouldn't? It's up to you to dig a little deeper. Engage these considered vendors in some casual conversation and throw in a question or two that's not related to reference checking. "Has anybody had really good results with HTML email? Has anybody learned something the hard way about it? Really? Who was that?"

Another way to find out about other customers is to ask the customers. Sometimes they know. When you *do* get one on the phone, you can ask them negative questions until you're blue in the face, but you won't get far. Nobody likes to admit they made a bad choice. "That vendor? Oh, yeah, they were great. I never had a problem with them."

So ask the same question sideways. Ask them if they could change one or two things about dealing with this company, what improvements would they make? They'll tell you it might be nice if there was somebody to answer the phone, instead of a voicemail machine. They may admit that there was a time or two when the number of hits they recorded on their Web site and the number of hits the vendor reported were miles apart and they might like to see that improved. Asking a positive question yields better answers.

VENDOR SELECTION GUIDE

Vendor name: _____

Vendor URL, contact, and email: _____

Number of lists to choose from: _____

Overall number of names:

☐ 1–3 million

☐ 3–5 million

☐ 5–7 million

☐ 7–9 million

☐ 9–15 million

☐ 15–20 million

☐ > 20 million

Lists identified for this campaign:

1. _____

2. _____

3. _____

4. _____

5. _____

Email names are collected through (for each list):

1.	2.	3.	4.	5.
☐ opt-in only	☐ opt-in only	☐ opt-in only	☐ opt-in only	☐ opt-in only
☐ opt-out	☐ opt-out	☐ opt-out	☐ opt-out	☐ opt-out
☐ combination	☐ combination	☐ combination	☐ combination	☐ combination
☐ harvested	☐ harvested	☐ harvested	☐ harvested	☐ harvested

Specific opt-in language:

_____

_____

Qualification quality of registrants (for each list):

Low = contest applicants, screen saver downloads, T-shirt grabbers

Medium = free subscriptions, club memberships, announcement lists,
newsletters

High = white papers, seminar attendees, software downloads:

1.	2.	3.	4.	5.
☐ low	☐ low	☐ low	☐ low	☐ low
☐ medium	☐ medium	☐ medium	☐ medium	☐ medium
☐ high	☐ high	☐ high	☐ high	☐ high

List validity. For every mailing, the percentage of undeliverable messages:

1.	2.	3.	4.	5.
☐ 0–1%	☐ 0–1%	☐ 0–1%	☐ 0–1%	☐ 0–1%
☐ 1–3%	☐ 1–3%	☐ 1–3%	☐ 1–3%	☐ 1–3%
☐ 3–5%	☐ 3–5%	☐ 3–5%	☐ 3–5%	☐ 3–5%
☐ 5–10%	☐ 5–10%	☐ 5–10%	☐ 5–10%	☐ 5–10%
☐ > 10%	☐ > 10%	☐ > 10%	☐ > 10%	☐ > 10%

List churn. For every mailing, the percentage of unsubscribes:

1.	2.	3.	4.	5.
☐ 0–1%	☐ 0–1%	☐ 0–1%	☐ 0–1%	☐ 0–1%
☐ 1–3%	☐ 1–3%	☐ 1–3%	☐ 1–3%	☐ 1–3%
☐ 3–5%	☐ 3–5%	☐ 3–5%	☐ 3–5%	☐ 3–5%
☐ 5–10%	☐ 5–10%	☐ 5–10%	☐ 5–10%	☐ 5–10%
☐ > 10%	☐ > 10%	☐ > 10%	☐ > 10%	☐ > 10%

Historical response range:

1.	2.	3.	4.	5.
☐ 0–2%	☐ 0–2%	☐ 0–2%	☐ 0–2%	☐ 0–2%
☐ 2–4%	☐ 2–4%	☐ 2–4%	☐ 2–4%	☐ 2–4%
☐ 4–6%	☐ 4–6%	☐ 4–6%	☐ 4–6%	☐ 4–6%

☐ 6–8%	☐ 6–8%	☐ 6–8%	☐ 6–8%	☐ 6–8%
☐ 8–10%	☐ 8–10%	☐ 8–10%	☐ 8–10%	☐ 8–10%
☐ 10–13%	☐ 10–13%	☐ 10–13%	☐ 10–13%	☐ 10–13%
☐ 13–16%	☐ 13–16%	☐ 13–16%	☐ 13–16%	☐ 13–16%
☐ 16–19%	☐ 16–19%	☐ 16–19%	☐ 16–19%	☐ 16–19%
☐ > 19%	☐ > 19%	☐ > 19%	☐ > 19%	☐ > 19%

List price: _____ per thousand

Select price: _____ per select for (category) _____

Select price: _____ per select for (category) _____

Select price: _____ per select for (category) _____

Select price: _____ per select for (category) _____

Total number of selects:

_____

Number of test runs included in the price:

_____

Number of names included in the test:

_____

Test-to-rollout sequence:

_____

_____

_____

Time lag from copy delivery to execution:

_____

To:/From: requirements: _____

Header copy required by vendor: _____

Footer copy required by vendor: _____

Customer references (other clients of this vendor):

    1. _____

    2. _____

    3. _____

Scoring based on phone interviews

On a scale of 1 to 10 the vendor:

	Cared about our campaign	Was easy to reach	Corrected problems quickly
Customer 1	1 2 3 4 5 6 7 8 9 10	1 2 3 4 5 6 7 8 9 10	1 2 3 4 5 6 7 8 9 10
Customer 2	1 2 3 4 5 6 7 8 9 10	1 2 3 4 5 6 7 8 9 10	1 2 3 4 5 6 7 8 9 10
Customer 3	1 2 3 4 5 6 7 8 9 10	1 2 3 4 5 6 7 8 9 10	1 2 3 4 5 6 7 8 9 10
	Avg. score: _____	Avg. score: _____	Avg. score: _____

Overall vendor average score: _____

The best reason to find a good opt-in list vendor to work with is to add new names to your own database. Surely you're keeping track of more detailed information about your own customers than would a third party, aren't you? Aren't you? If not, to quote AT&T, "You will."

Making Your Own List

Nothing draws better than a list that's made up of people you already know. In the first place, they already know you. In the second place, you can start to collect information about them to make your message more targeted. Therefore, it's more meaningful and more response evoking.

Call it database marketing, call it customer service, or call it customer relationship management. It's simply a matter of knowing more about your customers and then using that knowledge to provide your customers more relevant information and to boost your profits.

How do you begin to collect email addresses? Start up a newsletter, as described in Chapter 7, "E-Newsletters, E-Promotions, and OPEmail." Start up a contest. Add a spot on your warranty card. Make sure your customer service representatives ask for it. For professional help, turn to an email management software or service company. Or simply get them to register on your site. And, at every step of the way, ask for their consent.

Registration

There are three broad categories of information/transaction you can offer on your Web site: free, trade, and pay.

The free stuff includes everything you want them to know about your company and what you sell. It also includes something of value to make a site visit worthwhile. Maybe there's a product configurator. Maybe there's a return-on-investment (ROI) calculator. Maybe there's a white paper or two.

The third category is filled with things for sale, things you'll trade them for money. But the second category contains things that you'll trade for information. You may offer a screen saver, a discount coupon, or a trial copy of your software. When they sign up, you learn a lot.

TeamAgenda from Teamsoft (www.teamsoft.com) is "a realtime, cross-platform features rich application that helps individuals, small businesses and larger workgroups coordinate their projects and optimize their time management." You can download a trial version, if you're willing to divulge the following:

(Fields marked with an asterisk [*] are required.)

Mr./Ms.

First Name*:

Last Name*:

Title:

Company:

Address 1*:

Address 2:

City*:

Prov./State*:

Postal/Zip Code*:

Country*:

Telephone*:

Fax:

Email*:

Web Site:

In what sector will you use TeamAgenda*:

Business

Home

Education / Non Profit

Government / Public Sector

Reseller

Filemaker Consultant

How many potential users of TeamAgenda are there at your location*:

1

2 to 9

10 to 49

50 to 99

100 to 1000

Over 1000

Indicate the trial version(s) you require*:

Windows, Macintosh, Windows and Macintosh

Please add any comments or questions:

When you first show up at the Tektronix Web site (www.tek.com), you are greeted with a pop-up window that wants to customize your visit (see Figure 5.8).

When you are trying to choose a printer, their Interactive Product Selector asks the same sort of questions a helpful retail salesperson might when you enter their store:

How will you primarily use your printer?

Graphic Design (brochures, comps, layout, . . .)

General Business Printing (word processing, presentations, spreadsheets, . . .)

Engineering/Scientific (AutoCAD, 3D-modeling, architecture, . . .)

What is the largest paper size you need to print on?

A4, A/Letter

Legal

A3 (297 × 420mm) / Tabloid (11 × 17in)

Poster (A0, 3¢ × 6¢)

Which statement best describes your printing needs?

Can't afford color now, but want an easy conversion to color later.

Need an outstanding all-purpose black & white and color workgroup printer.

Already have a black & white printer. Need to add a fast, high-quality color printer.

Based on your answers, the Web site offers several product suggestions. However, Tektronix knows that educated shoppers want to see the goods. They want to look at

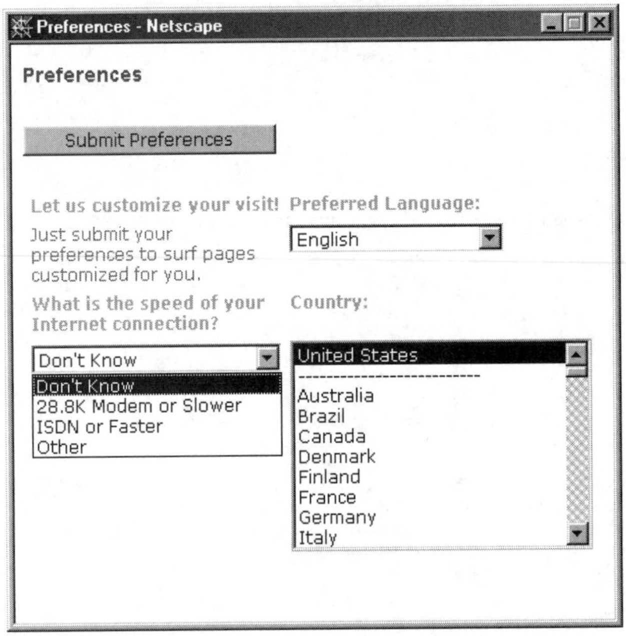

Figure 5.8 Tektronix will tailor your Web visit depending on your language, location, and connection speed.

the actual output on paper. That's something you can't do on a computer screen. So they offer to send you free samples.

FREE SAMPLES AND INFORMATION

Thanks for taking the time try our Product Selector! If you'd like to get detailed information and sample output for the recommended printers, just fill out the form below to let us know what you need.

Designing Web pages that can be viewed by anybody, anywhere, as often as they like is well worth the one-time expense and ongoing maintenance. But sending a literature package costs money each time you send it. That means Tektronix wants to use this survey to qualify their prospects. The questions are a bit more pointed.

What is your primary application for a printer?

GENERAL BUSINESS

DESIGN AND PUBLISHING

ENGINEERING/SCIENTIFIC

FINANCE/INSURANCE

RETAIL

IT

EDUCATION

GOVERNMENT

Which of the following best describes the principal business of your organization?

ADVERTISING/GRAPHIC DESIGN

PUBLISHING/NEWSPAPERS/MAGAZINES

COMMERCIAL PRINTING

HIGHER EDUCATION

K–12 EDUCATION

STATE & LOCAL GOVERNMENT

FEDERAL GOVERNMENT

ENGINEERING ARCHITECTURE / R & D

AEROSPACE

MANUFACTURING

CONSTRUCTION

TRANSPORTATION

UTILITIES

PHARMACEUTICALS

RETAIL/WHOLESALE

HEALTH/MEDICAL

FINANCE/SECURITIES

REAL ESTATE

INSURANCE

OTHER

Are you planning to purchase a color printer

Within 30 days

Within three months

Within a year

More than one year

What budget price range are you considering for each printer?

Less than $1,000

$1,000 to $2,000

$2,000 to $5,000

$5,000 or more

How many color printers are you considering purchasing?

1

2–10

11–25

26+

First Name
Last Name

Company

Street

Address

Suite/Mailstop

City

State/Province

Zip/Postal Code

Country

Daytime phone

Email

Email is Optional. Providing it indicates agreement to receive future informational emails from Tektronix.

Please check if you are a reseller of printers.

With that sort of information, Tektronix can now plug you into a sophisticated system of contact and relationship management systems.

They can also send out emails that are a lot more personal than those that start, "Dear Xyz1234@hotmail.com."

Contests are another great way to collect information. All of this personalization can be heady stuff and it can be quite valuable. You just need to do it carefully.

Personalization

The power of the computer spells the ability to remember everything about every customer. Using that power has its rewards as well as its risks.

Books and books have been written about one-to-one marketing, and you should read a couple of them. The Peppers and Rogers books are a great place to start:

The One to One Future: Building Relationships One Customer at a Time (Bantam Doubleday Dell, 1997)

Enterprise One to One: Tools for Competing in the Interactive Age (Doubleday, 1999)

The One to One Fieldbook: The Complete Toolkit for Implementing a 1 to 1 Marketing Program (Bantam Books, 1999)

The main thrust is very simple and is based on a handful of premises. First, it's cheaper to sell something to a current customer than to find a new one. Next, the more you know about each customer you have, the easier it is to cater to their needs. And finally, as you learn more and more about each customer, they become more and more locked in to buying from you. After all, who wants to have to break in a new vendor?

As simple as these ideas sound, using them as the foundation of your business and building relationships with individual customers on top of them are not simple. That's why Peppers and Rogers have a rapidly growing consulting business and lots of good information at www.1to1.com (see Figure 5.9).

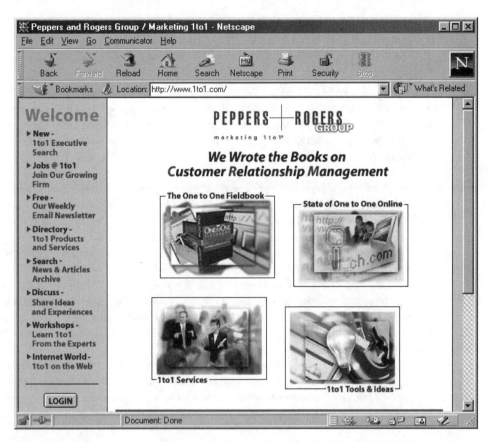

Figure 5.9 Peppers and Rogers' Marketing 1 to 1 Web site offers valuable information on getting to know your customers very well.

In the beginning, there was the email address and it was alone on the face on the database. And lo, there came to pass some nifty ideas to get people to reveal more and more about themselves. And soon the database filled two by two and the data went forth and multiplied. And the result was a rich wealth of knowledge that spread joy upon the vast reaches of the marketing department. And they saw that it was good. Because it could be used to get people to buy more stuff.

Collecting Attributes

Starting with the humble newsletter, marketers are finding ways of encouraging people to reveal more and more about themselves. The first thing you can do is watch people while they surf your site. When they give you their email address, you give them a cookie.

From *World Wide Web Marketing, Second Edition*

PERSONALIZING WELL

Don't you hate it when somebody you've never met comes up to you and says, "Oh, Hi! You must be Jim! Your wife has told me *so* much about you!" My first reaction is to be grateful that my wife is one of those discreet people and is not inclined to babble about my song selections when I sing in the shower. My next reaction is that I don't even know if I'm going to like this person and why are they acting like a long lost friend. They say familiarity breeds contempt. I say over-familiarity is far worse.

American Express learned this when they started using caller ID. People didn't like it when AmEx seemed to use ESP to recognize them before they spoke. Answering the phone with, "Hello, Mr. Smith, this is Sally at American Express. How can I help you?" was repeatedly met with disdain, distaste and distrust. The advent of caller-id did not delight the caller. It was only a matter of time before AmEx allowed callers to identify themselves first. "My name is John Smith and I have a question about my bill."

"Yes, Mr. Smith, I have your account records in front of me now." That turned out to be quite a coup. Customers got the impression that AmEx's computers were blindingly fast. More importantly, it provided the customer with that all-important feeling of being in control of the conversation. Turns out the correct answer to "Do you know me?" is "Not until you introduce yourself."

We all prefer to shop without being hovered over. Nobody wants to walk into a store where the clerks follow your every move and note each item you glance at. At first, it's a desire to be left alone to contemplate the merchandise. Then it's a matter of negotiation dexterity. Frankly, I don't want the car salesman to know that I've already decided to buy a car and this afternoon is the only time I have to do so. I want to hold up my end of the illusion of being a savvy, aloof buyer for as long as possible. I don't want the saleswoman in the antique store to know that I'm a meerschaum pipe fanatic. That makes bargaining much more difficult when they know they have a live one on their hands.

A wonderful cautionary tale appeared in the *Harvard Business Review* (January–February, 1998, page 42). In it, Sandra Fournier, Susan Dobscha and David Glen Mick suggest ways for "Preventing the Premature Death of Relationship Marketing."

They warn about asking customers for too much. Just how many times do I have to give the guy at Radio Shack my address? I was just in here last week buying. You really need my address again so I can buy this telephone cable? They warn that there are too many companies that want to bond with an individual and the resulting flood of "personalized" postal mail is overwhelming. They warn that savvy customers are feeling put out because they are not Gold Club Members or Platinum Card holders.

I was on a United Airlines flight once and the captain came back into the cabin to seek me out. When I agreed I was the one he was looking for (desperately worried that the only reason he'd leave his seat to look for me was to deliver some very bad news), he handed me his business card and said, "Thanks for flying with us so often." On the back of the card was a handwritten note, "My crew and I wanted to let you know we really appreciate your 100,000 miles on United. Thanks!" and was signed by the captain.

My first thought was pleasure for being singled out. My second thought was noticing the dirty looks from the guys on either side of me. I felt good. They felt crummy. That's two to one. Those *Harvard Business Review* people were on to something.

As interesting as those cautions were, the one tale stuck in my mind. It was from an interview they did with a consumer who had ordered some gifts from a catalog. They send annual reminders to their customers, figuring the gifts were usually birthday, anniversary or holiday related. They're right. I have purchased gifts from the Harry & David catalog for several years in a row and in November they send me a printout of what I bought and the ability to check the ones I want to re-send. If you buy lots of fruit baskets for lots of office staff, it can be quite handy. Good thinking.

But this gentleman had a problem. He had bought gifts for the physicians and nurses who had taken care of his mother during a medical emergency. It was a very unpleasant time and now, every year, he gets a cold, calculated reminder of it.

A little knowledge is a dangerous thing. Use your knowledge wisely.

Taking the train from London's Waterloo station to the Gare du Nord in Paris is great. You get there faster and you don't get seasick. But, you also don't get to enjoy the wind in your hair, see the sights or smell the sea air. You are sealed in a metal tube which plunges you beneath the English Channel and you don't see a thing until you pop out on the west coast of France.

When you profile somebody, you can guess what they might be interested in next. But you also put them on a straight and narrow track with blinders on all sides. Adroit retail practice places the staples at the back of the store to force customers to walk past aisles and aisles of impulse items.

Infoseek President and Chief Executive Officer Robin Johnson feels that search engines should keep queries in context. In *Information Week* (10/14/96) Johnson said, "If you do a lot of business searches and type in 'chicken stock,' we're not going to direct you to a bunch of gumbo recipes." But what if gumbo recipes were exactly what you had in mind? How can a computer decide you are either an investor or a chef, but never both?

Sometimes you go to the store as a mother of a sick child, and sometimes as a plumber with a leaky faucet. The "milk" you're looking for might be for breakfast, might be baby formula and might be coconut milk. What if you're trying to find a present for your wife? Will the Sears site not show you the softer side if you spend too much time looking at Craftsman tools?

The trick is to be knowledgeable about your guests without being overly familiar. Be attentive without being fawning. Helpful without pigeon-holing people into such small categories that they have to fight your system to find the products or services they want. It's a dance. It's a mutual exchange of data. I don't mind that the woman at the dry cleaner knows my name and phone number. I don't mind that my bank knows my savings balance. I don't mind that Amazon.com knows what kind of books I like to read. But I do mind if that information is used callously.

Cookies: The Short Course

When an individual shows up at your site for the first time, you look to see if they have a *cookie* from you. That's a small text file stored by their browser that contains an identification number you would have given them on a previous visit. Since this is their first appearance, they have none, so you plop one down on their hard drive. You don't know who they are. You don't know their name. You don't know anything yet, except that they stopped by your homepage. From this point on, you track what they look at on your site.

For the long course, take a look at www.wdvl.com/Authoring/Languages/Perl/PerlfortheWeb/cookies.html.

Track What They Click On

With the cookie, you can keep an eye on what they look at. You can keep a log of which products they look at and which they ignore. If they have consented to receiving email from you, then you can send them notices about products they may have missed but should know about.

If they come to your travel products site and look over the currency calculator, the dual-zone travel alarm clock, the European translation dictionary, and the laptop cases, you might shoot off an email inviting them to consider the international electric plug adapter and the international internal modem surge protector.

Track What They Buy

If they come to your audio component site and look at the wide variety of speakers you have on display, you might take an automatic peek into your customer files to see which amplifier they bought and send the automated order confirmation with an up-sell suggestion.

```
Thanks for your order! We're sure your [sic] going to enjoy your Bose 701
Direct/Reflecting speaker system, but we'd like to make a suggestion.
Since you have a high-end amplifier (Purchase Order #02355097), we'd like
to point out that the 901® Series VI Direct/Reflecting speaker system
might be a better match. If you upgrade before we ship the 701's to you
tomorrow, we'll split the difference in price with you. You get better
speakers at an awesome price, and we get a customer with a happier pair
of ears. Want to take advantage of this offer? Click here: Sounds Great!
```

Learning about people by following them around is useful, but it's a long-term job. Do it if you can, but take some proactive measures as well.

The Outright Survey

Your database should keep track of the last time you sent each individual a message and which one it was. Not only do you ensure you don't send duplicates and that you don't send too much to one customer, you get to see who's ripe for another survey.

Just come right out and ask them to give you a hand. Offer them a prize for their participation? Certainly, if you must. But this is a different kind of survey. This isn't a bunch of questions about the features they want added to your fax machine. You're not asking them to rank the reliability of your food processor against those of your competitors. This isn't about how often they eat pizza out versus having it delivered. You're asking them about what they like and dislike. This is personal.

Make it clear from the get-go that you're bothering them in order to provide more tailored information:

WOODAUCTION (WWW.WOODAUCTION.COM)

WoodAuction will never provide your membership or purchase information (including personal data, bid information, or products purchased) to any outside organization for marketing purposes.

We will use the information in a secure environment to communicate special WoodAuction news, promotions, and deals to you on a regular basis. WoodAuction will also use this information to personalize and improve the service we offer to you.

MACZONE (WWW.ZONES.COM)

Confidentiality—We may use some information to communicate special offers, promotions and contests to you on a regular basis, unless you indicate that you do not wish to receive the messages. The MacZone will use this information to personalize and improve our online service for you. If you would not like your personal information to be included in our promotional distribution list made available to third parties, please call Customer Service and our operators will take care of your needs.

What do you do with this personal information besides offering very personal special sale offers? You make very personal special newsletters—in Chapter 7, "E-Newsletters, E-Promotions, and OPEmail."

The Occasional Question

Ask a single question of your customers every now and then. Just one.

When they come to your site, you might hit them with a single question—a pop quiz. You get to analyze the aggregate opinion of your clients *and* you get to store one more datapoint about each one.

It's a fairly common practice and it's interesting to your site visitors as well. CMP, publisher of more than 30 technical magazines (www.cmpnet.com), wanted to know if consumers care about Microsoft's troubles with the Department of Justice (see Figure 5.10).

When you visit McArthur Business Systems (www.mbsinternet.com) you might get a pop-up window with a new Instapoll in it (see Figure 5.11).

When you send out email, include a question. Make it dead-bang simple to answer. They can hit Reply, type an X in the right spot, and hit Send. The easier it is, the greater the response you'll get. The greater the response you get, the more you know about each of them.

Enhanced Targeting

Want to get a tighter focus on these people who are coming to your Web site, registering for your newsletters, and downloading your screen savers? Then overlay your list with traditional database information (demographics).

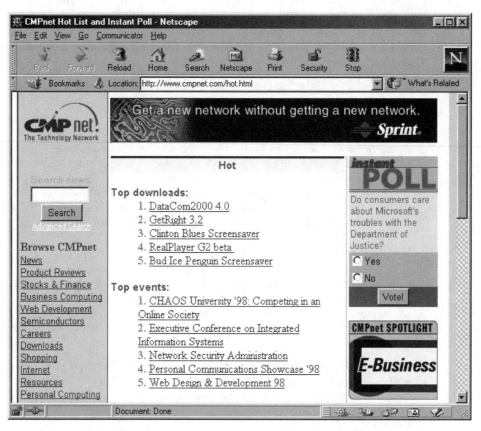

Figure 5.10 CMP pops a one-time question.

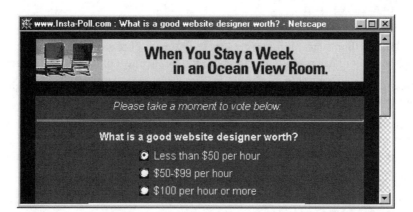

Figure 5.11 This Web shop wants to know how much they can charge people.

FirstLogic (www.firstlogic.com) offers database enhancement and cross-referencing services to those with large direct marketing needs. Catalog companies rely on them to verify addresses, correct spelling mistakes, supply missing data, fix transposed zip codes, and provide updates on people who have moved. In more formal terms, First-Logic:

- Parses all elements of customer names and business names, even floating, unfielded data.
- Standardizes professional titles, postnames, maturity postnames, business suffixes, and much more.
- Appends customer demographics, phone numbers, geocodes, gender codes, and much more.
- Performs data search-and-replace functions.
- Corrects and completes addresses, including updating addresses of customers who have moved.

If you want to verify thousands of customer-entered names and addresses, automation is the way to go. Or would you like to go a step further?

Abacus Direct (www.abacus-direct.com) has the selling history of somewhere around 900 catalogs, which represents something to the tune of 88 million U.S. households. That means they can match your name and address with the sorts of things you like to buy. Add a touch of statistical modeling and they have a pretty good idea of what you might be interested in buying. If you have a name and an address, data from companies like Abacus can vastly improve the pitch you offer to each individual.

Data Mining and Customer Relationship Management

On the very high end of complex customer attribute collection, storage, and use are data mining and customer relationship management.

Data mining is the science of trapping every bit of information that comes into your company about all of your customers and analyzing it to learn new insights about your marketplace. A white paper at DMReview (www.dmreview.com), written by Information Discovery, Inc., defines data mining as "a decision support process in which we search for patterns of information in data." It's a different way of looking at your customers in order to see them in a new light.

Customer relationship management (CRM) is the art of using every bit of information that comes into your company about each particular customer as a means of tailoring your communications with them on a one-to-one basis.

Both of these topics are covered in more detail in Jim Sterne's *Customer Service on the Internet* (John Wiley & Sons, 2000). For immediate information, see the Peppers and

Rogers Group (www.1to1.com), Personalization.com (www.personalization.com), and CRMCommunity.com (www.crmcommunity.com).

Between the things people say (explicit) and what they do (implicit), and the information you can learn about them through other sources, you can build profiles that will help guide your email marketing efforts. But even perfect aim won't help if you don't get the message right.

CHAPTER 6

Writing an Email Masterpiece

Shakespeare, Faulkner, Emerson, Fitzgerald, Virginia Woolf, and Dostoyevsky—all literary giants. These are the names that come to mind when the term *literary masterpiece* is mentioned. These are the towers of erudition we can only aspire to emulate. These are the scholars whose words have shaped the very culture we live in. These are the men and women who never had to decide between paper or plastic, Windows or Macintosh, or ASCII and HTML email. Life was simpler then.

As Alan Rosenspan, creative director of Bronner, Slosberg, Humphrey, puts it:

> Direct mail is almost like sending a sample of your company to a potential customer. How it looks, how it feels, its very presence, all communicate a certain image in a tangible and involving way. In fact, it may be the only part of your company that people will ever hold in their hands.

Yes, email is very different from an envelope or a postcard. It's not tangible; it's not held in anybody's hands. But it definitely has a presence. It definitely represents you and your company to an audience. It is very involving. You'll have to do your level best to make sure your message gets its due between the moment it shows up in the in-box and the next, when it's deleted to the trash folder.

Before embarking on creating the *great American email*, however, you're going to have to make some mundane choices about the format in which it is to be delivered.

Format

You have one major decision to make right up front. Do you write your email in straight ASCII text or HTML? There are a handful of minor issues you'll need to resolve, but this one has the biggest impact on how you go about creating your masterpiece.

ASCII according to C/Net (www.cnet.com)

Bland, unformatted text files are best saved in American Standard Code for Information Interchange, or ASCII (pronounced "askee") format. But ASCII is more than a text file format—it's a standard developed by the American National Standards Institute (ANSI) to define how computers write and read characters. The ASCII set of 128 characters includes letters, numbers, punctuation, and control codes (such as a character that marks the end of a line). Each letter or other character is represented by a number: An uppercase A, for example, is the number 65, and a lowercase z is the number 122. Most operating systems use the ASCII standard, except for Windows NT, which uses the suitably larger and newer Unicode standard.

HTML according to C/Net

As its name suggests, Hypertext Markup Language, or HTML, is a collection of formatting commands that create hypertext documents—Web pages, to be exact. When you point your Web browser to a URL, the browser interprets the HTML commands embedded in the page and uses them to format the page's text and graphic elements. HTML commands cover many types of text formatting (bold and italic text, lists, headline fonts in various sizes, and so on), and also have the ability to include graphics and other nontext elements.

ASCII versus HTML

If you could email a Web page to somebody, why wouldn't you? If you could make use of all those graphic artists who have painstakingly learned PhotoShop and Adobe Illustrator and send out a little bit of electronic artwork, why would you even consider sending a plain old Courier 12 message that resembles a World War II Western Union telegram from the War Department that starts out, "We regret to inform you . . ."?

If you could send out an email that looked as good as the *ClickZ Today* newsletter (see Figure 6.1), why wouldn't you?

You'd consider holding off on the HTML tricks for the same reasons you waited a couple of years before implementing JavaScript on your homepage. For the same reasons you still don't offer a streaming video of the CEO's last luncheon speech on your homepage. Not everybody has software that can display HTML email, and not everybody wants to wait for it to download.

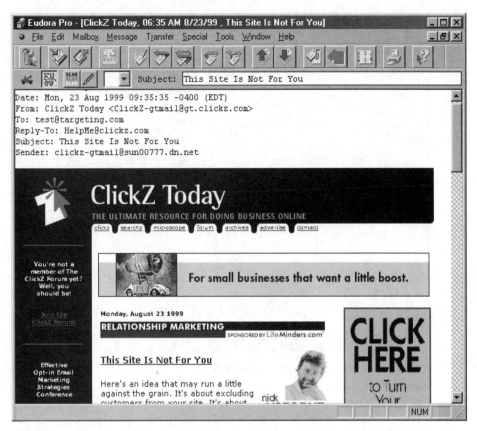

Figure 6.1 HTML email can look very professional.

Even playing with the text formatting of some email programs can cause trouble. This bit of spam (see Figure 6.2) is much easier to read in black and white than it was in Eudora Pro 4.1.

That's the way it looked with the Eudora option set to use its own viewer. If the user had selected the Microsoft Viewer option, the message would have looked considerably different (see Figure 6.3).

While the latest versions of Netscape and Internet Explorer display HTML email messages just fine, there are plenty of people using older versions, plenty of people still using Pine and Elm, and plenty of people using sophisticated software like Eudora, with the HTML feature turned off.

Of the 50 companies they interviewed that are using email for marketing, "Lack of HTML-capable clients holds most to text," according to Forrester Research's March 1999 report, *Opt-in Email Gets Personal.* Interviewees said most customers were asking for ASCII.

In the June 24 issue of his excellent and highly recommended newsletter, *Iconocast* (www.iconocast.com) (see Figure 6.4), Michael Tchong described the results of a survey performed at his first Web Attack! conference on June 17 and 18, 1999.

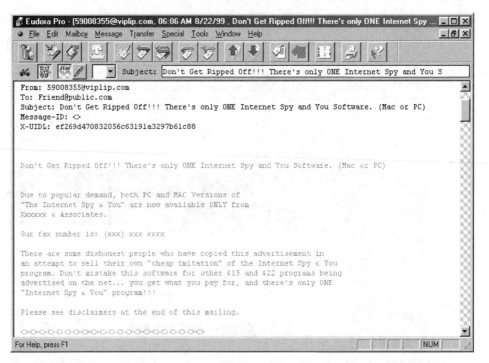

Figure 6.2 This message showed up with turquoise text on a white background. Impossible to read.

```
Email Marketing
***************
```

There were a few surprises in the session that brought day one to an end. The first item that stood out was a poll that asked the audience's preference for either HTML or plain email. Contrary to two earlier surveys, cited in "CMP Email List Gets Results" (ICONOCAST 22-Apr-98), and "Email Standards" (ICONOCAST 04-Feb-99), this group voted 54% to 46% in favor of HTML email.

This was quite remarkable given that a January I-Sales Digest survey found only 23% preferring HTML. This does suggest that the move to HTML email is in full swing, with more users switching to HTML-friendlier clients.

When the crowd demanded that we divide the question into two parts to detect a possible difference between home and work email habits, the results showed a stronger preference for HTML email at work, reflecting perhaps the presence of better bandwidth and software at work:

```
+-------------------+--------+--------------+
| Email Preference  | HTML   | Plain-text   |
+-------------------+--------+--------------+
| Overall           | 54%    | 46%          |
| At work           | 69     | 57           |
| At home           | 31     | 43           |
+-------------------+--------+--------------+
```

Source: Jun. 1999 ICONOCAST Inc./Web Attack! poll
    by Audience Response Systems

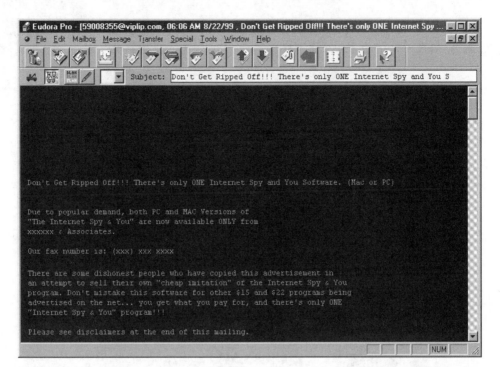

Figure 6.3 Turquoise text on a black background hides all of the header information but doesn't help much with readability.

In the July 1 issue, Tchong printed a follow-up from Infonautics director of product management, Michael Holland:

"I thought you might like some 'free stats.' We currently send out almost 200,000 emails every day for such Sleuth products as Company Sleuth and Job Sleuth and here's the most recent email data:

```
+-------------+-----------+
| Email type  |  Percent  |
| Text        |    65%    |
| HTML        |    16%    |
| AOL         |    20%    |
+-------------+-----------+
```

Source: Jun. 1999 Infonautics

"We detect AOL members from their email address and send them a specialized text version with live links, and bold and italics, given that AOL doesn't support key elements of our HTML version (mainly tables)."

Edit.: Sleuth's email use represents historical data, i.e. what people do *now* with email. We asked Web Attack! attendees what they *preferred*, which tends to deliver more predictive answers.

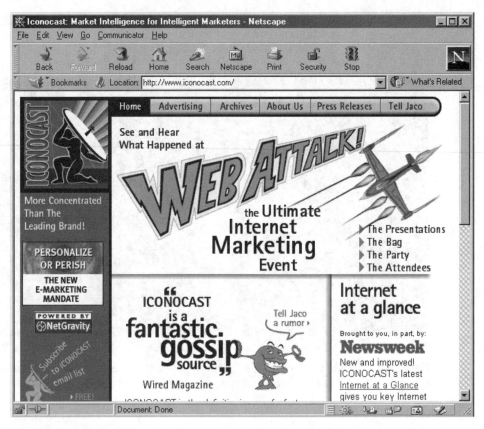

Figure 6.4 *Iconocast* is an excellent resource. You should subscribe.

Embedding HTML in emails can be tricky and the results can be downright ugly (see Figure 6.5) and can give your brand a technical black eye if you're not 100 percent up to speed (see Figure 6.6).

The bottom line? The market isn't quite ready for HTML. So why would you consider sending HTML messages? Because according to the opening paragraph of Forrester's *Opt-in Email Gets Personal:*

> Outbound email marketing messages sent to voluntary recipients drive sales and site traffic. But personalized HTML email will evolve into a central point of contact with rich interactivity and anywhere, anytime delivery.

Besides, HTML email recipients are two to three times more likely to respond, according to interviews done during 1999 by Michael Tchong of *Iconocast.*

Another advantage of sending HTML email is the ability to determine whether the message has even been opened. An embedded HTML tag can report back to the server. Now you can tell if your subject line is working. More on that in Chapter 8, "Testing Your Talent, Reckoning Your Response, and Managing Your Email."

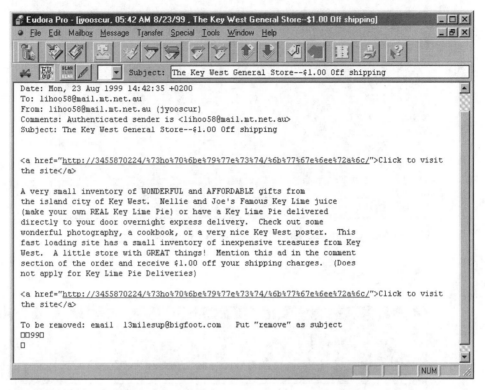

Figure 6.5 That link actually worked, but you wouldn't want one in *your* message.

Just be ready to design your HTML a whole lot differently than you do your Web pages. They have to be shorter, they have to be narrower, and they have to be smaller in file size. They also have to instantly show the offer/benefit/call to action because deleting email is much easier than moving the mouse over to the Back button on a browser.

Remember how much fun it is to create Web pages that will work with multiple browsers? Well, you just walked into a quagmire of unbelievable choices when it comes to email clients.

For an introduction to the technical side of creating HTML email, take a look at Hotwired's Webmonkey (www.hotwired.com/webmonkey). See Figure 6.7.

To Each His Own

If you are a Web marketing connoisseur, you automatically consider a truth we hold to be self-evident on the Web: Let the customer control his or her own destiny.

The whole idea of one-to-one marketing is remembering details about each customer. Put them in control of the relationship. Let them decide which format they'd like. Let them tell you which email client they're using.

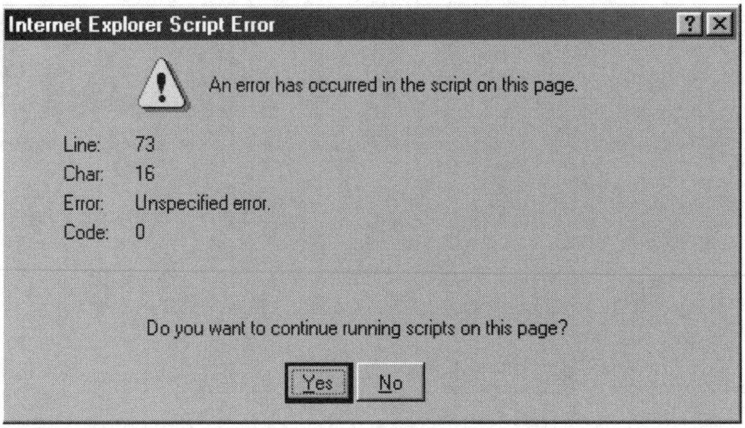

Figure 6.6 Getting too fancy with HTML is asking for trouble.

Figure 6.7 Webmonkey is a great place to start when it comes to sending HTML email.

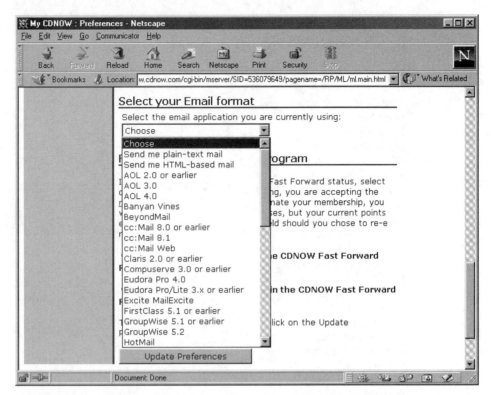

Figure 6.8 CDNOW wants to make sure it matches its format with your ability.

And then work like hell to ensure their wishes are respected. That's what CDNOW (www.cdnow.com) does (see Figure 6.8).

See the 19 choices CDNOW offers on its sign-up page? Sounds like a lot? Try 47. Here's the list of email clients they let you choose from:

Send me plain-text mail
Send me HTML-based mail
AOL 2.0 or earlier
AOL 3.0
AOL 4.0
Banyan Vines
BeyondMail
cc:Mail 8.0 or earlier
cc:Mail 8.1
cc:Mail Web
Claris 2.0 or earlier
CompuServe 3.0 or earlier
Eudora Pro 4.0
Eudora Pro/Lite 3.x or earlier

Excite MailExcite
FirstClass 5.1 or earlier
GroupWise 5.1 or earlier
GroupWise 5.2
HotMail
Juno 1.49 or earlier
Lotus Mail 4.5 or earlier
Lotus Notes 4.5 or earlier
Lotus Notes 4.6
Microsoft Exchange
Microsoft Internet Explorer 3.0
Microsoft Internet Explorer 4.0
Microsoft Internet Explorer 5.0
Microsoft Internet Mail 3.0
Microsoft Outlook 97
Microsoft Outlook 98
Microsoft Outlook Express 4.0
Microsoft Outlook Express 5.0
MSN Mail 2.5 or earlier
Netscape 2.x or earlier
Netscape 3.0
Netscape 4.0
Netscape webmail
Pegasus 2.54 or earlier
Prodigy/Net
Pronto97 4.01 or earlier
ProntoMail
Quickmail Pro 1.5 or earlier
RocketMail
USANet Netaddress
Yahoo! Mail
Zmail Pro 6.1 or earlier
Zmail for Unix

Does each of these different versions of email clients require its own formatted email? No, there's a lot of commonality. But rather than put the strain on customers to figure out what they can and cannot read in their particular versions of email software, CDNOW simply has them identify which package they're using.

A Wide Variety of Attachments

Since it's as easy as pie to attach a file to an email, some companies have tried sending attached commercials. The easiest are the simple postcards. Head over to Fox Broadcasting (http://foxworld.com/postcard.htm) and send your friend a postcard from your favorite show. Sadly, there are a few speed bumps in this seemingly simple scheme.

First, the message arrives (see Figure 6.9). Not a very captivating message, except that it's from somebody you know. No telling what it is. No branding. What a waste.

Next, you click on it to open it up, but, alas, it's been misnamed so you can't (see Figure 6.10).

Once you've selected the proper application to view the postcard, you find it underwhelming (see Figure 6.11).

What if it was more than a card? What if it was an all-singing, all-dancing attachment?

@loha

One of the first companies to try email marketing through attachments was Media Synergy with their @loha offering (www.goaloha.com). As a demonstration, they offer holiday cards. The following series of screen shots (see Figures 6.12 through 6.14) captures portions of an animated greeting card that displays when the recipient clicks on the link within the email.

This type of attachment requires recipients to download the @loah PlayPro player, configure their email system to recognize that application, and, perhaps, restart their email system. There's even a page that gives instructions on how each email system might handle this (see Figure 6.15).

This is something like sending your dad a coded Father's Day greeting that has to be translated from Estonian after being deciphered.

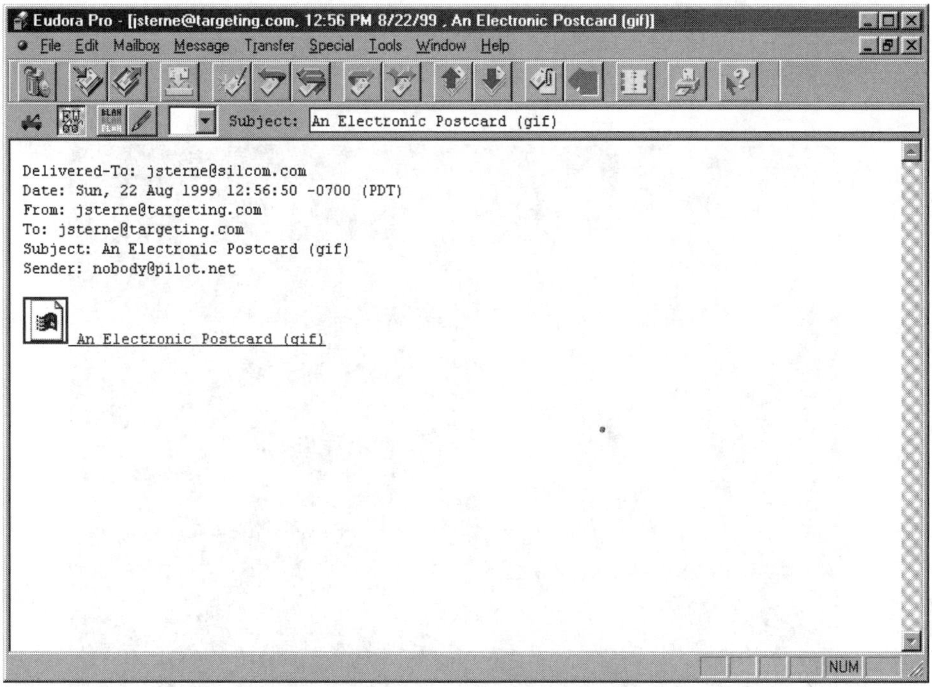

Figure 6.9   A Foxworld postcard is delivered to your email system.

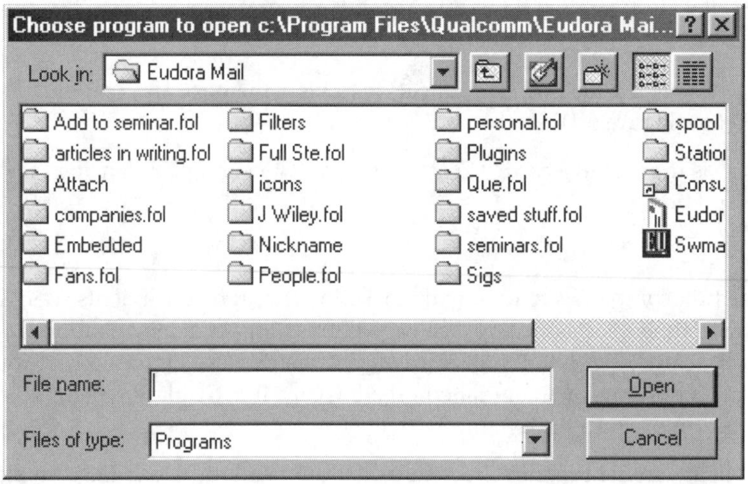

Figure 6.10 — window content:

Choose program to open c:\Program Files\Qualcomm\Eudora Mai... ? X

Look in: Eudora Mail

- Add to seminar.fol
- articles in writing.fol
- Attach
- companies.fol
- Embedded
- Fans.fol
- Filters
- Full Ste.fol
- icons
- J Wiley.fol
- Nickname
- People.fol
- personal.fol
- Plugins
- Que.fol
- saved stuff.fol
- seminars.fol
- Sigs
- spool
- Station
- Consu
- Eudor
- Swma

File name: [ ]

Files of type: Programs

Open / Cancel

Figure 6.10 Had Fox named the file with "gif" on the end instead of "(gif)," the file would have opened of its own accord.

Nevertheless, response rates using this sort of marketing can be significant. In their December 1998 report, *Direct Email: Winning Long-Term Consumer Attention,* Jupiter Communications described a campaign SportsLine (www.sportsline.com) ran using @loha email as part of their Nagano Winter Olympics promotions. Special offers, special merchandise, and the ability to view the latest event scores and schedules were sent to 20,000 addresses. Within two days, 73 percent clicked through to the Sports-Line site and fewer than 100 unsubscribed.

Figure 6.11 Not worth waiting for? That's a branding problem for Fox Broadcasting.

Figure 6.12 An @loha greeting opens in the @loha player . . .

Figure 6.13 . . . plays . . .

Figure 6.14 . . . and will eventually display the personal greetings from the sender.

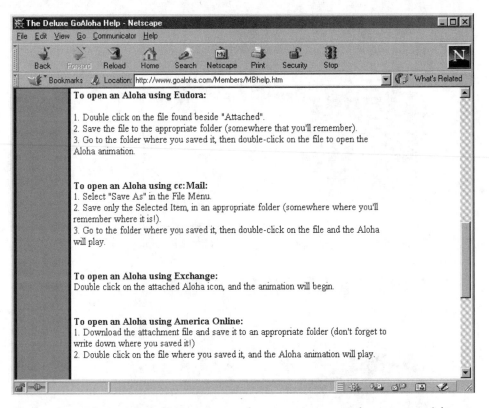

Figure 6.15 When you need instructions on how to open an attachment, you might not be dealing with the best marketing tool on the planet.

RadicalMail

Jim Sterne received a request for advice from the general manager of a radio station. Since the general manager was his brother, he gave the best advice he could. The question came up with an attached executable file that showed the picture of a competitive DJ, and played a vocal invitation to a concert.

```
At 12:23 PM 7/28/99, Doug Sterne wrote:
>james..what was your suggestion about an alternative to this
>gimmick....as I recall your concerns were file size and unsolicited
>files from unknown sources.

Another problem is the scare about viruses. People shouldn't open exe-
cutables that show up in their email - it's dangerous.

Alternatively - make a short but very sweet offer and drop in a link
back to your pages. It's nowhere near as kewl, but it will probably get
more/better response.
```

```
Here's the caveat: if your audience is hipper than hip, and your brand is
filled with Trust, then people will *want* you to be technologically cool
as well and will blindly execute any software you want to send them.

Lemmings--- gotta love 'em.

Soooo.... if you really want to do the multi~media thing, take a look at
http://www.RadicalMail.com.

In a nutshell, you send out an email that's only 2k or 3k. When they
open that message, the RadicalMail server starts streaming the email
content - audio, video, fill-in-the-form, you name it.
```

Yes, it's simply streaming media, but one doesn't expect it in one's email (see Figure 6.16).

At the end of the day, even something as careful and straightforward as RadicalMail can run into problems. Chris Donaldson, one of RadicalMail's founders, posted the following to the ClickZ Forum in August 1999:

> RadicalMail relies on HTML to provide media rich messages to its audience. But with all the email clients out there, sometimes our messages just don't get through. And though we can kick non-HTML clients directly over to a text message that can say anything our clients want it to, link included, there're still some people out there who don't want HTML even if they are so enabled, under any circumstances.

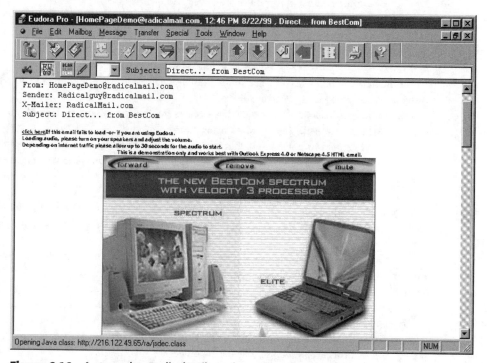

Figure 6.16 A streaming RadicalMail can be quite a surprise.

How do we get around this? By offering a "remove" button in plain sight that's simple to use. Even with this, though, we have to ultimately ask for forgiveness and ensure they never hear from us again.

Email? Yeah, it's a beautiful thing. But as marketers, we have to manage this segment carefully and responsibly. Otherwise, we'll all be looking for jobs.

Forrester Research thinks that browsers and email software and functionality will all merge by 2001. So your worries about HTML-enabled email readers will disappear over time. Of course, there's still the growing specter of all those other gadgets out there that people are using now and will start to use more and more.

In the last chapter of this book (Chapter 10, "A Look toward the Future"), we'll talk about the future of email marketing. One thing you can be sure of is that people will be getting their email everywhere and anywhere and on lots of different kinds of devices. So remember to ask your customers if they want to get your messages on their cell phone, their pager, or their wristwatch.

From *Full Sterne Ahead*, May 1999

My in-box got a big surprise this month. I received a RadicalMail.

OK, OK, so Mark Gibbs from Network World sent me a way-cool email with the subject "I've been thinking..." using HTML, with a dark blue background and an animated gif of himself rubbing his chin in that pondering way. That made me smile and nod in recognition of his new-found plethora of spare time. Does the man never sleep?

But the RadicalMail I got made me sit up and imitate Sparky—the dog that looks into the gramophone listening to His Master's Voice.

In a nutshell, RadicalMail is a service that streams multimedia into an email with no plug-ins. The results are all-singing, all-dancing emails.

Dedicated to an opt-in-only model, this company makes it possible to send a 2k email message that reaches out to the server when it's opened and streams whatever you choose.

It's very easy to drop a link into an email and ask people to click on it to go to a Web site. But this simply hits you between the eyes.

Want to know when your favorite manufacturer comes up with a new laptop? Want to know when the video store has a special on *Saving Private Ryan*? Open the email and see a mini commercial.

Now comes the part that makes my little marketer's heart sing: Everything is trackable. They know how many emails they sent out. They can know how many were opened. They know how many were forwarded. The mail can include HTML forms so they know if people clicked for more info, and how many made the purchase—all from inside the email client.

Not good for non-Americans who don't stay online to read their mail? All in good time.

I wrote RadicalMail a note about giving email the branding power of television and they put me in their brochure. How interactive can you get??

General Elements of Style

This is not the place to lay down the well-worn rules of effective business writing. A quick search on Amazon.com will return more than 75 books on the subject and more are coming all the time. But please pay attention to the little things like grammar and spelling.

In *The Guy Kawasaki Computer Curmudgeon* (Hayden Books, 1992), the author figured email was not the place for such rigid rules:

> Using email saves time because careful editing and proofing are not necessary or appropriate. Email is supposed to be fast, tit-for-tat communication. You ask. I answer. You ask. I answer. You're not supposed to watch the sun set, listen to the surf pound the sun-bleached sand, and sip San Miguel beer as Paco dives for abalone while you craft your email.

One look at the date he wrote that book is enough to back off of giving Guy a black eye. He was speaking of personal email. This was well before commercial interests overran the Internet back in 1994. That was back when email was the playground of the technically gifted.

But that's still no reason for the individual writing a personal e-note to throw etiquette to the four winds. People still judge you on how well you communicate. It affects your opinion about the writer when you receive an email like this:

```
i WANTED TO LET YOU KNOW ABOUT jOHN'S NEW cHEVY bLAZER... oh damn! There
goes that caps lock again and I hate it when that happens. Anyway, about
John's new ride...
```

Add to that errors in spelling and punctuation and it gets worse. Commercial email represents your company and your brand. There's no room for excuses.

In this day of built-in spell checkers, we are constantly amazed by spelling errors in email and on Web sites. Show a little respect for the recipient and proof your work! (Our crystal ball shows a flood of emails happily pointing out spelling and grammar mistakes in *this* book.)

It's all a matter of respect for the reader. If you won't take the time to proof your work, why should we take the time to read it?

Strunk and White

When it comes to the basics, you cannot go wrong following the advice of William Strunk and E.B. White in their classic, *The Elements of Style, 4th Edition* (Verve Press, 1999). For seven bucks, you owe it to yourself to keep this one on hand. Don't follow this treatise word for word—heavens, you're writing advertising copy here—but do read through it in one sitting to give yourself the right perspective on putting words together.

For suggestions on how to write well for email, try a different couple of authors.

Angell and Heslop

The Elements of Email Style (Addison-Wesley, 1994) is a good read as well. Also a general instruction book and not focused on the commercial use of email, this book has a wonderful chapter called "Tone, Rhythm, Persuasion—and Flame Control."

> Your writing style is a subconscious sum of its mechanics that is larger than its parts. The rhythm of your writing and the attitude you convey play major roles in how the reader responds to your email messages. Readers respond, consciously or unconsciously, to a false tone or awkward writing. This chapter explains ways you can use tone and rhythm to make your messages more friendly and more lively. It also explains tactics and tips for writing persuasive messages and for responding to flaming messages.

After defining style as the tactic you use to establish tone, Angell and Heslop give some specific advice for nonspecific communications:

- Use contractions to make your message friendly.
- Avoid hedging.
- Write positively.
- Create sentence rhythm.
- Make smooth transitions.

They also spend a lot of time on general grammar as it applies to the modern world. This book represents another $13 well spent.

Given that the people writing your emails have attained some level of education in the art of stringing words together in a way that can be understood by others, let's narrow our focus to the medium at hand.

Getting Their Attention (the Header)

In the world of direct mail, the only thing that matters is the envelope. The envelope has only two reasons for being. One is branding, and the other is to make the recipient want to open it. Nothing else matters—at that moment. Once they open it, a whole new set of priorities takes over. For now, it's just the envelope.

The envelope tells us who the mail is from, who it's to, and—if we're lucky—what it's about. Seeing a folded piece of paper in your mailbox with "APR 2.9%" on it is an instant giveaway and allows you to toss it out without another thought. You have plenty of credit cards already. If it says "Department of Water and Power," you know it has to go in the bills pile. The one rule that holds true for all email is that it's very hard to send or receive if they've cut off your electricity.

With email, your envelope shows a few things: who it's from, when it was sent, and what it's about. Different email clients are going to show varying other tidbits such as how big it is, what the priority level is, whether there are attachments, and so on. For now, we need only concern ourselves with the From: field and the Subject line.

From:

In looking for answers about "How Consumers Deal with Impersonal Email Messages," Jupiter Communications had NFO Interactive talk to 2222 email users. Almost 16 percent of them said they throw out any emails that come from people they don't recognize. If it's not a friend, a family member, or a coworker, they hit the Delete key. A little over 17 percent said they would open an email if it came from a familiar company. (Branding is important.)

That means one-third of the people you're trying to reach will make a yes/no decision about reading your message based on how you identify yourself. And it's no wonder.

Take a look at the spam you usually get to learn what not to do. Over the course of one week, we got spam from the following "people":

sqmvzajswfyajadv@aol.com—*Gobbledygook at AOL. No thanks.*

shoppingnews@shopitall.com—*Obviously a sales message. Delete.*

6046083328@www.inetdata.com—*A bunch of numbers? No thanks.*

RealSuccess@cnam.fr—*From France? The associated Web site says it has "over 500 courses for industrial and service fields." It's unlikely that they're spamming. But it also says, "Every year, more than 70,000 adults all over France take CNAM courses." Yes, it's very likely one of 70,000 students thinks this is a good idea.*

SuccessQuest—*Obviously a make-money-fast company.*

32229457@31326.com—*You've got to be kidding!*

So where are the real people?

In the same week, newsletters and announcements came from bona fide companies. These people aren't afraid to tell you who they are. They know they *belong* in your inbox because you invited them.

The Motley Fool

InformationWeek

PeppersAndRogers@1to1.com

ZDNet's Software Library

BlueSkies@allergy-relief.com

Interactive Week

WebPromote Weekly

ClickZ Today

Microsoft

United Airlines Mileage Plus

eFax.com

Iconocast@iconocast.com

So tell it like it is. If you're in a position to handle the response you're going to get, use your own name. If you expect a lot of reply emails, then use a generic name, but use one that is clearly from your company.

This becomes a very important issue when dealing with companies that send mail out for you. Make sure your name is the most prominent—if you are the one with the relationship.

If you are renting a list, go with a company like yesmail.com. People on that list have signed up with YesMail to receive offers that come through YesMail. The YesMail name is the one they'll recognize. It's the company to which they gave their permission. This is akin to walking up to the speakeasy and telling them Joe sent you. They'll let you in if you're a friend of a friend. They'll let you in if you're Joe.

Nick Usborne described it this way in a ClickZ article entitled "More About Writing Emails":

> When someone comes to your web site, they're in your place of business. They're your guests. Hopefully, you'll be a good host.
> But when you communicate via email, you're a stranger turning up at their home, knocking at the door and letting yourself in.
> That changes everything.
> First of all, like any good neighbor, you shouldn't just turn up uninvited. Hence the difference between an "opt-in" list and Spam.
> Spam is like a stranger just walking right on into your home and launching into a sales presentation. Not good.
> Does this mean that the only time you can ever email someone is if they have invited you? Not necessarily. A little imagination is allowed.
> I have a client who wanted to reach a large group of very targeted individuals. The client didn't have an opt-in list for that group. But he knew someone who did. So our email went out accompanied by an introduction and endorsement from the list owner.
> That's ok. It's like a friend of yours turning up at your door, coming in and saying, "Hey, I hope you don't mind me bringing Frank along. He's a good friend of mine."
> Mind you, even if you're my good buddy and I'm used to you turning up at any time, I'd appreciate it if you announced your arrival.
> "Hey Nick, it's Larry. May I come in?"
> There's a couple of things you did right here. First, you called me by my name. That tells me right away that you're not a stranger.
> Here's the email equivalent.
> "For Nick, Web Marketing Today Links, Issue 52"
> That's the subject line of an email that I received from Dr. Ralph Wilson recently. And when I look to see who sent the email it says, "Dr. Ralph F. Wilson, wct@wilsonweb.com."
> Dr. Wilson is being a very courteous and smart guy.
> He's announcing his arrival by calling out my name, so I know he's not a stranger. And he lets me know that the email is from him, Dr. Wilson, a person. A lot of companies would have put the company name in the "From" line.
> He's saying, "Hey, Nick, it's me, Dr. Wilson. May I come in?" Sure he can, any time he likes. Even if I'm sometimes too busy to read everything he sends me, his email is always welcome in my home.
> However, things change. Last year's good friend may become this year's occasional acquaintance. So even if I opt in to your list, you should always give me the opportunity to change the agreement, shift the relationship.
> That's why you always say, "May I come in?"

Now that the recipients have made some serious delete/save/read decisions based on about a half a second of looking at the From: line, they're going to look at the reason for the message.

Subject:

What's it about? Can I tell her the reason for your call? Why are you bothering me?!?

Here's your chance. This is your shot. You get one opportunity to make them open that electronic envelope and this is it. What are you going to say?

The first step in knowing what to do is to take a close look at what not to do. One week of spam brought the following subject lines. We've taken the liberty of grouping them. (And removing the ones for XXX sites. Is it just us, or does it seem those are getting fewer and farther between? Let's keep our fingers crossed.)

Meaningless

```
I'll take 1
VERY IMPORTANT Announcement !
Pls Support us
[ADV]Secure, Safe, and Easy
Important Message!
YOUR Top Secret!
attn President
PUBLISHERS CD-ROM
AMERRICANS: Fed UP with Big Brother WATCHING like a Hawk?
```

Vague offer:

```
Super software sale
For Serious Marketers ONLY
Technical assistance available . . .
CAN BULK EMAILING WORK FOR YOU??
Federal Government Property Sale 99'
AMERICANS: Get the IRS Off Your Back—LEGALLY!
Free Software!! Plus much more
Increase Sales w\4 Powerful Words
"Work Smarter, Not Harder!"
Are you looking for a gift for a special person?
PUBLISHERS CD-ROM
Protect Your Health
```

Make money fast:

```
Own your own HOME SECURITY BUSINESS for less than $1000.00
$4370.00 A MONTH FOR LIFE!!!!
Earn $50,000 In The Next 90 Days—AUQK
Great Mortgage Leads
Only 14 Good reps needed!
We'll Pay Your Debts!!!
Leverage YOUR Time and Capital . . .
Get paid for surfing the Internet, 4 levels deep!
```

```
EBIZ = 1,2,3 . . . 4 CASH
**Increase Sales w\4 Powerful Words**
Start Earning Money While You Are Sleeping
Free travel, Check me out! Big Income$
$100,000.00 and Beyond.......
MASS MAILING CAN WORK 4 U—TRY IT!$$$$$$$$$$
Interested in working from home?
Accredited Investors Only!
MAKE BIG PROFITS WITH NEW PERSONAL POSTCARDS!
Just sharing a fantastic opportunity, it's working for me!
Just sharing a fantastic oppurtunity, it's working for me!!!!
KEEP 100% OF THE REVENUE YOU GENERATE!
HOT NEW BUSINESS OPPTY.—PERSONAL POSTCARDS!
How a $5.00 investment can save you THOUSANDS of $$!
A Great Opportunity
BEWARE OF BUSINESS OPPORTUNITY SCAMS!!
1000 Envelopes=$4000.00
$1000.00 CASH GIVEAWAY
Don't Get Ripped Off!!! There's only ONE Internet Spy and You S
```

Pretend newsletter:

```
iNet News—Editor's Choice News
Club Shopitall Summer Shopping News
```

Fake component:

```
Hi
Re: how are you doing?
Fw: The Ultimate Internet Marketing Tools
"As Seen On World News"
Protect Your Health
Re: Lawsuit (this is unsolicited email)
```

Spam:

```
We are a clearing house for targeted email lists, general lists
defined -targeted..leads—EC..technology
Email--Leads-- ...reaching your internet clients
Released 8/4/99! Millions CD Vol. 5A
```

Real-sounding offers from no-name spammers:

```
WIN AUGUST'S PENTIUM 550MHz GIVEAWAY!!
Great New Book—Men Enjoy Sex More—dywtj
link your email account and telephone number together
The Internet Spy! Find out anything on everyone!
FRAMELESS BUILDING CONSTRUCTION
Free Web Site Analysis
Publishing Company for Sale!
Name$: Quit Smoking In 7 Days Or Your Money Back!!—MVFY
$7.95 for a 45 MB NT Hosting plan
Stop Getting Ripped Off !!!! $9.95 Web Hosting
Quality Inspection Services in the Far East
```

```
Internet boom going wireless !
LOSE 30 POUNDS IN 30 DAYS, GUARANTEED!
CHEAP Dental-Optical insurance!! $2 a week!!!!
UNLIMITED Long Distance Calling for only $25/month
```

Based on these and other dumb mail we've all seen, we can get some of the more obvious rules out of the way.

No Exclamation Points

Not even one. Save them for exciting stuff like "It's a Girl!" or "IPO Today!" Definitely not more than one. One of the first spam filters anybody sets up has a rule that says if it has more than one exclamation point, it is automatically routed to the trash, untouched by human hands.

No $$$

Dollar signs are in the same category. After sending the third email looking for payment of an old, old invoice, I got a call from a client in London. Hadn't I received his replies? I looked through my email archives and found none for the dates he had claimed the messages were sent.

```
"And I just sent another one about an hour ago. What's wrong with your
email?"
"Maybe the dates are wacky. What's the subject line?"
"Need your address to send your $$$"
```

Sure enough, the message was right there in the trash folder.

No Free

This one's a tough call. Nothing in life is free but the Internet has changed that just a little. There are free email accounts, free horoscopes, and free Web pages. But for the most part, the only things that are offered for free are things that seem too good to be true. You don't want to be painted with the spamming brush, so don't overuse the word, but if you're starting with a well-known, trusted brand, "Free" might be your most powerful ally.

NO ALL CAPS

Yes, this is shouting. If the email filter were smart enough, it would recognize an all-caps subject line and send it to the vaporizing unit at once.

Instead of ALL UPPERCASE letters, instead of all lowercase letters, and instead of Using Title-Case letters, use standard sentence case. Start with a capital and leave the rest lowercase except for proper names. Why? Because it's easier to read.

Email is starting to make people wish they were born with Evelyn Wood's reading skills. They are glancing at subject lines in order to make as quick a determination as possible. It's easier to read lowercase letters than title-case. Case closed.

Be Brief

Even if prospects have their email program window open as far as it'll go and have each message open as far as it'll go, a subject line like "Don't Get Ripped Off!!! There's only ONE Internet Spy and You S" gets truncated by one of the systems along the way. It could be the mail sending system, it could be the ISP gateway, or it could be the email client.

Angell and Heslop figure the first 25 to 35 characters are all that end up getting displayed. So keep it short and to the point.

Don't Pretend

If you're trying to make an offer, make an offer. Getting people to open your message by subterfuge might work—it might get them to open the message. But then you're faced with the enormous task of getting them to forgive you for the ruse and get interested in your offer.

Motivate Them

Much better to use the subject line as a hook for your offer. Make them want to open the message so they can learn more. Come up with three to five words that sum up your pitch.

A subject line is most effective when it can accomplish four things:

1. Solve a problem.
2. Solve that problem quickly.
3. Solve that problem for what appears to be a small or reasonable amount of money.
4. Create intrigue.

Angell and Heslop like the idea of using actions in your subject line. Tell recipients what you want them to do. Rather than just saying "20% Discount on radial tires," you might encourage them to "Take 20% off radial tires."

Writing Effective Email, by Nancy Flynn and Tom Flynn (1998), is part of the "Fifty Minute Series" of books by Crisp Publications. It's brief, to be sure, but the section entitled "Writing a Subject Line with Real Oomph" makes a very important point.

REMEMBER THE HIDDEN READER
When messages are forwarded from one reader to the next, the original subject line often is left intact. This gives you the opportunity to attract a broader audience of unintended readers to your message.

Follow-on readership is an important enough issue with email to warrant its own section (see *Word of Mouth*). But it's not too soon to consider these hidden readers while you're writing your subject line.

When Little Things Mean a Lot

Ron Richards, the president of ResultsLab (www.resultslab.com), once found himself losing sleep about one word in an email subject line he wrote for an online publisher.

ResultsLab is a San Francisco agency that specializes in optimizing the persuasion elements in email campaigns—the strategy, the words, and the pictures. They're obsessed with results. When I described Ron in my book, *What Makes People Click: Advertising on the Web,* I said he was "a curious mix of creativity and scientific analysis. Imagine a genetic lab mixture that produced a clone from the DNA from David Ogilvy and Thomas Edison." I stand by that description, but now I get to add that he's been applying his *persuasion engineering* skills to email marketing in the several years since *What Makes People Click* was published.

The word that kept Ron awake was already in the email and repeated on the site. The line read:

```
Subject: Readers' Choice of Twelve Must-Read Articles From Past Issues
```

Ron's client, the publisher, was after one thing: daily pageviews. The more pages visitors wanted to read, the more ads they showed, and the more money they raked in.

The next morning, Ron changed the line to read:

```
Subject: Readers' Choice of Twelve Must-Read Articles From Recent Issues
```

Most of us would ignore that one word, "Past," almost at the end of the line. But these guys really are obsessed with the deep psychological impact of every element. Ron thought the word might imply that those articles were old hat. Knowing the articles were all from the past six months, and quite relevant, he decided it was just as honest and more powerful to change the word to "Recent."

Pageviews increased by 17 percent.

In ResultsLab's work in optimizing email, banner ads, and Web sites, they sometimes find dozens of these little improvements that matter. Sometimes the hidden poison elements cause response to hover around zero. Ron loves to point out that if ResultsLab finds six elements that multiply results by 1.3 times each, the compounded effect is fivefold.

Michael McCarthy, the president of IDG's online technical magazine division, agrees. "That very first ResultsLab letter pulled a far higher response than we'd ever seen. The degree of gain surprised everyone until Ron explained the dozen subtle reasons it worked so well." I've seen him do it and you can read how it works in "The Multiplier Principle" at the ResultsLab Web site. Ron lives and breathes human motivators.

First, Catch the Rabbit (First Line of a New England Rabbit Stew Recipe)

Ron says an email's most critical grabbers by far are in the header: the Subject:, the From:, and the To: lines. "After all, the email won't get opened if any of those are poisoned; in fact, since everyone gets a lot of junk mail, those elements had better make opening the mail virtually irresistible."

What's irresistible? He says, "Some of the main qualities you want are: signaling a compelling issue, talking to fundamental human desire, uniqueness, urgency, news, and an offer of fascinating learning. Be very clear about the learning you're offering if someone opens the email. Never 'bait and switch,' by promising something the email doesn't deliver.

"On the other hand, don't fall into the trap of giving away the story or news. Curiosity and anticipation are key. When we train experienced copywriters and journalists, we find the 'give away' is one of their main pitfalls."

He gave us a few examples of subjects from his projects, with the principle involved:

DECISION HELP

Subject: Urgent upgrade decisions, and those to delay.

SOCIAL PROOF

Subject: Our number one-rated story in the past four months. Half of our visitors read this.

WORD OF MOUTH

Subject: Send this article URL to your whole team.

To:

You have two choices in the To: field. You can send your message to a collective name such as "Newsletter Subscribers," or "Lucky Customers," or you can send it to individuals.

The vast majority of spam comes from a fake address and goes to a fake address. Consider this space unusable for promotions. Sending your offer to "Prize Winners" feels just a little flaky, and chances are excellent that recipients won't even read it.

All legitimate emailers have legitimate addresses and should use them. You want your relationship to be with me. Calling me by name goes a long way toward making me feel like a member of the inner circle, rather than one of the nameless, faceless hordes.

Hide Your List

It's happened to the best of us. Somebody with an itchy trigger finger sends off a mass email to a carefully culled list of good, trusted customers and that very list ends up in the To: field or the Cc: field. The result? Everybody who gets it sees the names of everybody else who got it. It's not a pretty sight.

April 1999 was a bad month for email marketers. AT&T sent out an email to 1800 customers. And put them all in the Cc: field. Nissan sent out an update on its newest sport utility vehicle and did the same thing. Only this time, the number was 24,000. One can only assume that there was a Ford employee or two among them.

Before We Begin, Tell Them How to End

This is the rest of the aforementioned article by Nick Usborn:

> Being a courteous person, you always ask me if it's ok to come in. We can take a lesson from ClickZ on how to do that online.
>
> First, ClickZ announces itself:
>
> **THE CLICKZ NETWORK TODAY**
> The Internet's Leading Resource for Doing Business Online
> Thursday, February 11, 1999
>
> The masthead says, "Hey Nick, it's us from ClickZ."
> Then, immediately, follows:
>
> **HOW TO UNSUBSCRIBE**
> If you'd like to remove yourself from The ClickZ Network Today mailing list, go to http://www.clickz.com/subscribe.shtml and follow the instructions.
>
> This is the email equivalent of asking, "Is it ok if we come in?" Sure it is. I may not have time for you every day, but make yourself at home.
>
> What has this got to do with writing? The way we write depends so much on where our head is when we sit down to write.
>
> If you write email communications with a view to reaching a large mass of people and selling to them, I think your success will be limited.
>
> But if, while you write, you never lose sight of the fact that you're reaching someone in their space and owe them a level of simple courtesy, I think you'll do much better.
>
> You're never writing to 10,000 people. You're always writing to one person.
>
> Keep that person in mind as you write and look at what you're writing—and how you're writing it—through that one person's eyes.
>
> And never forget that with email, you're their guest for only as long as they want. Respect that.

Respect their desires when they've had enough of you. Make it as easy as possible to unsubscribe. Is unsubscribing really that important? AltaVista found 496,940 Web pages given that search term. You bet it's important.

Finding people is hard. Getting them to sign up is harder. Why would you want to let them go? Because this is their relationship. Make sure that each message you send includes the option to get off your list, and put it in a prominent position.

Voice mail may be one of the most annoying things ever invented by mankind. The worst "I'm not here" messages are the ones that go on and on about where they are that day; when they'll get back; whom you can call in the meantime; how to get hold of an operator; a list of their pager number, their mobile phone number, their dog sitter's pager number, and—oh yes—if you'd like to skip this message next time, just hit star, pound, ampersand, at, dollar sign. That's exactly what you feel like saying: "*#&@$!".

Why not make that clear up front, before launching into the Phone Directory of You? Same goes for email. Put the unsubscribe message in plain sight.

Leading the Way

The U.S. Postal Service has a whole Web site dedicated to helping people send better direct mail (www.uspsdirectmail.com). See Figure 6.17. One of the pages of advice you'll find there is called "Making Creative Work."

On their "Making Creative Work" page, the Postal Service offers some advice about the first thing a reader sees upon opening an envelope.

> There are several identifying features to a typical Direct Mail letter. . . . The first one greeting your target will be (if you choose to have one) a "Johnson Box." This technique was devised by a Direct Mail writer named Frank (you guessed it) Johnson many years ago.

Figure 6.17   The Postal Service wants to help you send better junk mail.

The Johnson Box is the "headline" at the top of your letter, set apart from the text and often encased by a solid line. Research has shown that adding a Johnson Box to a letter will increase response by an average of 40%. It should be short, one or two lines, at most, and include the main benefit, offer or anything else that might intrigue your customer to read on.

People want information and they want it now. They will not waste valuable time trying to figure out what you're trying to sell. That's why a short, snappy beginning will pull better than a long wind-up.

The first two sentences should tell who you are, what you want from the reader, and why they should care. You better make these lines count, because they are the only thing that will make people want to read more. Your lead is the top of the inverted pyramid to which journalists always refer. Put the most important information at the top. Save the elaboration for those you have successfully compelled to continue reading.

The lead should take four items into account right off the bat. Who is it for? Why did you single them out? What is it you're offering? What's in it for them?

For owners of pets with special dietary needs, our veterinarian approved dog and cat foods will give you peace of mind and healthier pets!

At a conference for distributors of Zebra Technologies' printers, Doug King from the U.S. Postal Service gave a wonderful presentation on creating direct mail. A lot of what he said applies directly to email marketing. One of the things he handed out was a list of "23 Key Appeals That Work with Direct Mail":

THE DESIRE TO GAIN:

Make Money
Avoid Effort
Save Time
Have Health
Be Popular
Experience Pleasure
Be Clean
Be Praised
Be Admired
Satisfy Curiosity
Satisfy Appetite
Have Beautiful Possessions
Attract Opposite Sex
Be an Individual
Emulate Others
Be an Opportunist

THE DESIRE TO AVOID:

Criticism
Lost Possessions
Physical Pain
Uncertainty
Premature Aging

Loss of Reputation
Loss of Money
Legal Trouble
Feeling Uneducated
Falling Behind the Trends
Losing Control of One's Future
Disease and Illness
Hassles and Time Killers
Embarrassment

Without writing an entire book on the finer points of direct marketing writing skills, suffice it to say that the lead is where you harp on one of these seven traditional human motivators and position yourself as the one company that can satisfy them.

THE SEVEN TRADITIONAL HUMAN MOTIVATORS

Need

Greed

Guilt

Fear

Exclusivity

Relief

Flattery

POSITIONING YOURSELF AS THE SOLUTION

Price

Value

Quality

Status

Uniqueness

Consider asking a question as a lead to your message. Get them to think *Yes* often enough and it'll seem natural for them to think *Yes* when you hit them with the call to action.

Grabbers, Grabbers Everywhere

Ron Richards knows how to optimize body headlines, subheads, lead lines, the letterhead, and the letterfoot. Remember his concept that six improvements that improve response 1.3 times each are equal to a fivefold gain? Ron lays out many more of the principles of creating great grabbers in four articles at www.result-slab.com. Our favorite is called "Grabbers Before and After," where he shows dozens of examples before and after ResultsLab rewrote them, and explains the principles involved.

Example number eight on that page shows *before*:

```
Book Excerpt: The best of the Netscape Plug-ins
```

and *after*:

```
Plug-ins: Tricks for finding, installing, and using the best
```

He then describes why the changes are important: "The revision puts the topic first, where it can better grab the eye of those interested in Plug-ins. But Plug-ins were old hat, so the new language offered learning of interest to a large audience whether new to Plug-ins, or very experienced. I call the technique a word-picture-cluster."

The first line or paragraph of the body copy is crucial, but ResultsLab has found that conventional wisdom advocating brevity has exceptions. For example, Ron believes that sometimes opening paragraphs can be more powerful if they're long, provided they're riddled with great grabbers. Here are two examples of email openings he wrote for an online publisher to prompt subscribers to come to the homepage (cover page) of the site.

First example:

```
I think we have a breakthrough to help you know in minutes which of the
28 articles in the November issue are for you -- exactly matched to your
current needs and interests.
We created brief descriptions of every story -- and put them all right
on the cover. By spending a few minutes speed-reading the story descrip-
tions, you'll know which are must-reading in your situation.
```

Second example:

```
Which articles do readers rate highest, rave about, and consider must
reading? In this letter, I'm including descriptions of the top 10% from
recent months--and what readers said about them.
```

He advocates keeping away from empty leads devoid of news, such as:

```
Greetings newsletter reader!
```

or

```
This is your email alert from the editors. The latest issue is ready for
you!
```

Body Building

The body of your email is the payoff. You got them to open your email by convincing them it was worth their time. Now make sure it really is. The competition here is much fiercer than in the paper world of the mailbox.

In another one of his ClickZ articles (August 6, 1999), Nick Usborne made us marketers walk in the email recipients' shoes for a few miles.

BEWARE LONG BRAINLOAD TIMES

Until now, it has been okay to put together your direct response email in a fairly casual sort of way. It's been okay to mix up a few ideas, throw in a couple of links, slop it all around into one big mess and email it out to 50,000 people.

After all, an email is a pretty simple thing to figure out. Start at the top and keep reading. It's not like a web site with hundreds of pages. Architecture, navigation and the organization of content are just for the web. Right?

Well, that approach may have been okay before, but I don't think it works any more. It doesn't work because your customers are being flooded with an increasing volume of email each day. And that means each individual email will receive a little less attention. And if your email receives less attention, you're going to have less time in which to catch and hold your reader.

How come? Because of "brainload time."

On the web we are all very aware of download times. The longer the download time, the fewer the number of visitors who will bother to hang around and wait for you.

On the web, we measure the time it takes for a page to download to the visitor's screen. I think there's an equivalent with email. It's brainload time. . . .

Brainload time is the time it takes for the recipient to figure out what your email is all about. (Assuming that they have bothered to open your email in the first place. But that's a different subject.)

Brainload time is the time it takes for someone to understand the reason for your email—plus the time it takes to decide whether or not they're even remotely interested in what you have to say—plus the time it takes to work out what you want them to do.

Let me break that down into a list of deliverables, from the customer's point of view:

What is this about? Do I care? What do they want me to do, and how do I do it?

Those are three things your email has to achieve in order to get to the point at which the reader can choose to respond or not.

Now for the big question: How much time do you think you need in order to cover those points? How long will the average email reader give you? What's the maximum brainload time?

Here's my guess. I think that from the moment someone opens your email you have three or four seconds. Max.

Why is this less than for a web page? Because customers can get in and out of their email messages much faster. It's easier to navigate from one message to another.

On a web site I may have committed five minutes to finding a site. If that site takes 10 seconds to download, I'll probably wait—because I have already committed a lot of time to find out what's on that page. With email I can get in and out of messages much faster. Lower commitment all around.

So. You have four seconds.

Four seconds in which to make me think, "Ah, this is about xyz."

Plus . . .

"Sure. That interests me."

Plus . . .

"Here's the link that tells me more."

That's not much time.

So you'd better start thinking "above the fold" in your emails. You better think about organizing the content of your emails more deliberately and more carefully. You'd better increase the quality of the writing so that what you want to say is communicated quickly and clearly.

Because in "killer-app land" the honeymoon is over. And slow brainload times will kill your response rates.

We all live in a world of information overload. Your message better be good.

Format Revisited

To start with, keep it simple. Don't use fancy colors or bold or italics or any other special font that may not be displayed the same way on different email clients. Give up on fighting for control of how your message looks, because you do not have control. You have to lay your messages out pretty carefully to make sure they display well, given the limitations of all the email reader software out there.

Keep your sentences short. They're easier to understand. Keep your lines short so they don't wrap wrong. Keep your paragraphs short and (maybe) your whole darned message short.

Line Length

This is the one time in your life that somebody is going to advise you to think *inside* the box. In this case, it's the box your email is going to show up in. Angell and Heslop warned against creating words nobody could see:

> Keep your line length less than 80 characters. On some terminals the lines might not wrap at all and the last 20 characters of a 100-character line will not be displayed.

> Keep the line length to less than 60 characters if your message is likely to be forwarded. Forwarded messages are often indented by a tab character, which is usually 8 characters in length.

Most email programs are pretty good about wrapping, but the result is a truly ugly message. The real problem comes when a hard carriage-return ends up on the end of each line. If Amazon.com were careless, their messages might end up looking like Figure 6.18 or Figure 6.19, rather than Figure 6.20.

Paragraphs

Most email systems also put a greater-than sign (>) in front of each line of the forwarded message: Each time it's forwarded, another greater-than sign is added. When counting line length, don't forget your follow-on readership.

Email Attention Deficit Disorder dictates short blasts of communication. Think in terms of trying to get your point across to somebody in a serious hurry. People are staring intently at the screen, trying to make sense out of your message. Make it as easy as possible for them to understand what you're offering.

White Space

When we first started reading, we had books with lots of pictures and a few words. As we got older, we faced those fat tomes with no pictures at all. On the page, there's nothing quite so daunting as one large block of text. Try to break it up a little.

Andy Bourland kicks off an Andromedia seminar invitation with some fairly blocky paragraphs (see Figure 6.21).

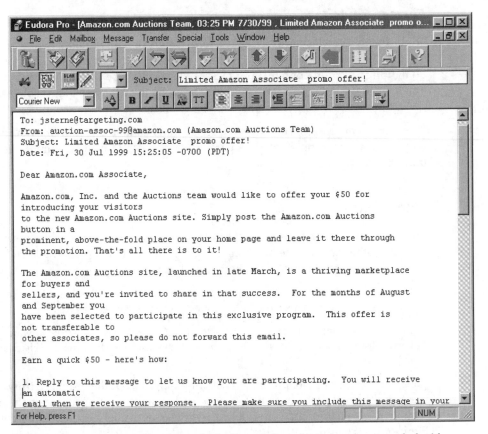

Figure 6.18 Hard returns at the end of a line work against you when coupled with an email client that wraps as it should.

Reading too much of this sort of text is hard work and the copy must be scintillating to get the reading to continue. That's why Andy decided to use a little formatting below the fold (see Figure 6.22).

ASCII Graphics

Smart direct marketers break up their postal mail letters with some sort of graphic element. You can do this with headlines acting as a design element as well, breaking up a text-dense message and making it easier to read. Or you can try using ASCII characters as graphic design elements.

There's a serious fifty-fifty split on this issue—it's simply a matter of taste and common sense. Common sense says not to use special characters. Use special characters? No way. Nothing looks worse than weird characters showing up in the middle of your message because you forgot to turn off Microsoft Word's Smart Quotes. Copyright and trademark symbols, long dashes, and a host of other non-ASCII characters can get you in trouble.

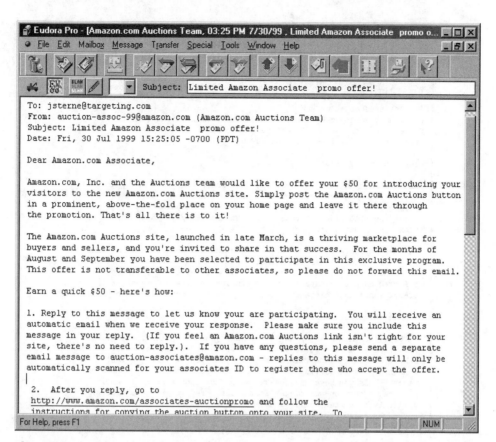

Figure 6.19 With no hard returns, the message is correct; it's just very hard to read with such long lines of text.

Taste says some emphasis is critical to a marketing message, and ASCII is the right way to go. Don't use a special bullet; use an asterisk. Good suggestion. If you wish to emphasize something, do it with an asterisk on either side to make it *stand out.* But you can also:

```
Underline important passages with the caret symbol.
     ^^^^^^^^^^^^^^^^^^^

              CENTER HEADLINES
              FOR MORE ATTENTION

#############################################
##                                         ##
##    Draw a box around critical points!   ##
##                                         ##
#############################################
```

But you can run into trouble using these devices. That trouble is proportional to the degree you rely on them to get your message across. If the whole world used the same font, life would be simple. The world doesn't, so life isn't.

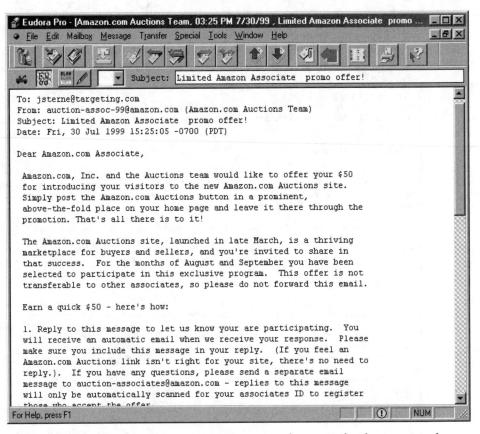

Figure 6.20 In reality, Amazon.com was smart enough to use a hard return to make each line less than 56 characters long.

If you create some fancy ASCII artwork, you could end up confusing the heck out of people (see Figures 6.23 and 6.24).

If you feel it's really important to communicate with your customers via ASCII art, take a look at Email Effects from Sig Software (www.sigsoftware.com). According to their Web site, "Email Effects is a program for getting the most out of email. With it, you can send pictures, drawings, and tables using simple plain text. It is also the world's premier ASCII art creator and great for creating vivid comments in source code."

Smileys

We find the occasional wink ;-), consisting of a semicolon, a hyphen, and a right parenthesis, to be useful in chatty emails between friends and relations. But in a business communication? Only if your brand can stand it.

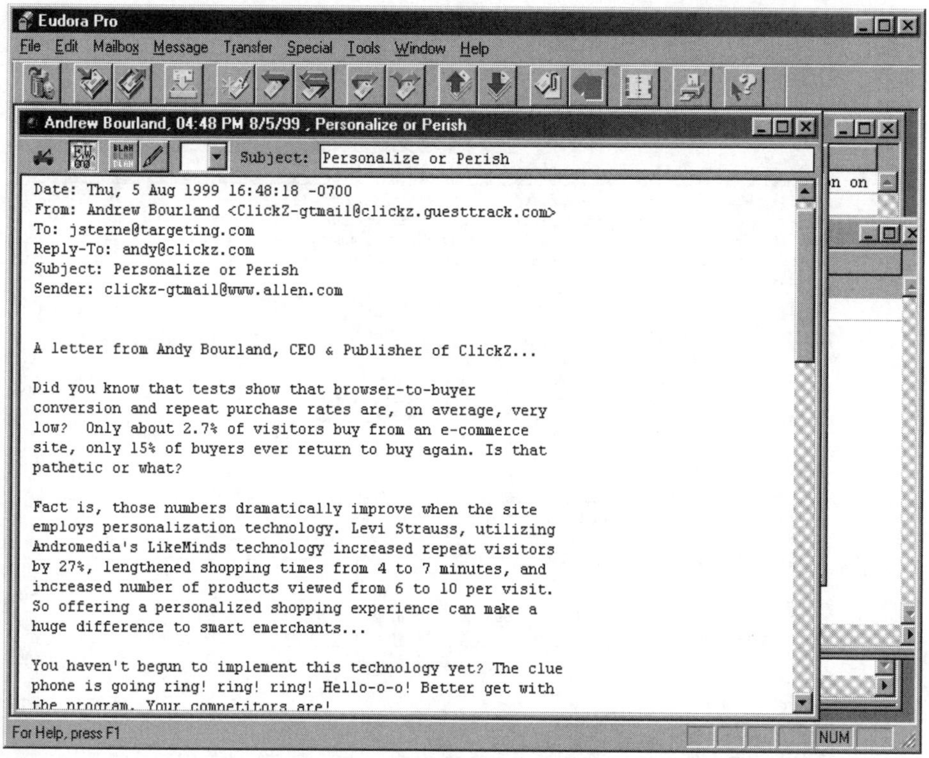

Figure 6.21 This seminar invitation is made up of pretty standard block paragraphs.

An email from IBM with a smiley in it is a little unnerving. If we got one from Charles Schwab, we'd find a new place for the IRA account. But a message from Comedy Central with a few funny faces? No problem. Nevertheless, there's one very good argument for not using the little ASCII emoticons, and nobody better to argue it than Network World's Mark Gibbs.

The Long Form or the Short Form

There's another universe of debate over whether direct marketers should indulge in a tell-all, sell-all style of writing. The tell-all long form gets the entire story in front of the prospect. It lets you address every benefit, conquer every objection, and sell, sell, sell.

If you think you can hold somebody's attention to their computer screen and get them to scroll and scroll and scroll, and sell them in one go, then you are welcome to give it a try. Let us know how it works for you. For the rest, we recommend keeping it short—three or four paragraphs.

You want to tell the whole story? Give 'em a link.

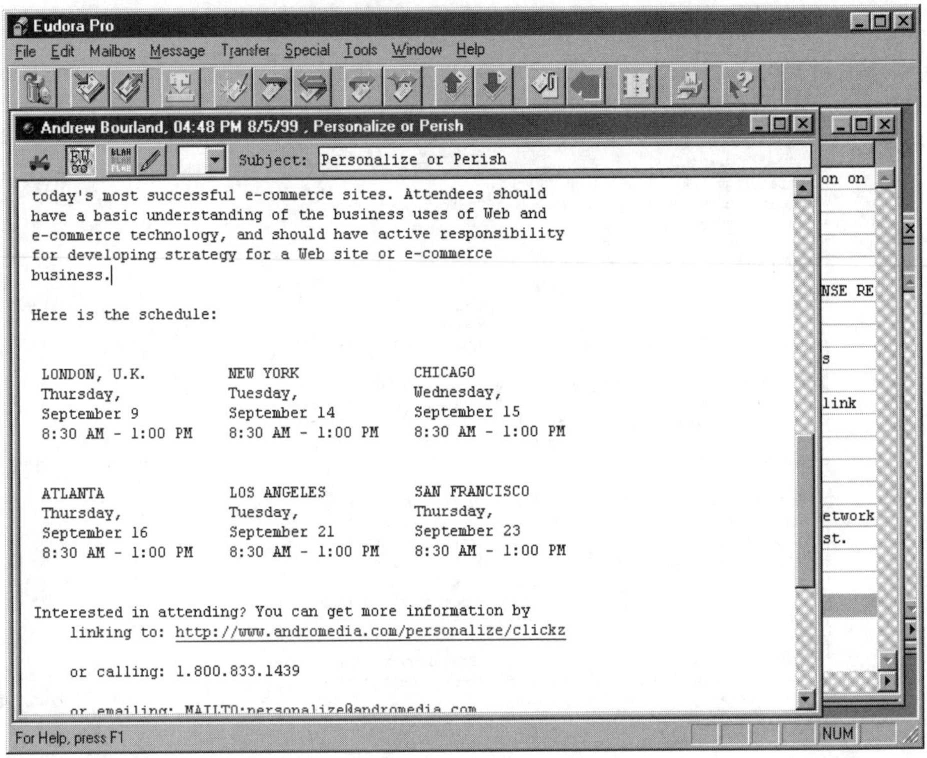

Figure 6.22 The schedule and contact information are much easier to read due to a healthy use of white space.

Walk into My Parlor

> *"Will you walk into my parlor?"* said the spider to the fly;
> *"'Tis the prettiest little parlor that ever you did spy.*
> *The way into my parlor is up a winding stair,*
> *And I have many pretty things to show when you are there."*
>   **Mary Howitt**

The only thing that matters when your email message shows up is getting them to open it and read it. The only thing that matters when they read your email is whether they click through to your Web site and complete the desired action.

Yes, you want them to read your words. Yes, you want them to have a positive brand impression. Yes, you want them to want to know more, see more, and do something about it. Clicking on a link to your Web site is one of the best ways to get them to the end goal.

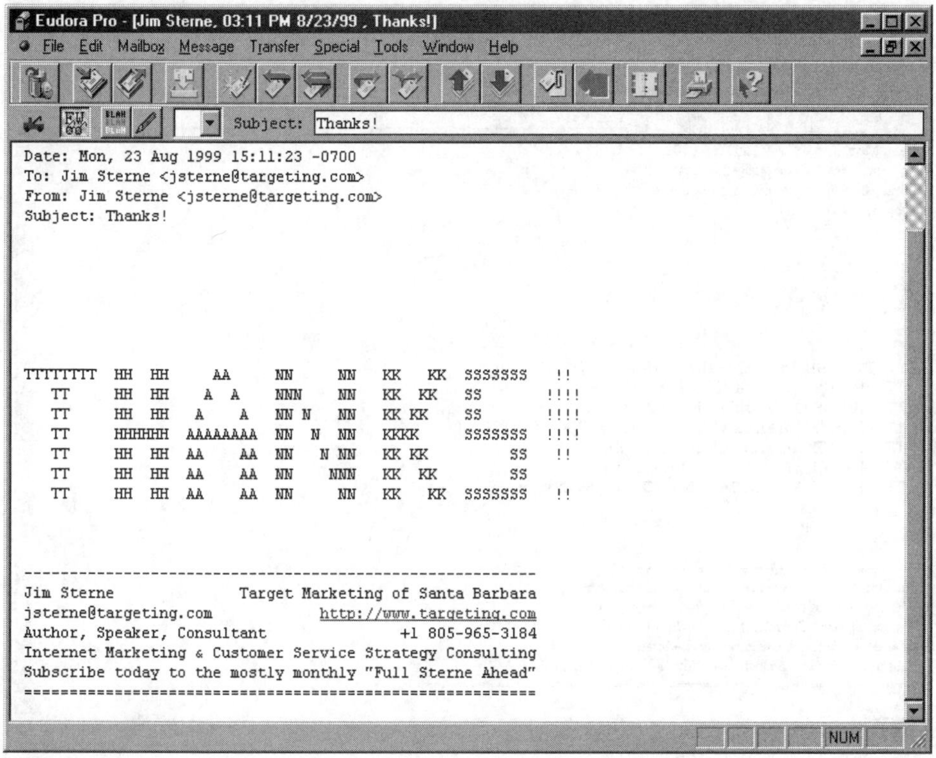

```
 Eudora Pro - [Jim Sterne, 03:11 PM 8/23/99 , Thanks!]                    _ □ X
  File  Edit  Mailbox  Message  Transfer  Special  Tools  Window  Help      _ ⑤ X
```

```
Date: Mon, 23 Aug 1999 15:11:23 -0700
To: Jim Sterne <jsterne@targeting.com>
From: Jim Sterne <jsterne@targeting.com>
Subject: Thanks!




TTTTTTTT  HH  HH     AA      NN    NN  KK   KK  SSSSSSS   !!
   TT     HH  HH    A  A     NNN   NN  KK KK    SS       !!!!
   TT     HH  HH   A    A    NN N  NN  KK KK    SS       !!!!
   TT     HHHHHH  AAAAAAAA   NN  N NN  KKKK     SSSSSSS  !!!!
   TT     HH  HH  AA    AA   NN   N NN KK KK         SS  !!
   TT     HH  HH  AA    AA   NN    NNN KK KK         SS
   TT     HH  HH  AA    AA   NN    NN  KK   KK  SSSSSSS   !!



-------------------------------------------------------
Jim Sterne          Target Marketing of Santa Barbara
jsterne@targeting.com        http://www.targeting.com
Author, Speaker, Consultant         +1 805-965-3184
Internet Marketing & Customer Service Strategy Consulting
Subscribe today to the mostly monthly "Full Sterne Ahead"
=======================================================
```

Figure 6.23 A fun ASCII *Thank You* looks great if everybody who receives it is using a fixed-width font.

Click Here

Don't make them guess. Don't make them wonder. Don't make them highlight your domain name from your email address, put a "www" in front and a ".com" behind in order to flounder their way to your homepage. Give them an active link.

This is the easiest call to action any marketer ever laid before a prospect. There's no charge for the call, no number to remember, no address to write to, no showroom to find, no parking lot to navigate, no salesperson to talk to. It's just a click. Just a simple, little click.

> "I'm sure you must be weary, dear, with soaring up so high;
> Will you rest upon my little bed?" said the spider to the fly.
> "There are pretty curtains drawn around, the sheets are fine and thin,
> And if you like to rest a while, I'll snugly tuck you in."

The best benefits you can imagine, the best promises you can fulfill, and the best offer you can make should be squeezed into a very few paragraphs so you can get that reader to click.

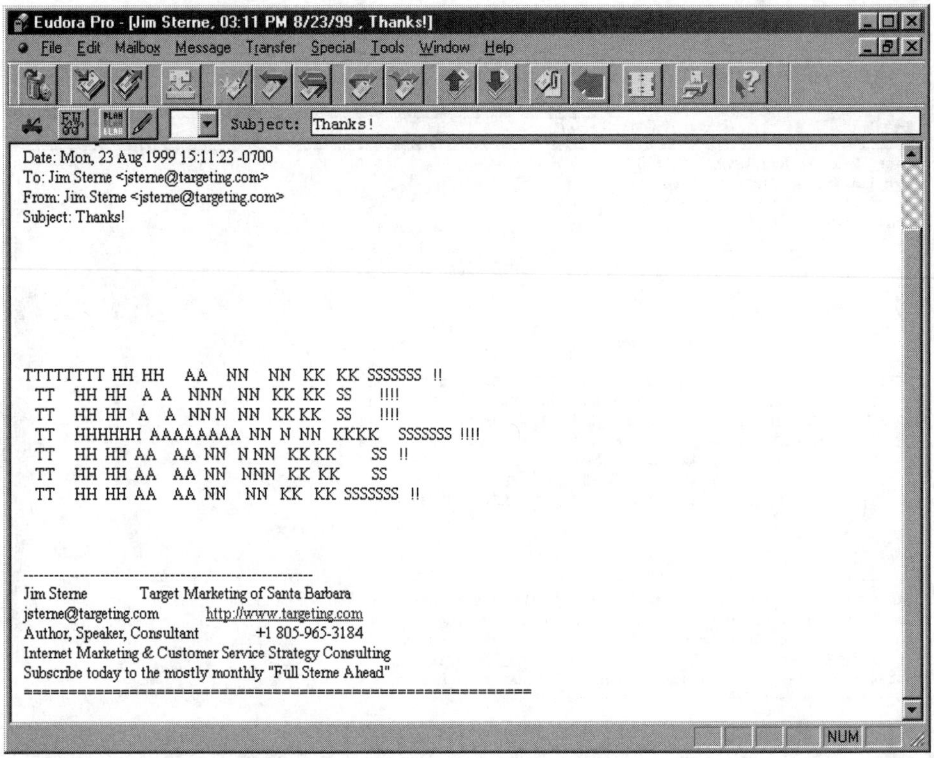

```
 Eudora Pro - [Jim Sterne, 03:11 PM 8/23/99 , Thanks!]
 File  Edit  Mailbox  Message  Transfer  Special  Tools  Window  Help
```

Subject: Thanks!

```
Date: Mon, 23 Aug 1999 15:11:23 -0700
To: Jim Sterne <jsterne@targeting.com>
From: Jim Sterne <jsterne@targeting.com>
Subject: Thanks!




TTTTTTTT HH HH  AA  NN  NN KK  KK SSSSSSS !!
  TT   HH HH A A NNN NN KK KK SS    !!!!
  TT   HH HH A A NN N NN KK KK SS    !!!!
  TT   HHHHHH AAAAAAAA NN N NN KKKK  SSSSSS !!!!
  TT   HH HH AA  AA NN N NN KK KK    SS !!
  TT   HH HH AA  AA NN  NNN KK KK    SS
  TT   HH HH AA  AA NN  NN KK KK SSSSSSS !!




------------------------------------------------------
Jim Sterne        Target Marketing of Santa Barbara
jsterne@targeting.com      http://www.targeting.com
Author, Speaker, Consultant      +1 805-965-3184
Internet Marketing & Customer Service Strategy Consulting
Subscribe today to the mostly monthly "Full Sterne Ahead"
======================================================
```

Figure 6.24 That same *Thank You* looks completely unprofessional when viewed with a proportional font.

> *"Sweet creature!" said the spider, "You're witty and you're wise,*
> *How handsome are your gauzy wings, how brilliant are your eyes!*
> *I have a little looking glass upon my parlor shelf,*
> *If you'll step in one moment, dear, you shall behold yourself."*

It's true that everybody's favorite subject is the same: themselves. The power of your product? The lowness of your price? The cleverness of your manufacturing process? The swiftness of your delivery?

None of these can hold a candle to how your product will make prospects feel about themselves.

> *He went out to his door again, and merrily did sing,*
> *"Come hither, hither, pretty fly, with the pearl and silver wing;*
> *Your robes are green and purple, there's a crest upon your head;*
> *Your eyes are like the diamond bright, but mine are dull as lead"*

The call to action isn't merely to click. The call to action is to click here for a knockout new look, click here for the book that will make you smart, or click here for the magic that will make you the envy of your peers.

Don't Say It with Smileys

By Mark Gibbs

Network World, 08/09/99

If we were standing face to face and I said something along the lines of, "I absolutely disagree with you, and I think you're an idiot," and then I smiled, what would you do? You would probably think "smug b*#$*%d" and attempt to smack me around the head.

So what I can't figure out is why people are willing to do in email what they won't do in person? Why do people feel no compunction about insulting me online and following it up with a smiley face?

Smileys are those concatenations of ASCII characters that are supposed to convey emotion in plain text messages, as in :-). I find it impossible to believe that Network World readers don't know about smileys, but just in case, :-) is supposed to imply lightheartedness as in "I can't find the 'any' key :-)." Thousands of smileys have been invented for all sorts of things. There are smileys for sadness, :-(, smugness :->, resoluteness :-|, a prognathous jaw :-], a lolling tongue :-P and a pointy nose :^).

These were once funny, but now they have descended to the nether regions of cultural hell alongside "Precious Moments" figures and Day-Glo velvet pictures of Elvis.

<confession> Out on the Internet there are far too many Web sites that have endless lists of smileys and their "meanings," and I must confess that I included a list of smileys in my book *Navigating the Internet.* <excuse> That was published in 1993 when the whole Internet thing was novel. </excuse> </confession>

In my "any" key example, using a smiley to indicate the lack of seriousness is obviously irrelevant, but you see the same convention used in messages such as "I absolutely disagree with you :-)."

Now ask yourself what that message really means. I contend the message means, "I absolutely disagree with you, but please don't get serious about it." That's a pretty reasonable request, so why beat about the bush? Come right out and say it.

But, of course, context is everything. If the message were in reply to, "Do you think the logo should be in blue?" then the sender would probably not be too upset. But in response to, "You have to marry my daughter, you swine," the result would, most likely, be quite different, particularly if someone toting a shotgun delivered the message.

So how are smileys used badly? Many people add smileys to be cute, so "Am I trying to be cute?" should be one of the first questions to ask.

If the answer is yes and the recipient isn't your mother or a paramour who doesn't mind a dose of saccharine, then go ahead and look like a half-wit if you wish.

On the other hand, if you are trying to take the sting out of a comment that you can't figure out how to rephrase and you think a smiley is the way to go, save the message and lie down in a dark room until the impulse subsides. Chances are, you will soon realize that you were attempting to be duplicitous. <digression> People write terribly when it comes to email or, for that matter, business correspondence in general. I recently heard of a large organization that retains a staff of four writers just to rewrite memos created by vice presidents so they can be understood! </digression>

Continues

Don't Say It with Smileys *(Continued)*

So when you receive a message containing a smiley, ask yourself what the sender is really trying to say, and assume that the sender is being deceitful. When you feel tempted to use a smiley, ask yourself what it is you're trying to say, whom you are saying it to and what the purpose is. After you choose your smiley, don't use it. Learn to say what you mean.

> *Alas, alas! how very soon this silly little fly,*
> *Hearing his wily flattering words, came slowly flitting by,*
> *With buzzing wings she hung aloft, then nearer and nearer drew,*
> *Thinking only of her brilliant eyes, and green and purple hue*

Yes, you're going to treat your prospects better than the spider treated the fly. You're going to do it from the very beginning by sending them to the next logical step in the buying process and not dumping them on your homepage to fend for themselves.

Point Them to the Right Page

The link in the Andromedia seminar invitation (see Figure 6.22) brings the recipient for a smooth landing on a page all about the seminar (see Figure 6.25)—a landing page.

If the link had taken the reader to Andromedia's rather busy homepage (see Figure 6.26), the prospective seminar attendee might have had trouble with registration.

In about three blinks of an eye, you can find a rather prominent button. Unless, of course, your monitor is set to 800 × 600. In that case, you can see "Personalize or Perish, The New E-Marketing Mandate," but you can't see "sign up for a FREE seminar today." That wouldn't be so bad, if it weren't for the fact that the second phrase is clickable and the rest of the graphic is not.

In the meantime, there are confusing things you *can* click on, such as "Product Tour," "Live Demo," and "Events." In the grand scheme of things, bringing people from an email to this homepage would not have been an egregious error, especially when compared to how hard it is to find things on most Web sites. But Andromedia didn't want prospective seminar attendees to be confused for even three blinks of an eye. Neither should you.

Give Them More than One Link

Consider multiple links, but don't confuse them. Don't give them a link for more information, a link for the order form, a link for the press release, and a link for marketing partners. Give them multiple opportunities to click on the same link.

Provide one link near the top and one near the bottom. You want people to be able to click when the impulse strikes. Don't make them scroll to find the URL.

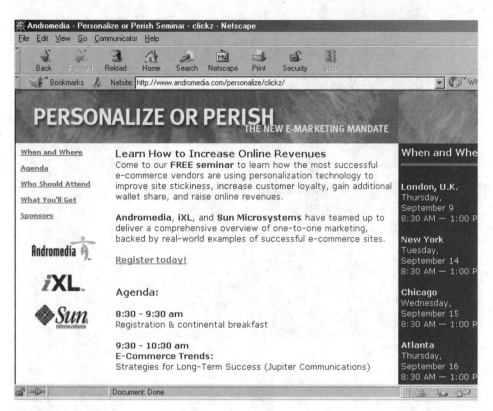

Figure 6.25 The email invitation is for the seminar and not the product—yet.

If you want to get a head start on personalization, you might consider breaking the aforementioned "don't confuse them" rule. You might give them three choices for getting to the ordering page:

1. Click here for the Deluxe Package.
2. Click here for the Super Deluxe Package.
3. Click here for the Super Deluxe Series with free delivery.

But a word of caution. Don't make the email intimidating. You don't have much space and you don't have much time. Once they get to your Web site, you have a lot more freedom.

Personalize the Landing Page

As you send out individual emails to individual people, consider embedding some sort of identification into each message. Why? So when they click through to the landing page it already has some information about them on it.

Want them to fill out a form? Help them along. You know something about their preferences? Let it show. This makes moving from the very private space of their email to

Figure 6.26 Quick, where's the Personalize or Perish Seminar link?

the more public space of your Web site a lot smoother and gentler. They'll feel welcomed, and they'll feel more like buying.

Avoid Email Black Holes

ResultsLab has discovered that you can have an email that is, in a sense, too compelling. Ron Richards, president of ResultsLab, explains how this can happen and how to solve the problem:

> Emails often contain news of an exciting new area on the site, or some product augmentation. For example, suppose you have a community portal of some sort and you add EWallet, giving your members the ability to have one-click ordering on the top 100 commerce sites. You hope that will irresistibly cause new visitors to click through to the site and enroll. Sure enough, it increases traffic to your home page. There, visitors find the EWallet offering, find it fascinating just as you hoped, and click through to the EWallet pages, leaving your site, never to return.
>
> But what's more common, is that marketers draw too much attention to something ancillary on their own site. Your desire to add lots of exciting augmentations to your emails, and your site can draw people into a whole range of areas that use up their time and never return them to your main mission. Your visitors could use up their unconscious, implicit budget of attention and time, and not reach the goal you had set. They get pulled into the black hole, and never come out!
>
> ResultsLab's solution is not to give up the powerful email promotion that led to the black hole on the site. Nor do we want you to remove that area on the site. Instead we modify what would have been a black hole to turn it into a sling.
>
> A sling is an area on your site designed and written so a visitor thinks "This is great. And now, I've learned enough to satisfy my curiosity without additional detail, and I'm ready to continue on to the other areas of interest on this site."
>
> Notice that even the email itself can contain a black hole. If it's so full of news that someone puts it aside until they have time to read it, they won't click through to your site now—while your implanted context is fresh on their mind.
>
> It's a fine art to make things irresistibly appealing while also keeping people on the main path of action, and the first step is being aware of the need to do both.

P.S.

There are no figures on the power of the P.S. online. In the direct marketing world, the P.S. might as well stand for Premium Spot. After the outside of the envelope and the headline in the Johnson Box, this is *the* place to get a prospect's attention.

Online, it's at the bottom where one would have to scroll to get to it. That means it's not going to have as much impact as it does just above a signature scribed in a flourish of blue ink. But readers have been trained over the years to look for the special offer, the last-chance-to-close, the final enticement down there, so don't pass it up.

ResultsLab is a big advocate of keeping away from email closings that thank the reader. Ron Richards says, "Closing with thanks suggests a bad polarity—that the writer is a pleading seller rather than a giver who gets thanked. There are better ways to be gracious, build rapport, and prompt action."

One ResultsLab email filled with news of updated client site features closed with:

```
Come share the adventure!
```

And from a letter that led with "Don't miss out on what your peers will be discussing," ResultsLab closed with:

```
Remember, your colleagues and competitors are reading this. Be ready to
discuss the new articles with them.
```

Write your message well and you'll get more clickthroughs. Write it *very* well and it becomes mathematically possible to get more than a 100 percent response.

Word of Mouth

It's often said that when somebody has a great experience with a company, they tell a couple of their friends. When they have a bad experience, they tell a dozen of their friends, who then turn around and tell several of their friends. This works the same way on the Internet, but multiplied several times over.

When somebody wants to share an experience online, they have a lot more reach. There are forums and chat groups. There are newsgroups and discussion lists. If they like, they can put up their own Web site announcing their feelings to the world.

So if you come up with an offer that really tickles somebody's fancy, the word-of-mouth effect online is enormous. Don't forget to encourage it. "Please feel free to forward this message to others and let them know about the special offer they can take advantage of at www.YourCompany.com!"

Keep your writing ear tuned to the follow-on reader. Create that email so it can move from screen to screen without losing anything in the translation. That's one of the reasons all your messages should come with a signature.

Sign Your Work

Possibly the simplest and most powerful traffic-driving tool that every person with an email account has at their disposal is the signature file. Every email software package allows for the inclusion of additional text as a signature. You set up your signature file once, and every time you send a message, your signature is rubber-stamped at the bottom.

Nowhere on the Internet is it unacceptable to have a signature that simply identifies the sender. It is only proper to identify yourself with the acknowledgment of your name, title, phone (with voice mail or answering machine to get all incoming calls), fax, email address, and Web site address. This simple courtesy provides ample avenues to make certain that recipients can always get a message to you without too much work and can research your online presence at their own leisure. Disclosing this information assures the recipient that you are a real entity and that you welcome an open dialogue with them.

But seeing as how you're creating a special message and seeing as how it's already a promotion piece, creating a special signature only makes sense. What attributes make a well-rounded and effective signature file? Make it memorable. Make it brief. Make it work for all types of email readers. Make it lead them to more information.

Whether you separate your signature from the body of your message with a horizontal line or enclose it with a box of asterisks is a personal matter. Just be sure to delineate it from the body of your message, giving it its own presence. Don't go to the opposite extreme.

Some have gone so far as to turn their signature files into attempts at artwork, or are misguided by the belief that abundantly applying dollar signs ($) to their signature file will make a lasting impression. In reality, these tactics, even though applied with the best of intentions, act to quickly categorize you into the spammer category.

If you can supply all of your contact information in five or six lines, then you have a winning combination. You have only a limited amount of time to make an impression, so use it wisely. Part of being memorable is being brief. We all remember "Intel Inside."

Provide a hypertext link to both your email address and your homepage in case readers have a question about something aside from your offer. Even if the suffix of your email address corresponds to your URL, you should not leave it to chance that the recipient of your message will go to the trouble of finding your online location.

Be certain that no punctuation, such as parentheses, is placed in front of or follows your URL. This may render it unclickable. Some email client packages require that you add the "http://" in front of your "www."

Ensure that your email signature file works properly by sending yourself a test message with the signature file in place. Then send it to friends and colleagues who you know are using different email systems on different platforms. That cool-looking signature of yours in your Netscape browser may not look right in Outlook or Eudora.

Examples

Reaching into the mailbag is one of the best ways to see what works and what doesn't. We'll look into several email marketing campaigns and their response rates in Chapter 9, "Stories from the Front Line," but first here are a few worth dissecting.

You might consider getting a separate email account at Yahoo! or Hotmail and subscribing to announcement lists whenever you see a major company publishing one. That way you can start collecting the good ones and the bad ones to see what you like and figure out why you like them. Here are a few to get you started.

eFax Scores 8 out of 10

```
Date: Wed, 25 Aug 1999 00:06:53 -0700 (PDT)
To: jsterne@targeting.com
From: news@info.efax.com (eFax.com)
Subject: Edit The Faxes You Receive!

Dear Jim,

Your eFax number (954) 301-6399 allows you to receive faxes in your
email in-basket.
Have you ever wanted to edit a fax document you've received?

With eFax Plus, you can receive fax documents as text that can be edited
in Word or any word processor. Sophisticated OCR (optical character
recognition) technology converts your faxes at your request.

eFax Plus also includes easy fax sending from your PC, even Web pages,
in just a few clicks, Web storage of your faxes (250 fax pages), a way
to preview the first few pages of long faxes, and unique ways to auto-
matically distribute faxes.

All for one of the lowest prices available.

To find out more and register for eFax Plus, go to:
http://info.efax.com/r/r0.4?lztgoC1biNBV9iU2E58yqWJ82EJLJ2GmtHYxU-Wd0a

Sincerely,

Scott Quinn
eFax Product Manager
------------------------------------------------------------------
You've received this message because you are registered as an eFax.com
member. If you wish to cancel your eFax service, please go to:
http://info.efax.com/r/r0.4?lztgoC1biNBV9iU2EIHYDKtHkrtRtkQVGM4oswK009
```

This message came from a trusted source and delivered an instant benefit in the sub-ject line. There was no guessing about why I might want to open this document. Either I'm interested in editing faxes or I'm not.

Besides using my name, they show my account number—proof that there's an active relationship and this is not spam. Then they used a bold font to hit the high spot, and they put it in the form of a question. Would I like to edit faxes? Sure! How much?

They were ready for me. Knowing that would be my first question, they prompted me with "lowest prices available," but no pricing. Why? Because they want me to click, and click I do. The result is more detail, the answer to my question, and an easy way to accept (see Figure 6.27).

This message is from news@info.efax.com, but it's signed by a human being. That's great. It gives the whole message a warm touch. Everything is right on the money . . . so far.

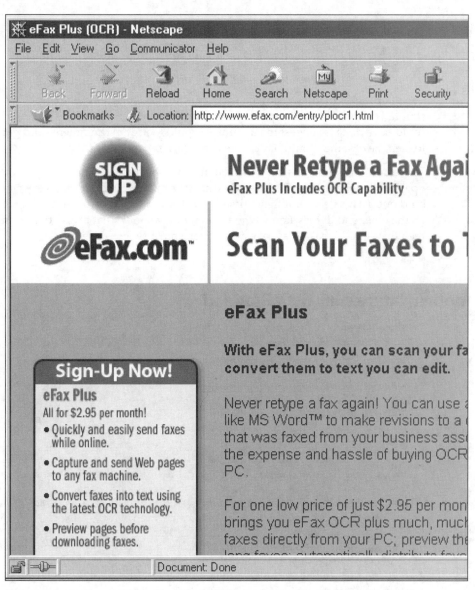

Figure 6.27 eFax provides the right payoff when the embedded link is clicked.

This mailing goes off the track in two ways. There's no person behind the signature, and there's no database behind the clickthrough.

When I sent a message to Scott Quinn, praising him on his business acumen and asking about response rates, my message was bounced.

```
THIS IS AN AUTOMATED RESPONSE -- PLEASE DO NOT REPLY TO THIS MESSAGE

If you have questions about any aspect of your eFax service, need techni-
cal support, or have any other questions please go to our help section at:
```

```
http://www.efax.com/help/index.html
To remove your name from our mailing list and cancel your eFax service,
please click the following link and select Cancel eFax Service in the
Subject Area:
http://www.efax.com/help/support.html
```

The offer was lovingly signed, but there was no real contact there. Instead, I'm shunted off to a technical support page and invited to unsubscribe. The least they could have done is suggest that a human would look at my comments and get back to me. The best they could have done is forward my message to Scott.

They finish the whole thing off with an unsubscribe message and link. Like the sign-up link, it's a messy one. It's messy because they're keeping track of every email they send out. That's good. But they missed a beat when they didn't prefill the order form on the other end. If they know who I am and they know what my account number is, then they should make it as easy as Amazon.com's 1-Click ordering.

MotherNature.com Gets Branded

```
From: YesMail <subs@my.yesmail.com>
To: jsterne@targeting.com
Subject: $20 Off from MotherNature.com
Date: Tue, 24 Aug 1999 21:37:52 -0500
----------------------------------------------------------------------
This message is brought to you by YesMail. We appreciate your member-
ship. To modify your member profile, please see "Member Services" below.
----------------------------------------------------------------------
Save $20 off your first order of any MotherNature brand product. We are
the largest online retailer of natural products ranging from vitamins,
minerals and supplements, to pet supplies as well as products for weight
control, nutrition and even our own line of organic coffee. Visit Moth-
erNature.com (http://mothernature.ym0.net/re2.asp?OID=516&UID=00000) now
and take advantage of this limited-time introductory offer.

Your $20 discount is our way of thanking you for trying Mother-Nature
products. We're sure you'll come back to MotherNature.com again and
again after experiencing our high quality, extensive selection, personal
service and in-depth online health information.

- Everyday discounts up to 50% less than retail on popular natural reme-
dies.
- FREE shipping with any order over $50.
- A range of products from health, to home, to pets and beauty.
- Complete product information, health news updates and an online nat-
ural health encyclopedia.

It's fun, informative, and ordering with MotherNature.com is always
secure!
```

```
So whether your goal is to lose weight, slow the aging process, decrease
fatigue or just to feel better, visit
http://mothernature.ym0.net/re2.asp?OID=516&UID=00000 today and cash in
on your $20 discount.
------------------------------------------------------------------------
*MEMBER SERVICES*
To unsubscribe from the YesMail Network send an email to
subs@my.yesmail.com with the word "unsubscribe" in the subject line.

Feel free to forward this email to interested friends, family and asso-
ciates. To find out more about the YesMail Network, visit
http://www.yesmail.com.
------------------------------------------------------------------------
```

The subject line delivers both the offer and the brand name. When scanning a list of incoming email, the brand name jumps out and makes an impression. The sales pitch is simple—dollars off—so this merchant spent the copy selling the virtues of the store itself. Everyday discounts, free shipping, variety, encyclopedia, and shopping security are all highlighted.

But for sheer branding, this message gets the message across. The MotherNature.com brand is mentioned no less than eight times. Yes, those words, buried in the URL *do* count.

In their efforts to attract first-time buyers and increase brand awareness, Mother-Nature.com sent out close to a million special discounts to categorized prospects. Like a lot of marketers who are being successful with a new technique, they aren't publishing their results far and wide. As Jeff Bezos from Amazon says, "Why should we help them write their business plans?" MotherNature.com will concede that they have significantly decreased customer acquisition costs.

Andy Sends a Personal Message

```
From: YesMail <subs@my.yesmail.com>
To: jsterne@targeting.com
Subject: Get New Stuff, Dirt Cheap at Andy's Garage!
Date: Wed, 25 Aug 1999 00:14:05 -0500
------------------------------------------------------------------------
This message is brought to you by YesMail. We appreciate your member-
ship. To modify your member profile, please see "Member Services"
below.
------------------------------------------------------------------------
Howdy, friend!

Andy's my name, and savin' you money at
http://andysgarage.ym0.net/re2.asp?OID=568&UID=00000 is my game! My wife
Gertie and I live here in Minnesota, the Land of 10,000 Lakes (and
10,000,000,000 mosquitoes!). We've been in business now for over four
```

```
years and take pride in workin' hard to find you eye-poppin' bargains on
top-quality products for your home and family.

Just in at the Garage, we're featurin' a Super Summer Blowout Deal! For
a limited time only, get a Winnebago(R) 10-1/2' Screened Gazebo for
$29.99 -- that's over $90 off! The mesh screen walls are great for
keepin' the bugs out and the shade in, so don't let summer pass you by
without spendin' some quality time with Mother Nature.

Enter to win our $25,000 Ford Explorer Sport Sweepstakes, and you could
be laughin' at all kinds of inclement weather from the inside of a brand
new SUV. Get an AUTOMATIC ENTRY with your order, but no purchase is nec-
essary to enter and win.

Get a rub-your-eyes bargain on first-rate sunglasses at my Shade Shack!
You'll save up to 85% off the manufacturer's retail price from famous
brands like Ray-Ban(R), Killer Loop(R), Revo(R), Serengeti(R) and
Nikon(R). Visit today for the best selection!

Plus, we've got lots of other nifty stuff you'll want to check out: Big
Deal of the Day - below-cost bargains specially handpicked by Gertie or
me!

Andy's Auctions — where YOU'RE the boss when it comes to the price!
Top 20 Liquidation Deals - posted each and every Friday for your shop-
pin' convenience!

Hot Buys - thousands of products at unbelievable savings!

The garage door's always open, so don't be a stranger. Deals galore are
waitin' for you at http://andysgarage.ym0.net/re2.asp?OID=568&UID=00000 !
Andy
----------------------------------------------------------------------
*MEMBER SERVICES*
To unsubscribe from the YesMail Network send an email to
subs@my.yesmail.com with the word "unsubscribe" in the subject line.

Feel free to forward this email to interested friends, family and asso-
ciates. To find out more about the YesMail Network, visit
http://www.yesmail.com.
----------------------------------------------------------------------
```

Andy goes for style first and hard selling second. Apostrophes, exclamation points, contests, brand names, colloquialisms, and his wife Gertie are all thrown into the mix.

But Andy's no country hick. Andy's Garage is owned and operated by Fingerhut (www.fingerhut.com), which is owned by Federated Department Stores. Fingerhut employs approximately 10,000 people from their Minnetonka, Minnesota, headquarters and they send out email to 10 times that many people each week, but not all about Andy's Garage.

Fingerhut can be found on the Internet through its three proprietary sites—www.fingerhut.com, www.andysgarage.com, and www.thehut.com—and through its Internet partner sites—www.pcflowers.com, www.figis.com, www.mountainzone.com, www.skiresorts.com, www.freeshop.com, www.roxy.com, www.pcscentral.com, www.satellite.com, and www.handtech.com.

The company pioneered database marketing and, with its sophisticated proprietary management information systems, maintains data on more than 30 million customer households. Up to 1400 data elements provided by customers are retained on customer files, including demographics, buying and payment histories, product preferences, and even birthdays and anniversaries. Fingerhut is recognized as a leader in information management and database marketing. Its world-class Data & Technology Center in Plymouth, Minnesota, helps Fingerhut maintain its leadership position.

Watch this company as one of the email innovators in the future.

Now that you've got the hang of the one-time, let's-tell-'em-about-our-special-sale message, it's time to turn your attention to getting in touch with them on a recurring basis.

CHAPTER 7

E-Newsletters, E-Promotions, and OPEmail

One of the things you try to teach to young salespeople is never to call a prospect without giving them something. Never call to ask, "Did you get the brochure I sent?" Never call to ask, "Did you sign the purchase order yet?"

While those are the right goals, they are the wrong tactics. Instead, you want your sales representative to offer something of value.

"I just read where your competitor is launching a new product line. Would you like me to fax it to you?"

"I'm calling to invite you to lunch with three other business owners in your industry to discuss government regulations."

"I wanted to see if I could bring those samples over tomorrow."

In each case, the prospect has something to gain by conversing with this salesperson. They come to learn that when this person calls, it's worth picking up the phone instead of hiding behind voice mail.

You want people to look forward to your communications as well. You want them to learn there will be something worth reading every time an email shows up from you.

The issue is one of branding. The point is to keep your name in front of people frequently enough to maintain mindshare without overwhelming them. In this chapter, we'll look into writing a newsletter masterpiece, sending out a promotional piece, and advertising in the section titled, *Other People's Email*.

E-Newsletters

Sending out announcements of sales and specials and the occasional product release is great. But to really make the most of this medium, it pays to publish on a periodic basis. Send out something once a week, once every two weeks, or once a month, rather than once in a while.

The Internet has made it possible for anybody to become a publisher. Do a search on Yahoo! and it'll find 50 categories and 4092 sites for newsletters. AltaVista? It found about 10,457,020 Web pages with the word *newsletter* on them.

You can call what you send all sorts of things. You can refer to it as an ezine. You can name it a news brief. You can say that it's the weekly alert or, perhaps, a thank-you note. You can even try to convince people it's a customer contact vehicle. But the fact that there are more than 4000 Web sites with, for, or about newsletters tells you two things right out of the gate: It's a very popular way to communicate, and yours better be really good.

Setting the Tone

Before you launch a bright and breezy newsletter to your customers and prospects, it's time to have a discussion with your corporate brand manager. For most of you, that means looking in the mirror.

Your company stands for certain principles. Whether those principles involve being trustworthy, loyal, helpful, friendly, courteous, kind, obedient, cheerful, thrifty, brave, clean, reverent, or just plain silly, you want to make sure all of your marketing efforts correspond to the corporate image. With that image in mind, it's time to decide what type of periodical you're going to send to people.

How you describe your newsletter will set expectation levels and further the branding process.

America On Lyme **newsletters.** A monthly emailed newsletter for education and support of people with Lyme disease, as well as their families, physicians, and friends.

American Health Line. A daily news briefing on health care policy and business published by National Journal Group Inc.

Balance Beam. A student health newsletter.

Ditherati. "Because digerati say the cutest things." A daily quote—from net.moguls, cewebrities, and new media hacks who should know better.

E-Commerce Tax News. Weekly email newsletter written by David Hardesty and covering taxation of electronic commerce. Site has archives of news articles.

Full Sterne Ahead. Contains the mostly monthly musings of Jim Sterne, author, speaker, and Web marketing consultant to business and industry.

Japan Internet Report. Newsletter featuring data, commentary, and analysis concerning Internet-related developments in Japan; available by email or through online archives.

Joke of the Day [joke-of-the-day.com]. Free service that sends original humor to sub-scribers by email every day.

Online Electronic Column. A weekly electronic column that covers shareware, book reviews, and online services.

SJI Sky and Space Update. Concise biweekly update for youths and adults interested in the night sky and space exploration, published by the San Juan Capistrano Research Institute.

Stick. Monthly newsletter for Web surfers. Each issue contains a giant list of World Wide Web sites, along with short descriptions for each one.

Universe in the Classroom. Resource for teachers, including topical updates and activities to enhance astronomy education.

WebPromote Weekly. The pulse of Web site promotion full of free information on the latest online promotion developments, opportunities, and tips to make your Web site more competitive.

Content People Will Like

You can spend a lot of money creating content for a newsletter. You can turn your small business or your product management team or your marketing communications department into a publishing company. You can hire a whole squad of outside stringers who round up tidbits to share with your customers. Alternatively, you can scour the news feeds online and populate your newsletter that way.

So what do you include? It depends. For the more informed opinion, we turn to Dr. Ralph F. Wilson, who has been dispensing Web marketing advice to small business in the form of his free monthly email newsletter, *Web Marketing Today* (www.wilsonweb .com/wmt) since 1995.

> What kind of content should you offer? A lot of this depends upon your industry. What do your readers want to know? If you have a computer games store, you'll want to offer cheat codes. You'll talk about graphics, and describe new products. What major trends are affecting the industry? Examine those. You could offer links to sites that provide more information.
>
> Many newsletters include briefs on the latest news in the field. Be careful, however, not to just snip out someone else's story and place it in your newsletter without permission. That's immoral and illegal, not to mention tacky. Always ask so you don't make enemies or expose your business to a copyright infringement suit.
>
> How-to articles are always popular. I spent several years engaged in biochemical research at Cal Tech in Pasadena, California. While I was a lowly research assistant, I would work alongside tireless grad students and post-doctoral fellows who our professor would refer to as "the local world's authority on . . ." and name their specialty. If you think about it, you're probably the local world's authority on something, at least your readers will think so if you explain the fine points to them in an article.
>
> Don't feel you have to write all the articles yourself. Ask others in your field to write an occasional article, or ask for permission to reprint something they have written. Perhaps one of your employees is an especially gifted writer. Use her talents.
>
> By this time you're probably getting an idea of just how much work a newsletter can be. I find it usually takes me a couple of days working hard to get a newsletter out.

Though the out-of-pocket costs are low, the time investment is substantial. I look at this as a marketing cost, and discipline myself to do it faithfully. I never have "time to do it," so I make time. It helps to look at the rewards. As you publish your newsletter regularly, you'll be establishing stronger ties with your customers, which will in turn build your online business substantially over a period of time.

How often should you publish a newsletter? Quarterly is a good goal at first. Get out a calendar and mark the days you plan to send out your newsletter, and then block out a couple of days prior to the deadline to prepare each newsletter. As you learn how to produce a newsletter, increase the frequency. I used to be amused that Mecklermedia's Web Week (now Internet World) came out every three weeks at first. Then it was every other week. Then every week. They started as their resources allowed and worked gradually to their goal.

Web Marketing Today, June 1, 1998

You want another content value tip? Go for a niche. The Web is the world's most niche-ified medium yet. Five hundred cable channels? That's nothing compared to the 50 million registered domain names out there. People have various interests, large and small, and companies like ABC, CBS, CNN, and Reuters do their best to stay on top of the larger issues of the day.

Finally, bearing in mind that people are more interested in themselves than anything else, ask them to respond. What did they disagree with in that last article? Do they have any hints, tricks, or traps to pass along? Have they had a similar experience? Do they have an opinion they'd like to share? Letters to the editor have always been well received on paper.

And, as always, start off each issue with instructions on how to unsubscribe.

Newsletter Formats

The rules laid out in Chapter 6, "Writing an Email Masterpiece," apply to newsletters. First and foremost, offer your readers a choice. ChannelSeven.com knows that people may also be enthusiastic about subscribing to an HTML newsletter, but may not be as happy to receive it. Up at the very top of their *Narrowcast Newsletter,* they offer an out:

ChannelSeven.com is pleased to present the daily Narrowcast Newsletter in HTML format. If you would rather receive the Narrowcast Newsletter in text format, or if you're having trouble reading this email, please send a blank email to narrowcast-text-on@lists.channelseven.com.

Let's leave the subject of HTML newsletters and turn back to Dr. Wilson, who knows whereof he speaks. He also knows that his readers have experience and opinions of their own.

THE "IDEAL" EMAIL NEWSLETTER WIDTH

After Larry Chase's comment last month about settling on 58-characters as the maximum width of his newsletter I asked for some feedback. Here are some of our reader comments:

It All Depends

"Our ezine, Canine Times (http://www.cfnaonline.com/caninetimes/) is heavily read by a consumer audience. Up until three months ago, we used carriage return/linefeed hard returns at line ends, which were set at 55.

"We did a survey and found that there were unspoken complaints about the narrow width. In particular, it impacted on the horrid long urls used by some associate programs. The newbies on the net simply don't know how to cut/paste and anything not immediately easy-to-use causes them to put it aside. Since then, we have changed to 65-character format, retaining use of hard breaks at each line end. Our readers have responded positively.

"IMHO, the decision should be based upon audience. A business audience is going to be using the hand-held devices more so than a consumer audience. Another thought is the content being delivered. Our readers are home readers. We've been told that many print out our ezine and relax on the couch in the evening to read it. Wow. They prefer the longer format.

Thus, my conclusion is deliver what the audience type prefers/needs and adjust accordingly when they are business versus consumer/lay audience."—Sunni Freyer, CFNA Inc: The PR Agency (http://www.cfnaonline.com), Pullman, Washington.

Too Long

Using the bottom scroll bar to read information on a computer screen is always a chore. Your 65-character lines are too long. Please revise to a 60- or 58-character line. —Tom, Hunter Employment (http://www.hunteremployment.com)

Our Conclusion

After thinking about this question for a month, I think we'll stay with our 65-character lines. Yes, it's too long for some like Tom. But since we use a great many URLs, many of them quite long, I think it would be wiser to have longer lines so fewer of them will wrap to the next line. *Web Marketing Today,* June 1, 1999

It's easy to make a text line run too long. But can it be too short as well? Not according to the writers at *Suck* (www.suck.com). Their newsletter takes the idea of a newspaper column and goes one better (see Figure 7.1).

They also decided HTML was the only way to go and they say so on their subscription page. "To get *Suck* delivered by email every day, you must use either a Web-based email service or an HTML-compatible email client like Netscape Navigator's In-Box Direct (version 2.0 or higher) or Microsoft Outlook Express. We recommend the following Web-based services: HotBot Mail, Hotmail, iName, RocketMail, MailCity, netMessenger, Netscape In-Box Direct, Microsoft Outlook Express."

When MaryAnn Pfeiffer asked the ClickZ Forum for the best formatting to accommodate "the variety of email programs, fonts, platforms, etc.," Richard Hoy, moderator and email marketing expert, shrugged his virtual shoulders and gave it his best shot.

I don't have a good answer for you. I can tell you what I do. I compose newsletters in a true text editor—either UltraEdit for the PC or BBEdit for the Mac. I do hard returns at 60 characters or less (both pieces of software let you reset the hard returns of a message in one swoop).

I stay away from formatting data in columns. And I left-justify everything. It never looks exactly as I hoped on the recipient's end, but there is enough flexibility built-in so it is reliable regardless of the font. (Or I think it is, anyway. I might have been fooling myself all these years! ;->)

What needs to start happening is:

1.) We'll have to screen for email client type on list sign-up forms, and start producing different versions for different email clients.

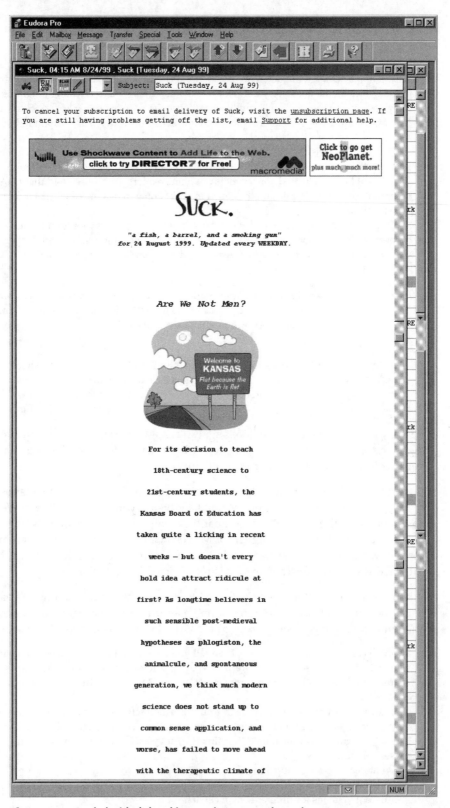

Suck.

"a fish, a barrel, and a smoking gun"
for 24 August 1999. *Updated every WEEKDAY.*

Are We Not Men?

For its decision to teach

18th-century science to

21st-century students, the

Kansas Board of Education has

taken quite a licking in recent

weeks — but doesn't every

bold idea attract ridicule at

first? As longtime believers in

such sensible post-medieval

hypotheses as phlogiston, the

animalcule, and spontaneous

generation, we think much modern

science does not stand up to

common sense application, and

worse, has failed to move ahead

with the therapeutic climate of

Figure 7.1 *Suck* decided the skinny column was the only way to go.

2.) Someone needs to document the idiosyncrasies of major email clients, just like we already do for Web browsers.

3.) Pray this fascination with text goes away soon and everyone converts to HTML email.

Yes, Richard, we can hope. We can also hope that someday we'll be able to get a cable modem or a DSL phone line to come to our house. In the meantime, we'll stick to formatting newsletters for those who want ASCII and send out the good-looking HTML pages for those who prefer it.

For now, we need to figure out how to get more of either to subscribe.

Getting Them to Sign Up

Some newsletters die on the vine and others take off.

Focus on Distributed Object Technology **(www.objectwatch.com).** There are now over 4000 subscribers to this newsletter!

Web Marketing Today **(www.wilsonweb.com/wmt).** A free, twice-monthly electronic newsletter about Internet marketing and doing business on the Web. Circulation passed 68,000 subscribers worldwide in July 1999.

Your WebScout (www.webscout.com). This popular searchable directory is designed, owned, and managed by Promethean. It features reviews of the Net's best Web sites and an email newsletter (over 12,000 subscribers).

Tennis Server INTERACTIVE **email newsletter (www.tennisserver.com).** You will join over 30,000 other subscribers in receiving news of updates to the *Tennis Server,* along with monthly tennis tips from USPTA pro Mike Whittington that won't be found on the Web site.

Beckett Collectibles Report **(www.beckett.com/newslet).** This newsletter now reaches 146,000 subscribers!

WebPromote Weekly **(www.webpromote.com).** *WebPromote Weekly* is the choice of over 400,000 Webmasters, Web publishers, marketing managers, and other Internet-savvy industry professionals who seek the pulse of Web site promotion.

A well-defined niche, a well-written newsletter, and a clear idea of what it takes to get people to sign up make all the difference. As with charity, newsletter sign-ups start at home.

Subscribe on the Homepage

"Jim, you're making a big mistake and missing out on a lot of readers." The best advice Cliff Kurtzman, president of the Tenagra Corporation, ever gave me was to put a subscription box for *Full Sterne Ahead* on the Target Marketing homepage. Before, the sign-up page was buried in the section listing articles I had written. At the time, I was getting three or four sign-ups per week. Pretty good for a monthly newsletter about my view of Web marketing.

Cliff had always given me good advice in the past, so I took a page from his book (see Figure 7.2) and put the subscription box on my homepage where it belonged (see Figure 3.7).

Figure 7.2 The *Tennis Server* is not shy about asking for subscriptions.

Overnight, my subscriptions went to four or five a day. I was thrilled. Little did I know there were more heights to be scaled.

Dr. Ralph Wilson, besides being an ordained man of the cloth, likes to experiment with success. "Once upon a time," he wrote in *Web Marketing Today*, "I was getting about 500 new subscribers per month. Then I added a newsletter sign-up form on every page of my extensive site. Subscriptions skyrocketed. Then I decided to offer a subscription opportunity two times per page, once in the left-side menu area, and another time in the text, and the subscriptions shot up again to about 2000 subscribers (net) every month."

Another way to get them to sign up is to give them a choice.

How Much Information Do You Need?

As a good marketer, you want to know *some*thing about the people on your list. That's the whole point, right? When people sign up for a newsletter, you have the ability to ask them a bunch of questions. If you want a lot of readers, you only ask for their email address. But people are generally willing to answer a few related questions.

DCDanceNet (www.dcdancenet.com) wants to know which style of dancing interests you. They want to know if you object to receiving only dance-related snail mail, and they want to know how you found the DCDanceNet Web site.

The Ski Santa Fe site (www.skisantafe.com) gives people a choice between the daily report and the special new-snow-only report (see Figure 7.3). Carlson Wagonlit Travel (www.cwt-allworld.com) lets you choose between two newsletters and how often you'd like to get them (see Figure 7.4).

The Sun picoJava and SPARC Technology Community wants to know whether you'd like information on the picoJava chip or the SPARC chip, and whether you're interested in using it for a set-top box, a Web phone, a handheld device, or an automotive system, or for network and data communications.

Besides name, company, and email address, Mad Tuna (www.madtuna.com) wants to know if you're interested in custom design, customer updatable sites, storefronts, software marketing, news sights [*sic*], or all of the above (see Figure 7.5).

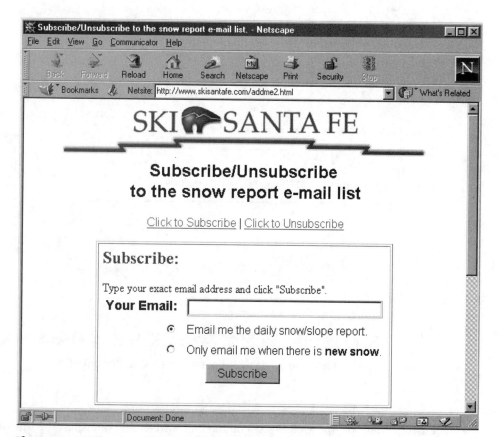

Figure 7.3   Giving the customer a choice of newsletters is the easiest way to learn the most from them.

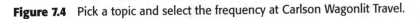

Figure 7.4 Pick a topic and select the frequency at Carlson Wagonlit Travel.

If you want a lot of power over relating the information you send out to specific customer and prospect interests, you have to start asking questions. Just be prepared for a sudden drop in subscriptions as you get nosier and nosier (see Figure 7.6).

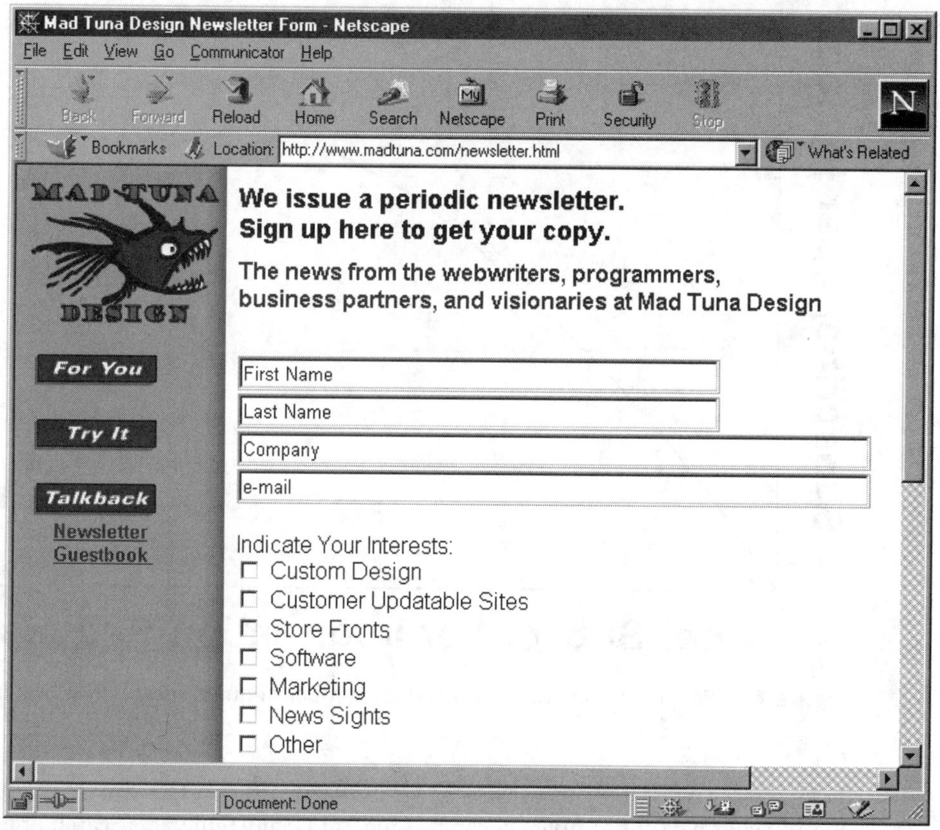

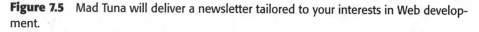

Figure 7.5 Mad Tuna will deliver a newsletter tailored to your interests in Web development.

National Semiconductor (www.national.com) makes use of their "Intelligent Agent" to keep customers up-to-date on product changes. "You specify your interests to the Intelligent Agent. When we add new information that matches your interests, the Intelligent Agent will send you a brief email containing a short description of the documents and the URLs to each one."

As a customer, it's up to me to decide what type of information I want, including 22 product categories and the ability to identify a specific part number (see Figure 7.7).

How many questions can you ask? It depends. If customers are getting some serious value out of their subscriptions, they'll tell you exactly what they do and do not want. It's your job to go out there and let them know it's available.

Promoting Your Promotion

Like all other things on the Web, the best way to get found is to go where people are looking. That means search engines. Enough has been written about search engines elsewhere; it's not necessary to go into it here. Suffice it to say that anything you need

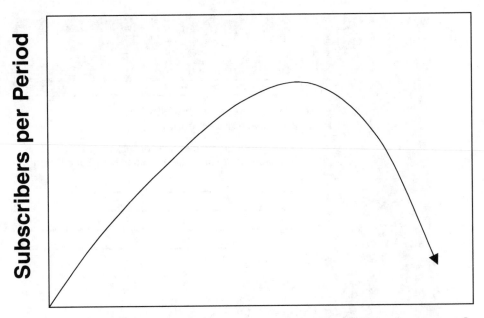

Figure 7.6 People will answer only a certain number of questions when subscribing.

to know about how they work, how to get ranked highly, and how to do it without tearing your hair out completely can be found at Danny Sullivan's Search Engine Watch (www.searchenginewatch.com) or RankThis! (www.rankthis.com).

There are, however, some other places people go to look for newsletters. Take newsletter directories, for example.

There are free newsletter directories like The EzineSeek Ezine Directory (www.ezine-seek.com), which is for email publications only (see Figure 7.8). It doesn't list Web-based ezines or email discussion lists unless those discussions have a digest, "thus making them more like an interactive newsletter."

There are also directories such as Newsletter Access (www.newsletteraccess.com), which will list your newsletter for $19.95 per year. This fee "entitles you to include an email address for automated subscription information requests. Visitors can contact you directly! It also entitles you to include your Web site URL, search keywords, and a description of your newsletter."

The E-Zine Directory (www.e-zinedirectory.com) takes a more pay-per-view approach and charges you 25¢ for every new reader they send your way.

Like anything else on the Web, promoting your newsletter takes time. Other books have been written about promoting Web sites, and everything in them applies to your newsletter as well.

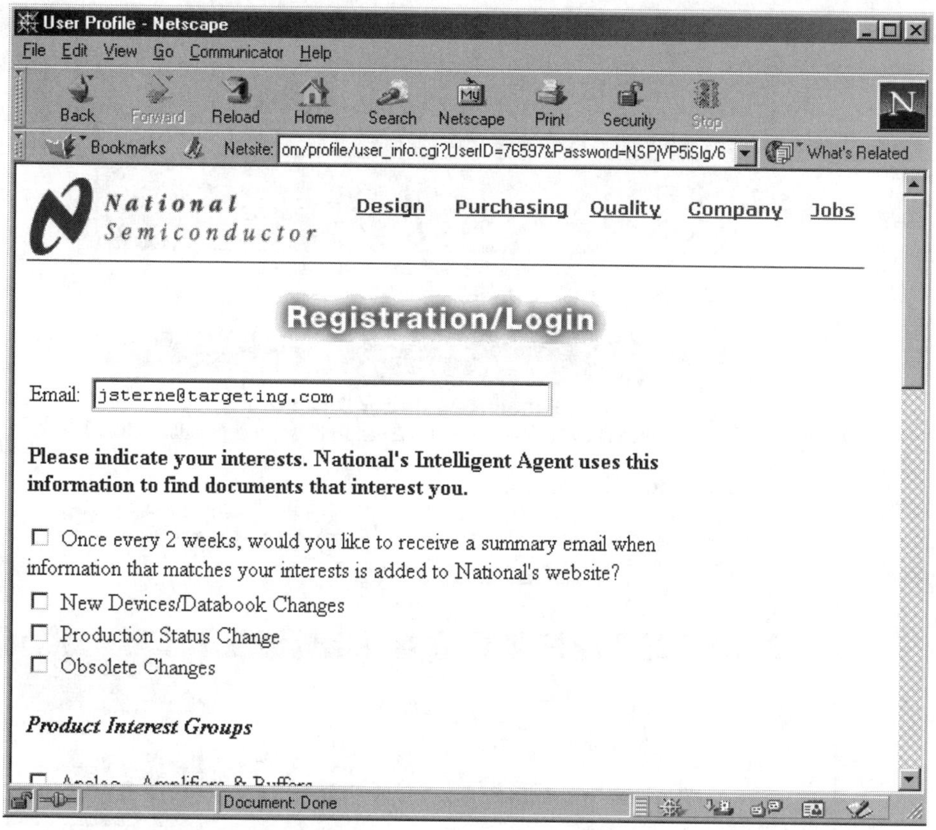

Figure 7.7 National Semiconductor lets customers configure their own newsletters.

Managing Your Subscriptions

The opt-in rules and double-opt-in recommendations apply to newsletters. The best recommendation we can make is to have you go out and subscribe to as many e-bulletins, e-journals, and e-dispatches as you can just to see what it's like trying to subscribe and unsubscribe.

Some make it very easy and some make it very hard. It's not intentional. It's not spiteful. It's not malicious. It's just not well thought through. You understand the process because you designed it. But that doesn't mean others will. Frankly, they don't want to understand it, they just want it to work as quickly and as well as possible.

Telling people to reply to any issue with "remove" or "unsubscribe" in the subject line is fine, if they are at the same address they had when they subscribed. Their email might be forwarded from a previous company or email service and they can find themselves unable to make the system acquiesce.

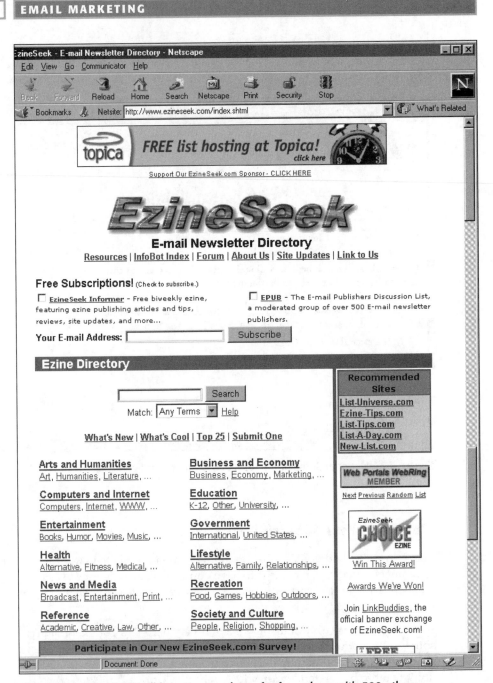

Figure 7.8 EzineSeek will list your newsletter for free, along with 500 others.

Make sure there are people in the loop. If your subscription system doesn't allow a subscriber to contact a person to help with a problem, you've got a problem that won't go away.

Archive Your Newsletters

Archive them and keep that archive current.

The magic of the Internet is that it is the most current medium of communication this side of live television or radio. Your prices changed? The catalog is out of date? Your headquarters moved? Customers can find the latest and greatest information on your Web site—if you keep it current.

Archiving is important because of the "I thought I saw that yesterday" syndrome. We all look at so many sites and read so much email that we have to be brutal about clearing the decks for the next batch of incoming info. It always seems that somebody asks you a question and you *know* the answer crossed your desktop within the past several days. You just can't put your finger on it.

You suddenly remember that electronic newsletter from last week and realize there was no reason to keep it at the time. Now, it could make a big difference to a friend, your boss, or a client. Time to go look for it.

Forget the search engines. They can't keep up with all the latest. It's just not possible. Instead, you head over to the Web site from which the potentially life-saving intelligence was spawned. There's the newsletter sign-up button. There's the archive page. And there's a very clear indication that the Webmaster has been worrying about other priorities for the past two months.

Try as hard as you can to post things on your site before you send them out.

Selling Ad Space on Your Newsletter

Here's a paraphrase to the introduction to a chapter on selling banner ads on your Web site, from *What Makes People Click: Advertising on the Web,* by Jim Sterne (Macmillan, 1997):

> Is your newsletter an ad for your company or is it a company in itself? If you're thinking that you could use a little extra income by selling ad space on a newsletter designed for marketing your own company, think again. If you're not dedicated to the business of selling ad space, you should probably stick to your knitting.

A newsletter is a great place for marketing, sales, and customer service. Marketing means educating people. Sales means transacting business. Customer service means solving customer problems.

The only way you're going to be successful turning your company newsletter into an advertising moneymaker is by deciding that advertising *is* the business you're in. If you're selling widgets and think you're getting enough readers to help defray the cost of publishing, you haven't thought about the cost of selling ad space. It is *not* a part-time job.

What's true for banners is true for newsletters.

Yes, you have a unique audience. Yes, they are all opt-in. Yes, email ads are easy to ship, style, and insert. But there are only two types of newsletters out there selling ad space. The first type got that way by design. The publishers built a business plan based on an advertising revenue model and they're making it work—or not. The other type started a newsletter for the marketing value (or the ego trip) and found people knocking on its door, dollars in hand.

If you're going to be a publisher, you'll want to have personal chats with people who are doing it successfully. If you are not, then wait until the buyers show up on your doorstep before selling your boss on the idea that your newsletter could take on a life of its own and be self-supporting.

And what do you say to marketers who want to rent your list? You speak very clearly and very slowly:

We send other companies' email only to people who have said it's okay.

That means our list of available people numbers only 750 and we lose 30 percent every time we mail.

We may refuse your creative endeavor if we don't feel it's right for our readers.

We have final say over how much gets mailed and when.

It's not a very compelling story. When your list of subscribers reaches 50,000 or 100,000, you'll have a much more interesting story to tell.

As for advertising in *other* people's newsletters . . . wait for the upcoming section entitled *Advertising in Other People's Email*. For now, think about protecting the privacy of your subscribers to the depth and breadth and height your Webmaster can reach.

Privacy: Rules, Laws, and Good Marketing

The European Union Data Protection Directive, which was supposed to bring down all of American international marketing data management, was supposed to go into effect in October 1998. It would have forced American companies to be a bit more careful than we're used to.

There are four basic rules:

1. You have to tell people you are collecting information about them and what you're using it for.
2. You have to allow people to decline to be tracked.
3. You have to allow people access to their data so they can correct it.
4. You have to ensure their data is safe from prying eyes.

That first one means you're not allowed to use personal data for anything except the purpose for which it was specifically acquired, unless you have explicit consent. In a nutshell, if you sell somebody a teapot, you're not allowed to turn around and try to sell them tea, unless they've signed a waiver.

If you're heavy into rules and regulations, you can find out more from Peter Swire, associate professor of law at the Ohio State University College of Law. He keeps tabs on the issue at http://osu.edu/units/law/swire.htm. But if you're simply into good marketing, you're going to follow these rules anyway. The fact is, if you treat people with respect, you can sell them more stuff. If you don't, you will be designated a data-Nazi.

Jason Catlett runs a company called Junkbusters (www.junkbusters.com) that covers personal privacy and the Web. With tongue planted firmly in cheek, he wrote the following example of target marketing run amuck:

> Dear Mr. Jones:
>
> Our research indicates that you have not bought condoms at SpiffyMart recently. (Your last purchase was 8 weeks ago.) Further, you have stopped buying feminine hygiene products, but have sharply increased your frozen pizza and dinners usage in the same time frame.
>
> It's clear that Ms. Jody Sanders and you are no longer "an item." (It's probably for the best—she consistently buys inexpensive shampoo, and it was obvious that the two of you were not economically compatible.) The Postal Service database confirms that she filed a change of address form.
>
> We at Hotflicks International offer our condolences.
>
> As the number-one vendor of hot XXX-rated videos, we want you to know that our products can help you through this difficult period. When you're feeling lonely, check out our unmatched catalog, there is guaranteed to be something that you'll want to purchase!
>
> Order from this catalog and we'll throw in an extra tape FREE!
>
> Yours Truly, Hotflicks Marketing Management

Convince your subscribers that privacy is important to you. If you collect all sorts of information about them, then your offerings can be more interesting to them. If you treat information about them with respect, they're going to feel much better about the relationship.

If they feel really good about it, they'll tell others.

Word of Mouth—Again

Inside 1to1, the Peppers and Rogers Group newsletter, counted their subscribers at almost 30,000 in April 1999. But their president, Bob Dorf, reported that random surveys revealed a pass-along readership in excess of 100,000 subscribers each week. Not bad.

Just after the good stuff and just before all the contact information of each and every *Inside 1to1* they write:

```
=========================================================================
We depend on word-of-mouth to spread the word about this newsletter. If
you enjoy reading INSIDE 1to1, please tell a friend or colleague about
it. Anyone can sign up for a free subscription on our Web site at
http://www.1to1.com/articles/subscribe.html or by emailing us at sub-
scribe@1to1.com .
=========================================================================
```

Pass-along is an important part of any publication. Spend a few bits to encourage people to share. *Information Week* keeps it simple:

```
Know anyone looking for a steady dose of IW Daily? To subscribe, go to:
<<http://www.informationweek.com/daily>>
```

Microsoft uses the long form:

```
THIS DOCUMENT IS PROVIDED FOR INFORMATIONAL PURPOSES ONLY. The informa-
tion contained in this document represents the current view of Microsoft
Corporation on the issues discussed as of the date of publication.
Because Microsoft must respond to change in market conditions, it should
not be interpreted to be a commitment on the part of Microsoft and
Microsoft cannot guarantee the accuracy of any information presented
after the date of publication. INFORMATION PROVIDED IN THIS DOCUMENT IS
PROVIDED 'AS IS' WITHOUT WARRANTY OF ANY KIND, EITHER EXPRESS OR
IMPLIED, INCLUDING BUT NOT LIMITED TO THE IMPLIED WARRANTIES OF MER-
CHANTABILITY, FITNESS FOR A PARTICULAR PURPOSE AND FREEDOM FROM
INFRINGEMENT. The user assumes the entire risk as to the accuracy and
the use of this document. This document may be copied and distributed
subject to the following conditions: 1. All text must be copied without
modification and all pages must be included 2. All copies must contain
Microsoft's copyright notice and any other notices provided therein 3.
This document may not be distributed for profit.
```

Not as encouraging as, say, Joke-of-the-Day (www.joke-of-the-day.com), which simply suggests you "FORWARD TO FRIENDS—Spread The Fun." If you subscribe at their Web site, they encourage you to pass along the good cheer on their Web site:

Tell Your Friends About Joke-of-the-Day in 4 easy steps!

Step 1: Enter Your Name Here

Step 2: Review a joke to send by choosing an icon below

Step 3: Enter the names and email addresses of the friends you want to send these jokes to. Name Email Address

E-Promotions

An article in *Business 2.0* (August 1999) reported that Amazon.com "generates two-thirds of its sales from repeat buyers—many of whom are pulled back to the site with friendly, well-timed promotions zapped to them via email."

This is the art of offering people something beyond an interesting compilation of news, weather, business, and sports in the form of a newsletter. You want to incite them to actually buy.

Discounts

Start by giving them a price reduction. If they're in the market, a low price is a great incentive. Offering a $100 off coupon certainly gets people's attention. Even if it's good only on the purchase of a $500,000 house.

This is the sort of marketing program you want going out to as many people as possible. You want to broadcast this in the truest sense of the word, advertising your offer on the radio, on TV, and on email.

Reaching as many people as possible through email means going where the addresses are. That's what companies like *Rolling Stone* magazine are doing. Let's dissect a recent email sent out in search of new subscribers. First, here's what the message looks like when it comes in:

```
From: YesMail <subs@my.yesmail.com>
To: jsterne@targeting.com
Subject: 4 Free Issues of Rolling Stone
Date: Tue, 24 Aug 1999 20:09:33 -0500
-------------------------------------------------------------------
This message is brought to you by Mpath and YesMail. You are receiving
this message because you have opted-in to receive special offers and
deals from Mpath's live communities: Mplayer.com or HearMe.com. Mpath
is now working with YesMail to protect your privacy and distribute
quality permission based offers to our members. We appreciate your
membership. To modify your member profile, please see "Member Ser-
vices" below.
-------------------------------------------------------------------
Rolling Stone magazine is pleased to bring you a special subscription
savings offer.

Subscribe right now and we'll send you the next 4 issues FREE.

If you find you like Rolling Stone, you'll get 26 issues in all for only
$12.97(including your free issues).

That's a savings of over $62 off the cover price.

If you don't like Rolling Stone, you pay nothing and keep your free
issues no matter what.

Click Here for 4 free issues!
http://RolllingStone.ym0.net/re2.asp?OID=575&UID=00000
-------------------------------------------------------------------
*MEMBER SERVICES*

To unsubscribe from the Mpath special offers list in the YesMail Network
send an email to subs@my.yesmail.com with the word "unsubscribe" in the
subject line.

Feel free to forward this email to interested friends, family and asso-
ciates. To find out more about the YesMail Network, visit
http://www.yesmail.com.
-------------------------------------------------------------------
```

Now, let's walk through this promotion one more time and take a closer look at each of its components. Why did they make some of the decisions they did?

```
From: YesMail <subs@my.yesmail.com>
To: jsterne@targeting.com
Subject: 4 Free Issues of Rolling Stone
Date: Tue, 24 Aug 1999 20:09:33 -0500
```

The header information tells us the email was sent to me as an individual and was not a suppressed list. That means they're confident I subscribed. It's from yesmail.com, a company I have a relationship with and recognize. The subject tells me who the advertiser is *and what the offer is.* I immediately know this is something I can take or leave without fear of missing some important news from my friends and family.

The very first paragraph identifies the senders as being both yesmail.com and Mpath, another company I have (or would like to have) a relationship with. It also contains a reminder about why I'm getting this offer, and tells me how to find out about changing my subscription profile, if I desire.

```
-----------------------------------------------------------------------
This message is brought to you by Mpath and YesMail. You are receiving
this message because you have opted-in to receive special offers and
deals from Mpath's live communities: Mplayer.com or HearMe.com. Mpath is
now working with YesMail to protect your privacy and distribute quality
permission based offers to our members. We appreciate your membership.
To modify your member profile, please see "Member Services" below.
-----------------------------------------------------------------------
Rolling Stone magazine is pleased to bring you a special subscription
savings offer.
```

Because I'm interested in music, I'm likely to be interested in *Rolling Stone.*

```
Subscribe right now and we'll send you the next 4 issues FREE.

If you find you like Rolling Stone, you'll get 26 issues in all for only
$12.97(including your free issues).

That's a savings of over $62 off the cover price.

If you don't like Rolling Stone, you pay nothing and keep your free
issues no matter what.
```

The offer is short, sweet, and to the point. The white space is generous because the publisher feels I'm already familiar with the product. This is not a product pitch, it's a price pitch, with a money-back guarantee.

```
Click Here for 4 free issues!
http://RolllingStone.ym0.net/re2.asp?OID=575&UID=00000
```

We'll look into funny URLs in Chapter 8, "Testing Your Talent, Reckoning Your Response, and Managing Your Email." For now, suffice it to say that tracking each clickthrough from each promotion is very important. Where the clicker ends up is important, and in this case, it's on an order page (see Figure 7.9).

Rolling Stone doesn't make an effort to sell here, either. The product and the offer ("If you don't like *Rolling Stone,* you pay nothing and keep your free issues no matter what!") are enough to carry the day.

Then comes the wrap-up housekeeping.

```
-----------------------------------------------------------------------
*MEMBER SERVICES*
To unsubscribe from the Mpath special offers list in the YesMail Network
send an email to subs@my.yesmail.com with the word "unsubscribe" in the
subject line.
```

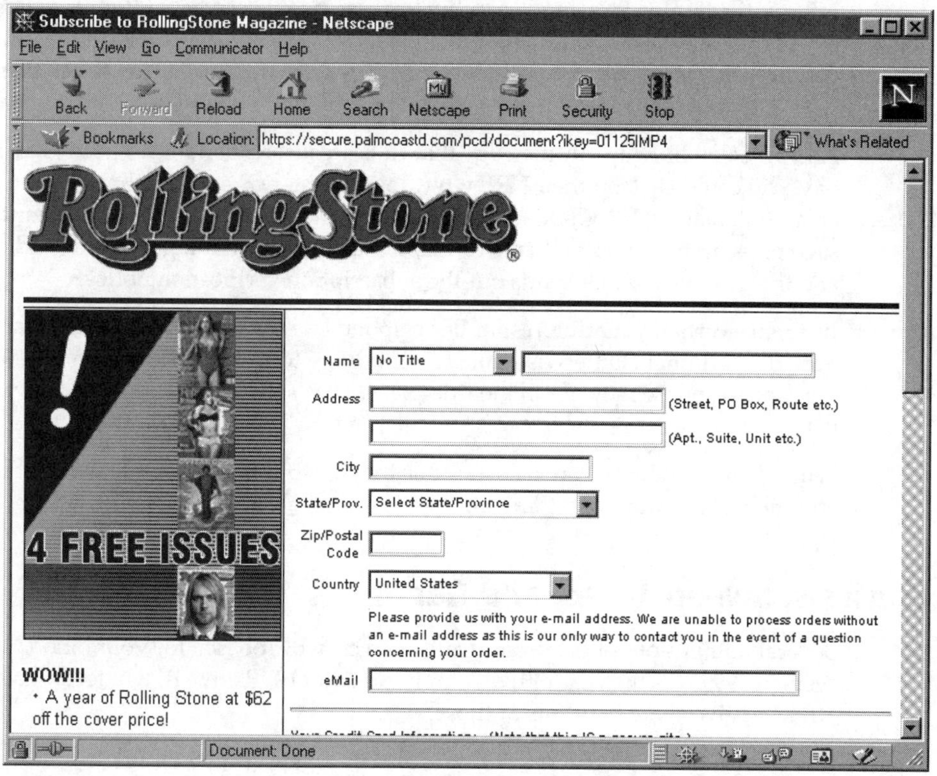

Figure 7.9 The landing page is an order form. No hunting and pecking.

If I get enough messages that do not tickle my fancy, I will unsubscribe. By keeping an eye on the numbers, YesMail has a very good idea of what people will like and what they won't. The voting happens very quickly.

```
Feel free to forward this email to interested friends, family and asso-
ciates. To find out more about the YesMail Network, visit
http://www.yesmail.com.
-----------------------------------------------------------------------
```

The finale encourages me to pass this along. Notice how helpful they are. Would I pass this along? Sure. The first people that come to mind are my friends—those who share my taste in music. But they suggest I consider my family as well. True, Dad and I don't have the same artists in our CD collections, but then neither do my nephew and I. Both of them, however, like to keep current and might enjoy a no-risk, check-it-out-and-see-if-you-like-it subscription to *Rolling Stone*. You never know.

But then they suggest sending this along to associates. That conjures up images of workplace colleagues and business acquaintances. That one phrase expanded the scope of my pass-along potential considerably.

If four free issues or a 10 percent off coupon won't get their attention, how about something for free?

Information is always a good come-on because people can get at it with a click. You send out a generic email; an unknown person clicks on a link, looks at the information on your page, and then wanders off. They win, you lose. Instead, ask them to type in their email address. Or go one step better and promise to email it to them.

Add an email link in your message that calls an autoresponder. To get a joke every-day, you could click on their URL www.Joke-of-the-Day.com, or click once on their email link mailto:JOIN@Joke-of-the-Day.com. The result is instant. A new email message pops up from you to them. You don't have to type a thing. Hit the Send button and their autoresponder sends out the subscription verification notice.

Just make certain your autoresponder responds with a Reply To: address that's connected to a human. Otherwise, subscribers trying to communicate with you will get the same response they got in the first place. That's the email equivalent of voice-mail jail.

White papers and jokes are nice as far as they go. But if you want to get everybody's attention, give away something big.

Contests, Sweepstakes, and Games

Several millions of dollars usually attracts a crowd. Too rich for your blood? It seemed 1999 was the year of the Palm Pilot, Palm III, Palm VII, whatever. You can afford to give away handfuls of those.

But the wonder of giveaways online is also its biggest problem. It's so easy. It's too easy.

No stamps to lick, no card to mail, no nothing. Click here and fill out a short form and you're done. Why's that great? You get lots and lots of people. Why's that bad? They might not be the kind of people you want.

If you're selling shoes and everybody is a prospect, fine. Build a huge database of email addresses. But what if you're selling swimming pool supplies? Do you really want a huge database of people who live in Nome, Alaska?

Marla Altberg is the senior vice president of marketing for Ventura Associates. They're the ones behind many of the random-draw, million-dollar, co-op sweep-stakes. Marla recently stated in *Target Marketing* magazine (www2.targetonline.com), "The chance to win something appeals to a basic human instinct. You can have parts of the sweepstakes pre-qualify the lead. It's perfectly legal to have consumers complete brief questionnaires that can help you determine what kind of prospect they are, just as long as you have an opt-out to let them know that they don't need to buy anything or be contacted as a condition of entry."

Don't have a million dollars sitting around gathering dust? Give away something that qualifies the people who might want to win.

Seventeen-year-olds aren't likely to sign up for a contest if the prize is a new set of air-conditioning filters for a commercial building. People who are not in the market are not likely to care for winning free installation of a downdraft bench for histopathology. But the people who *do* sign up to win 1000 meters of pneumatic piping are the kind of folks you want to talk to.

But do they want to listen?

Did They Consent?

When they send in their name, email address, and maybe even their postal address and phone number, they have given you permission to let them know if they've won. They have not necessarily said they wanted to hear from you for future contests or for product announcements.

If you are a Web marketing connoisseur, you automatically consider a truth we hold to be self-evident on the Web: Let the customer control his or her own destiny. When they sign up for the contest, make sure they have the ability to check the box that says, "Yes, I would like to receive invaluable information on inventive new uses for my used knuckleboom scrap loader."

Viral Marketing: Word of Mouth on Steroids

Viral marketing is simple. You come up with a promotional innovation that's so interesting other people want to pass it along. In the old days, this meant they would talk about it. If you were really good, they would adopt your innovation in everyday speech: Kleenex, Xerox, "Where's the beef?"

These days, when it takes only about an hour for a brand-new joke to make it to every high school student with a modem, you've got to be just a little more creative. That's not to say you have to go out and author the world's most memorable punch line. You just have to come up with another way of reaching out and getting people to touch one another.

Online it's a natural response to want to share something fun you've just discovered. It's so easy to do. Several of my friends have added me to their joke lists, and when they come across something that tickles their fancy, they send it to their jokester list rather than to each of us individually.

Shareware was the original viral marketing on the Internet. A useful piece of software is floated around with a request for payment built in. If enough people use it, some will send checks. Today's marketers have taken that concept and elevated it to high art.

Hotmail Proliferation

Hotmail figured out the best way to let people know that they could sign up for a free email account: they let their customers do it for them. At the bottom of every message a Hotmail user sends is the signature line:

```
Get Your Private, Free Email at http://www.hotmail.com
```

What could be simpler?

Instant Messaging

Instant Messaging was a surefire winner that couldn't be stopped. Friends tripped over each other to tell other friends how they could create buddy lists and keep track of when their friends were online—all in the desire to communicate more.

Associate Programs

When Amazon.com added money to the mixture, it became explosive. If you have a Web site, you can sell books.

What's that got to do with email? Everything, if you're from Barnsandnoble.com. You don't need a Web site—just an email account—and you can start collecting a 5 percent commission.

> Anyone with an email account can join our exciting new MybnLink Program! This new program enables you to sell books, music, and more to friends and family through your email, and to earn money for a favorite charity—or yourself! We provide you with quick and easy links and updated daily sales reports.
>
> No spamming—just email people you already know. This means friends, family, and colleagues: people who would welcome an email from you. You can't represent yourself as barnesandnoble.com. You are the author of any email that points your friends and family to our site. You can't use this program to promote hate mail, pornography, or anything illegal.
>
> Each email you send must include our basic legal disclaimer.

Then comes the legalese about spam.

> No spamming is permitted as part of the MybnLink program. You understand that, for the purposes of this Agreement, rarely should any one email be sent to more than 50 individuals comprising your group of friends, family and colleagues. You may not send Program Emails in any type of mass marketing attempt, including, without limitation, sending Program Emails to (i) any type of listserv or automated mailing mechanism, including, without limitation, any type of specialty group mailing list, (ii) any individual or group of people with whom you are not personally acquainted, and (iii) any third-party emailing list of any type. You may not post your Link on any web site or with any type of Internet newsgroup, message board, or bulletin board. By including Links in any unsolicited bulk, junk, or spam email communications, you shall become ineligible to receive any commissions hereunder, and this Agreement shall be subject to immediate termination by bn.com. Furthermore, and not in limitation of the foregoing, you agree that you will not send any emails to any individuals who have indicated in any manner for any reason that they do not wish to receive such emails.

We'll just have to wait and see how well they can enforce it.

HomeGoodies: Virus and Metavirus

Start with the belief that people like to get something for nothing. Continue with the idea that people like to share good things. Finish off with the fact that the Internet and email make sharing things incredibly easy. Exponentially, in fact. Mix these together and what do you get? If your name is Jay Steinfeld, you get HomeGoodies.

From *World Wide Web Marketing, Second Edition*

The concept is so simple as to be laughable and the implementation has been brilliant. You want to sell books off your Web site? Become a retail store front to the Amazon.com back-end delivery system.

Let's say you wrote a book called *World Wide Web Marketing.* Let's say you wanted to sell it from your Web site, but you didn't want to have to take orders, box books and open up an account with UPS. The Amazon Associates Program awaits. Just put up a link to their site from yours (see Figure 7.10) and they take care of the rest.

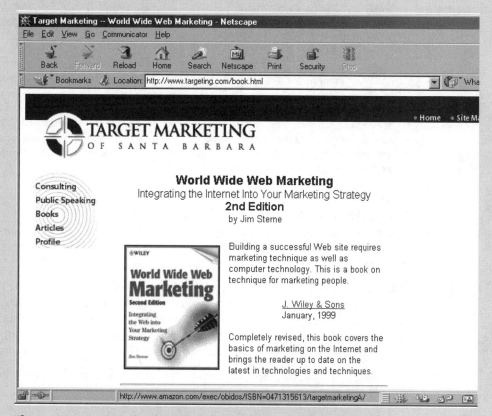

Figure 7.10 Buying a book from Target Marketing is just a click away.

Notice the URL at the bottom of the screen. One click will take the buyer to http://www.amazon.com/exec/obidos/ISBN=0471315613/targetmarketingA to buy the book. Notice the "targetmarketingA" at the end there. That means if you buy the book, Amazon.com can tell I was the one who sent you and will send me 10% to 15% commission at the end of every quarter.

It takes about ten minutes to sign up and start earning money as a retail book store on the Internet. It takes a serious out-of-box thinking experience to come up with something so elegant. So what would you like other sites to be selling for you?

Jay and his wife run a chain of Laura's Draperies, Bedspreads & More in the greater Houston area. Jay got into the Internet early on and created Laura's Online (www.lauras.com) to promote the stores. Since Laura's prides itself on custom work, Laura's Online could only service Houston. This frustrated Jay, who quickly saw the potential.

That potential was realized in a new Web site Jay called No Brainer Blinds & Shades (www.nobrainerblinds.com). Quickly recognized as an Incredibly Useful Site of the Month by *Yahoo!* magazine, No Brainer is a simple, easy-to-use site that, well, as Jay puts it on his About No Brainer page:

> You'll find detailed measuring and installation tips, including Quick Time movie tutorials. Plus, we've packed in decorating advice and product information enabling you to make informed decisions.
>
> But not all of you need our help in selecting, measuring, and installing blinds and shades. You just need super low prices, quality blinds and shades, and you want them FAST—without hassle. That's why you need No Brainer, and why we're so popular.
>
> The No Brainer concept is simple; low prices made possible by mammoth buying power, streamlined order processing using electronic gadgets, and next day manufacturing on most products. Our high tech means your low price. We've worked hard to eliminate all the usual overhead incurred by our mail order competitors. No costly catalogs and samples, and no commissions to our employees—so our costs are tiny. We pass along all these savings in the form of lower prices for you!

Okay, so where's the virus? It's coming.

Jay worked out all the bugs and No Brainer started being profitable quickly. It was a smooth-running, well-oiled machine. In fact, it became so smooth, Jay realized it could handle a lot more volume. But how to create that volume? The answer was a brainstorm.

What if, Jay reasoned, a bunch of vendors got together and dropped some coupons in a basket to hand out to people who were moving into a new home? What if those coupons were for home insurance, vacuum cleaners, alarm systems, bedding, and all that other stuff people need when they move? And what if it was an electronic basket? And what if it was free? The brainstorm was HomeGoodies (see Figure 7.11).

You click; you send; they get the goodies. This would be a no-brainer if Jay hadn't called his other business that already. The first message looks like this:

```
Date: Sun, 8 Aug 1999 14:12:29 -0400 (EDT)
From: homegoodies@homegoodies.com
To: jsterne@targeting.com
Subject: Great gifts from Jim Sterne

Jim Sterne has sent you some HomeGoodies homewarming gifts as a special
way to say, "Best wishes with your new home".

Your gift basket is absolutely free and you can pick it up right now at:

http://www.homegoodies.com/cgi-bin/get_basket.pl?id=1999080814xxxxx (You
can collect your gifts at the above web address for 90 days).
```

Figure 7.11 HomeGoodies is banking on giving things away.

```
    Enjoy your gifts and your new home!

    Warm regards,
    Jay


    <><><><><><><><><><><><><><><><><><><>
    Send FREE homewarming gifts to friends and family.
              That's right. FREE!
          http://www.homeGoodies.com
    <><><><>   Jay Steinfeld, President    <><><><>
```

One click, and the happy recipient gets to redeem the freebies (see Figure 7.12).

But wait, there's more. When you claim a goodie, you're invited to sign up for more special offers from that vendor. If you order the Oreck Power Brush (with headlight), you get the free eight-piece tool set and an order confirmation from Oreck that finishes up with:

```
    Oreck is now a sponsor of HomeGoodies at http://www.homegoodies.com.
    Visit and get free homewarming gifts for your friends and family.
```

Then there's the coup de grace. Jay sends a follow-up message to the recipient, hoping you enjoyed the goodies and inviting you to thank the sender by sending *them* a basket. And every basket contains a coupon for a free book called *What to Wear If You're a Window* and a gentle nudge back to No Brainer Blinds & Shades.

Now *that's* a virulent virus.

It's also an example of advertising in somebody else's email.

Advertising in Other People's Email

With so many newsletters, announcements, bulletins, and the like out there, it's not a great leap to imagine some of them would be advertising supported. That means you get to take advantage of the hard work others have done getting an audience together.

Audiences gather around subjects and they gather in a number of ways. The newsgroups kicked things off by providing an electronic gathering place. Then people discovered the ease of email discussion lists. Newsletters were quick to follow, and today we see a growth industry in professional audience gatherers: contests, shopping coalitions, coupon traders, and the like.

Caution: Here There Be Newsgroups

Newsgroup discussions offer a wonderful clustering of topic-specific interest. But remember, spamming got started in newsgroups and tolerance for mistreating people there is as close to zero as you can get.

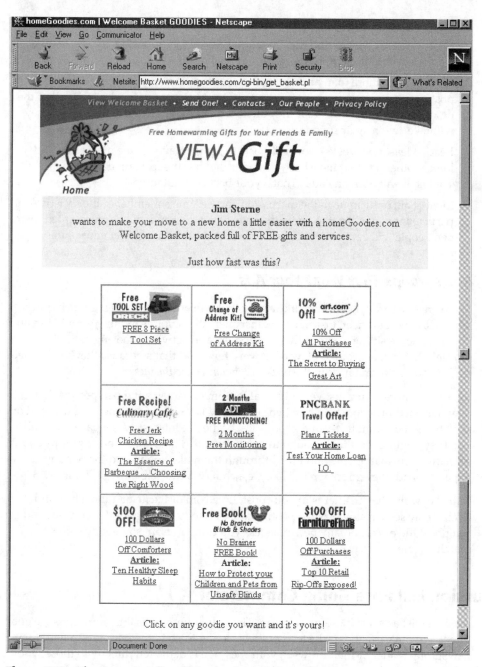

Figure 7.12   The HomeGoodies gift basket is ready for collection.

The Critical Rules of Newsgroup Advertising

Each newsgroup is a separate society with separate rules and customs, and an unspoken code of conduct. If you ignore these, you do so at your own peril.

1. Be certain your subject matter is on topic.

2. Go out of your way to find the Frequently Asked Questions document. Read it well regarding the acceptance of ads.

3. If you post to more than one newsgroup, cross-post rather than re-post. Cross-posting means your message is seen only once by somebody who reads all of the newsgroups you posted to. If they are faced with your ad again and again, they will take action against you.

4. Read at least two weeks' worth of posts to get the flavor of the discussion and look at other ads that have been posted. What has the reaction been to them? There haven't been any ads? That's your best clue not to post.

5. Most of all, participate in the discussion and become a member of the society. As a participant you will get to know the code of conduct and will be an accepted member. People will get to know you as a voice of reason and respect your opinion.

Newsgroups That Want Your Ads

There are newsgroups out there like alt.biz that will accept anything: get rich quick schemes, cure for cancer, insurance against alien abduction. Anything goes. Can you imagine people sitting down at their computers and actively choosing to read through that sort of group? A few do. A very few. And that's because they've finished reading about worm farms in the back of *Popular Home Businesses*.

But don't ignore alt.biz just yet. It has value from one interesting perspective that may make it worth your while. When somebody is looking for something unusual or something they want to get at a good price, or they're interested in a particular subject, they might go trolling through the newsgroups. There are so many groups and so many posts that people don't read through them like you would the Sunday paper. Instead, they go someplace like Deja.com (www.deja.com). See Figure 7.13.

If the keyword they're after is in your post, Deja.com or Excite or Yahoo! can find it. Alt.biz may seem a silly place to post, because nobody will read it directly. But you can't beat the price, and any new business you bring in from somebody using a search engine is gravy.

Discussion Lists Are Going Commercial

An email list acts just like a newsgroup. The only difference is that your message goes directly to the participants. Instead of their having to go to the newsgroup with their newsgroup reader or their browser, your message is delivered directly to those who subscribe to the list.

People subscribe to lists either in digest format or post by post. Digest subscribers may get one summary of posts per day, or one per week depending on the amount of traffic. Nondigest subscribers get each post as it's posted—all day long. If they have an opinion about something on the list, they hit Reply and their thoughts get delivered to all the other subscribers. When they do, your ad can go along for the ride.

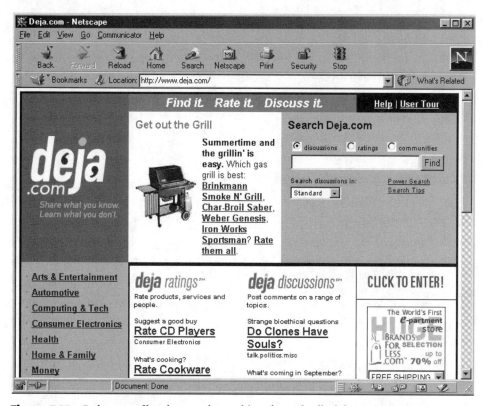

Figure 7.13 Deja.com offers keyword searching through all of the newsgroups.

A list subscriber doesn't look at postings during a free moment like the newsgroup reader does. The subscriber is barraged with messages all day long. People in large organizations who belong to two or three lists will routinely receive more than 100 email messages per day. Your advertisement comes right to their screen. It had better be on topic. List moderators will see to it.

Some of the best lists are heavily moderated. The list owner/manager reads every post and decides which to forward to the group. If you've said something that 27 others have already said, if you flame some list member without adding intellectual value to the mix, if you can't structure a sentence to save your life, then the moderator will act like an editor and make sure the quality of the posts stays high.

The Online Advertising list (www.o-a.com) has been active for several years. Here's an example of a single post from the middle of a discussion about personalization:

```
From: Ian Leicht <ian@inspiredarts.com>
Subject: RE: ONLINE-ADS Is personalization really personal?

CHRIS TOPPE WROTE:
Unless the number of items for sale exceeds the number of visitors, then
one-to-one advertising is impossible...
```

I don't think that your description of 1:1 marketing is a fair characterization. 1:1 marketing isn't just a tool for mapping your x products to y
customers. The goal of a 1:1 marketing implementation is to profile your
customers, employers, or partners as individuals and then match them with
information, services, and products that their profile indicates.

If you have 1M customers and 100k items, it would be very important to
profile those customers and deliver personalized service and recommendations based upon their stated preferences, purchasing history, and
observations about their actual browsing habits.

How does this mapping and segmentation happen? Does it have to be done
manually? No! Collaborative filtering technology such as Net.Percep-
tions, used by companies such as Amazon, demonstrates that automated
behaviors and assumptions can still be very valuable.

It will always be valuable to break your customers into various segments. However, as the technology improves, it will become possible to
push this forward to the next level. It isn't just about matching 10x
customers to 1x products. Different sorts of customers may be interested
in a variety of your products, and 1:1 marketing is a great tool for
cross- and up-selling.

Ian Leicht
Chief Technology Officer, Inspired Arts
Email: ian@inspiredarts.com
Phone: (619) 713-6201, (800) 851-4394x104
Fax: (619) 623-3534
Email paging: 6199543756@page.nextel.com
Web paging: http://www.nextel.com/paging/index.html

```
============================================================
------------------------------------------------------------
```
```
        This week's Online Advertising Discussion List sponsors:
                Flycast, AdKnowledge, and RadicalMail
```

AT FLYCAST WE ARE PASSIONATE ABOUT RESULTS. Not just branding. Not just
click-through -- results. Take the next step. Get the maximum number of
responses at the lowest possible CPM. Visit http://www.flycast.com/oa.
```
---
```
What is the brand effect of Web advertising? Only AdKnowledge goes
beyond the click to offer real answers you can act on. For details about
AdKnowledge eAnalytics, visit us at http://www.adknowledge.com
```
---
```
Interested in reaching opinion leaders in one of the most active discussion communities online? Try RemarQ at http:
//www.remarq.com/discussions/ad6
```
------------------------------------------------------------
============================================================
```

There were three sponsors of this list at this time and their messages also show up on
the thank-you-for-subscribing page when you subscribe online (see Figure 7.14).

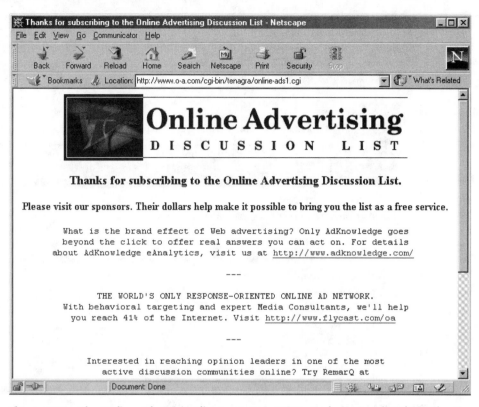

Figure 7.14 The Online Advertising list managers at Tenagra know to offer their advertisers yet another venue for their messages.

Cliff Kurtzman added one more twist to the list. When a new advertiser signs on, he sends out a short post to the list, thanking the advertiser in public and introducing them to the subscribers. Emphasis here is on the *short*. Cliff makes sure this isn't a blatant ad for the sponsor—they'll get plenty of those in each post. This is simply a way of acknowledging them. It also alerts people to a change in the sponsorship, in case they lost interest in the repetition of the ads.

The mechanics of subscribing are simple. As of August 1999, the Online Advertising Discussion List had 7,958 subscribers, and was growing at a net rate of about 40 subscribers per week. Approximately 80 percent of subscribers received the list as daily digests of all posts to the list.

They're careful about editing, so people don't get overwhelmed and the quality stays high. Approximately five to eight messages (or one digest) get sent to the list every business day. Sponsorship is sold in one-week increments and three slots are available each week.

Each sponsor can place a text banner that appears on the bottom of each nondigest post and on the top, middle, and bottom of each digest post. The text banner can change daily if the sponsor desires, provided that a week's worth of banners are sub-

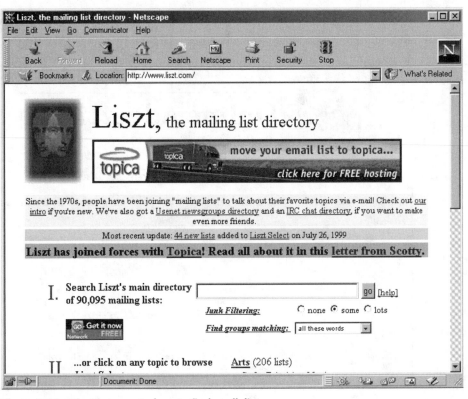

Figure 7.15 Liszt is a great place to find, well, lists.

mitted up front, and can be three lines at 70 characters per line, including spaces and URLs. Naturally, Tenagra maintains full editorial veto power.

Tenagra posts their schedule of available slots on their site so potential advertisers can see how soon they can get placed and choose specific dates if they like. As long as the ads are well targeted, the audience is served interesting words from sponsors, sponsors are getting their ads in front of the right people, and the Tenagra Corporation defrays some of the costs of hosting and managing the Online Advertising Discussion List.

Liszt at www.liszt.com is one of the best places to find lists on all topics (see Figure 7.15). A little digging will turn up the ones that accept advertising.

Newsletters Are Ripe for Advertising

We may have beaten to death the subject of creating and mailing newsletters, but maybe advertising in other people's newsletters is a good move for you. Because they come in all shapes and sizes, because they cover all sorts of topics, and because you may have neither the wherewithal nor the desire to publish your own, other people's newsletters could be the consummate spot for your ad.

Like any other sponsorship, your ad is going to appear to support whatever the newsletter editorial perspective might be. You are associating your company with the writers of this periodical for good or ill, so choose wisely. Naturally, the closer you can tie the content of your ad to the content of the newsletter, the more readers will find it of interest.

Text Ads in Text Versions

Take a look in their archives or have them send you a dozen issues so you can see how the formatting works. Ads in the aforementioned Online Advertising Discussion List are well defined and stand out pretty well.

HotWired's Webmonkey distinguishes its ads by surrounding them with the imitation HTML tags <advertisement> and </advertisement>. Not very distinguishing. The Motley Fool (www.fool.com) and *Interactive Week* take it a step further by surrounding ads with asterisks (see Figure 7.16).

The ClickZ newsletter uses a line of greater-than and less-than signs at the ad's top and bottom, like this:

```
>>>>>>>>>>>>>>>>>>>>>>>>advertisement<<<<<<<<<<<<<<<<<<<<<<<<<<<
```

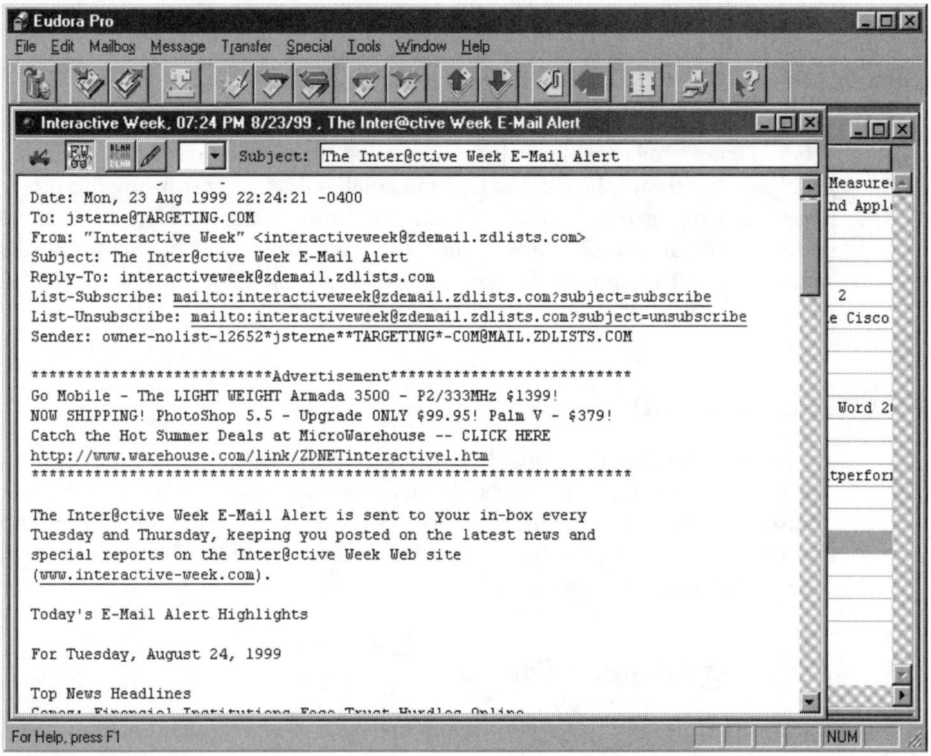

Figure 7.16 *Interactive Week* draws visual attention to their advertisers.

In January 1999, in an effort to promote systematization of text banners, ClickZ Publisher Andy Bourland called for text banner standards. He offered the following potential formats:

AD FORMAT	PROPOSED DEPTH	PROPOSED WIDTH
Small	4 lines	60 columns
Medium	7 lines	60 columns
Large	12 lines	60 columns

But ClickZ does something else by way of text ads—something unique, well worth paying for, and well worth asking others to imitate. It's something they call *spotlight advertorials*.

> An effective way to launch a new product or service is through the use of the ClickZ advertorial. One advertorial insertion includes 200–300 words written by a professional copywriter hired by ClickZ, leading to a call to action with links, telephone number and URL.
>
> One ClickZ Advertorial insertion includes: One week of home page presence on ClickZ.com One week inclusion in daily HTML and TEXT mailings to 43K subscribers.
>
> Specifications: 200–300 words Company logo URL, Email and Phone info included Custom written by ClickZ.

It's a real attention-getter. As an advertorial, it's not hype and it's not news. It feels more like the personal perspective of the author, without the negatives. If you throw in your company logo, it looks pretty good in the HTML version of ClickZ (see Figure 7.17).

Banner Ads in HTML Versions

When it comes to HTML newsletters, you have to switch your thinking from text to graphics. You'll find the sizes to be a tad smaller, but the results are the same as banner advertising on other Web sites. You'll go through the same creative process, development, and testing as Web site banner ads. You'll just be displaying them in a smaller space. Delving into banner ads would require an additional book's worth of analysis and we'll leave you to find the right book.

Professional Promotions

There are companies that run ad-supported email contests. There are companies that run ad-supported email joke lists. There are companies that hand out email coupons. There are companies that will pay people to read your email ad with points and some that will pay them in cash. These are professionals and their job is to push your message out to as many people as possible.

Targeting Coupon Clippers

Coolsavings.com is a destination site for consumer savings, and a direct marketing service for advertisers. Coolsavings.com has more than 2 million registered households (as of June 1, 1999), which are identified by key demographic and other house-

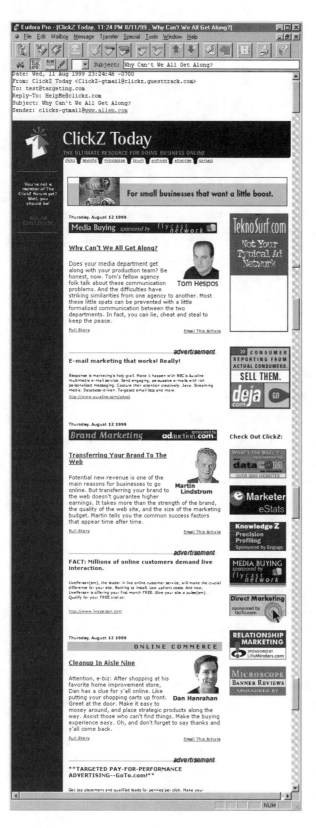

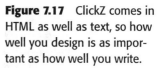

Figure 7.17 ClickZ comes in HTML as well as text, so how well you design is as important as how well you write.

hold information, with the guarantee that their identities and contact information will not be revealed to advertisers. Advertisers may target consumers with coupons, rebates, savings notices, samples, and trial offers.

Going beyond geographic and demographic registration profiles, the coolsavings.com system also tracks member shopping preferences as they clip, click, and view offers throughout the site.

They also send out to their subscribers five- and six-page emails filled with the latest in savings. For the 1999 holiday season, coolsavings.com offered advertisers email with a holiday theme. Each email contained a link directly to the clients' exclusive offers, and advertisers got to decide whether to go solo or join a group of cosponsors for a lower cost.

Playing Games

Gamesville.com offers games online. That's it. But they do it well enough that they get 200,000 people a day to come to their Web site and play.

It's no surprise that 26 percent of the gamers are between 18 and 24 years old. That sounds like just the sort of group you'd expect to register to play games like:

Three-Eyed Bingo. Bingo from Outer Space WIN $333–$3333 Cash.

Quick-Draw Poker. Poker on Steroids WIN $500–$1500 Cash.

CatchUp CoverAll. Fast Paced. High Stakes! WIN $300–$2500 Cash.

AceyDeucey. The Big-Ass Card Game WIN Realtime Cash Prizes.

The Bingo Zone. World's Biggest Bingo Game WIN Realtime Cash Prizes.

TV Crystal Ball. Predict the Emmy Awards WIN a 55-Inch Projection TV.

StockCar Madness. NASCAR Prediction Game WIN a Trip to Daytona 500.

March Mania. Predict NCAA Tournament Meet the Winners.

Pop Quiz. 5 Weekly Music Trivia Games WIN $150 Music Shopping Spree.

Roundball Madness. World's Biggest NCAA Office Pool.

But it *is* surprising that 38 percent are between the ages of 35 and 54. It's also interesting that 60 percent are female and 42 percent of *them* are between 35 and 54 years old. That makes for a compelling demographic.

Email goes out a couple of times a month to Gamesville players and ads may be targeted by gender, age, education, occupation, household income, marital status, city, state, country, zip code, SCF code, area code, Nielsen media regions, registered email domain, operating system, browser, date, and time.

The Gamesville registration database was boasting 1 million registrants in the fall of 1999, with 40 percent of those receiving the HTML version. Gamesville does HTML email sniffing. The first message a recipient receives comes with one invisible graphic in it. If the email client opens that graphic by sending an HTTP call to the server, then Gamesville knows that email software client will handle HTML.

The emails are all from Gamesville and they all have to be something special. "When people register, they're asked if they want occasional email specials from us," says Mark Herrmann, director of sales and marketing at Gamesville. "We work very hard to make sure the offers *are* special so people don't unsubscribe.

"We also have shopping online and keep track of people's buy-o-graphics. After a long period of time, we get a pretty deep profile of our players. And then we can overlay that data with other information from database companies like Experian. The result is very tight targeting if you want to send an offer to men between 18 and 34 in the greater Boston area who lease Saabs, own their own homes, expressed interest in a smoking cessation program and purchased a copy of the software game Trophy Bass 2 Deluxe."

Ads or Minuses?

From www.cybergold.com:

> Earn $75 cash back when you open an E*TRADE account with a minimum balance of only $1,000.
>
> Get $3 cash back when you request a FREE, no-obligation quote from Autobytel on any new car. Receive $500 in grocery coupons and $5 in Cybergold when you sign up for a 30-day trial membership in the American Homeowners Association.
>
> Get 3 days, 2 nights deluxe hotel accommodations in Hawaii or one of 8 other resort destinations FREE plus $10 from Cybergold. Simply switch to Qwest long distance with rates as low as $.05 per minute.
>
> Get $0.50 when you sign up for a FREE membership at YesMail, the revolutionary new way to shop on the Internet.

What is CyberGold? It's a company founded on the idea that the best way to get people to read ads is to pay them—in cash. Consumers can read ads, participate in marketing surveys, register at Web sites, sign up for services and more, and earn a buck here and 50¢ there.

It's based on a time-honored calculation. Take all of your spending for three months on advertising, marketing, and promotions and divide it by the number of leads you got. That's your cost per lead. If it costs you $5 in advertising to get somebody to ask for a price quote on a car, $3 from CyberGold is a real deal. If it costs you $200 to get somebody to sign up for a discount brokerage account, $75 is a steal.

The concept is very straightforward, even if it did cause George Guilder to proclaim it was proof that commercials were not added value when you had to pay people to watch them.

How to Write Email So Your Site Is Transformed in Their Eyes

Ron Richards wasn't sleeping well again, but this time it wasn't a suboptimum word in an email subject line that kept him up. This time, he couldn't sleep from excitement. He'd just figured out the answer to the most far-reaching puzzle in persuasion strategy he'd ever encountered.

He passed his breakthrough along to me because he knew it applied strongly to emailings and every other form of advertising—even though he'd discovered it in the context of Web banner ads.

For weeks he'd been studying data on how two different ads were getting the same clickthrough rates, but one was generating 10 times more sales. The people who responded could be identical populations, matched in every way (demographic, psychographic, product need, and so forth), and yet when the two groups got to the site their purchase activity could be an order of magnitude apart.

I share Ron's attitude that there's nothing so practical as a good theory. This one he calls the *implanted context theory* and you can take it to the bank. He emailed me this description:

> People coming to a site from two different emails no longer have the same eyes and mindset. Each email, whether intended or not, implants a context in the person's mind and establishes a structure for their experience in a surprisingly powerful way. It determines what they look for on the site, what questions they seek answers to, what organizing themes help the site be accessible. Even a brief ad or email can reframe their site experience totally, coloring the meaning of everything on the site for them.
>
> Here's an example of two emails and the contexts they implant: Email A: Our widgets are the best, but they're the least expensive. Email B: Our widgets do what all the other widgets do, but have 7 breakthroughs that make the other widgets obsolete, and make ours indispensable.
>
> People coming to your site from email A are browsing for verification that your widgets are cheaper. Those coming from email B are browsing for verification that your product is just as good in every way, and wondering what the 7 breakthroughs are. They want to know whether those breakthroughs are important in their situation, and whether your claim that your indispensable widgets obsolete your competitors can possibly be true.
>
> Email B is full of news and curiosity. It resets the standard and disqualifies the competitors (if it can be verified). But those persuasion virtues are not my point here. The new point is that it sets up questions, and the visitor is virtually *compelled* to search for those answers on the site.
>
> Both emails are driving traffic to the identical site. But if you interviewed visitors coming from different implanted contexts, they'd describe the site so differently, you'd think they'd been to different sites. The visitor is literally coming from a "different place."
>
> This theory of implanted context explains why many of ResultsLab's other principles have such big effects, in areas such as positioning, resetting the standard, and finding a great issue. It explains why the primary grabbers in ads and emails have by far the most effect on response. It sets the stage before people read the body copy, and click to other areas.
>
> Here are some of the ways ResultsLab uses implanted context to maximize results:
>
> Check to assure the email is totally congruent with the home page.
>
> Double check usability and persuadability to insure the answers to implanted questions can be found easily.

Have the email clickthrough go to a side door page (landing page) that
acts like a linear accelerator, to intensify the implanted context.
We now do everything to take advantage of the realization that each step
in the persuasion process is delivering a mind with a changed context to
the next step. It's a sequence of email, landing page, and sub pages.
Together, they have to be considered a persuasion *system*. They have to
be persuasion engineered in light of the fact that big effects seen at
the last step may in fact be due to big implanted context differences
during one or more of the prior steps.

Implanted context makes a whole bunch of old beliefs obsolete. We used
to think that the stats of email and ads, such as their clickthrough
rate, measured their power independently of what happened on the site.
And we used to think the site took full credit for the stats that happen
on the site, like pageviews, time spent, percent who purchase, and average size of purchases. Now we know that each step's effects can show up
mainly in later steps, and be large.

Rising to Higher Persuasion Levels: An Email Must

Ron says it became essential for ResultsLab to conceptualize persuasion levels to keep
clients away from pitfalls, differentiate them from low-level competitors, and take
them to the levels where they can achieve competitive dominance (see Figure 7.18).

"As you read the press, you'd think that advertisers and sites were constantly using or
considering unethical practices, the bottom level in our diagram," says Ron. "To us,
this is ridiculous. We find clients in companies large and small to be people proud of
their integrity, and quite aware that the unethical level would provoke anger, bad
word-of-mouth, and boycott. One key to that is purging any actual or *perceived* salesy
language, exaggeration, or hype. The language we use in grabbers is very strong, but
only because it signals hot news, or a new decision standard." To see the difference,
see the before and after examples in the Grabbers section of www.resultslab.com.

Next, Ron clarifies the different persuasion levels, why they're so important, and how
you can take advantage of them:

When we first look at our clients' emails and sites they (and their competitors) are almost invariably at the Typical level. Despite the work
of great agencies and inside copy writers, their communications are riddled with stumbles, open questions, and things that prompt qualms. The
readers are confused and frustrated, and that's bad enough. But then a
dangerous piece of psychology kicks in. Confused readers don't want to
feel dumb (which they're not), and they assume their confusion is evidence that the advertiser is being intentionally evasive.

We can fix all those stumbles, taking the email and site to the Competent level, but that doesn't differentiate it from thousands of other
sites, and still leaves our client vulnerable.

The real battleground begins the next level up, where the emails we
write and the site changes we make actively protect the visitors in some
way, and help them make better decisions. That generates trust. But

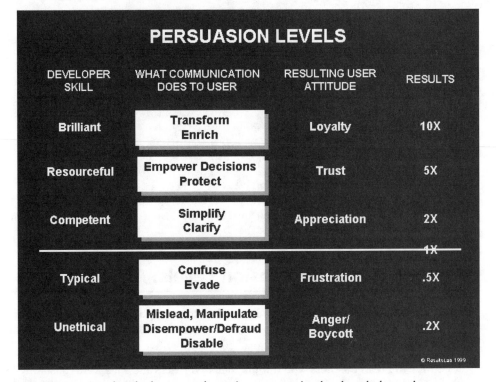

Figure 7.18 ResultsLab charts out the various persuasion levels to help marketers understand the difference between typical and brilliant.

we're not satisfied by just doing those things. We find ways to make it obvious we're doing it—so our client gets credit for it and, thereby, great word-of-mouth.

Finally, brilliant email, ads, and sites take the attitude toward their audience that you would take with your best friend or brother. Having established trust, they become active advocates for practices and products their audience didn't know about—things that are deeply in the audience's interest. Imagine being able to really come on strong, as you could with your best friend, without being accused of being pushy, or self serving.

Once we establish that top-level relationship, we can write copy with language like, "Three things to alert all your colleagues to tomorrow, and the consequences if you don't" or, "A must-read article that protects your IT purchases in ways no one else is talking about."

Rising to the top persuasion level in your email, ads, and site will multiply your results by 10-20 times. Even moving up two levels is worth a 5 fold improvement in final results.

No matter how expert you have been at moving up the persuasion levels, you can multiply your results by an order of magnitude if you take the time for some thorough testing.

CHAPTER 8

Testing Your Talent, Reckoning Your Response, and Managing Your Email

How's it going?

Things working out like you expected?

How do you tell?

If you need a few more sales under your belt to get that promotion, if you need a few more sales on the bottom line to make that IPO, if you need a few more sales so you can show the board why they shouldn't replace you with a 25-year-old, fresh-out-of-college Generation Y'er who *majored* in electronic marketing, then maybe it's time to take all of this seriously and get into some rigorous testing and finite measuring.

What's the best way to boost your rate of conversion from prospects to customers? Test, measure, and refine a campaign before you launch it wholesale. Oh, and don't forget to be ready when people come calling.

Testing

Testing means preparation. It means setting up a campaign in such a way that you'll have some interesting data to play with at the back end. And if you're good, you can turn that data into information that will add to your knowledge about what works, so you can run the next campaign with wisdom on your side.

Williams-Sonoma knew what they were after when they sent out a trial promotion of their bridal registry. They wanted people to sign up and they wanted to boost store traffic. They got a 5 percent success rate. They're very careful about their mailings.

"Our fall catalog can cost us a dollar. Email doesn't cost us anything, but it can cost us a relationship if we mail customers too much," says Pat Connolly, in charge of Williams-Sonoma's direct-to-customer catalog business. After a few tweaks, they sent out another test and scored twice as high.

It's all about setting goals and embarking on the never ending struggle of continuous improvement.

In smaller companies, testing advertising or testing direct mail pieces has just been too expensive in both financial and human resources. It takes a long time to roll out a new mailer and get it printed up. Create two? Three? Four? Not likely.

But the cost of creating an email message is very small. The cost of renting an opt-in email list is small. The cost of delivering those messages to that list is very small. So it makes sense to spend a bit of your budget making sure your messages are hitting their mark and having the desired effect.

You get to test under real marketplace conditions in real time. With email, the initial response measurements may only take several hours. The final statistics, due to pass-alongs, people on vacation, and people playing save-it-for-later, may take a few weeks. All told, it's a fast medium to test and to measure.

Gone are the heady days of "throw it up on the Web and see what happens!" The fast, loose, and out-of-control trial-and-error approach is being replaced by techniques for testing and measurement that are rapid and revealing.

Rapid, Continuous Improvement

ResultsLab's goal is always to increase results two- to fivefold beyond the client's best current persuasion tools. We can learn a lot from how they pull that off and got results that look hard to beat.

Their secret sauce is a strange combination of persuasion engineering approaches. They consciously apply 17 major persuasion principles and hundreds of smaller principles. They virtually beg their clients to say, "Why are you doing it that way?," and they always have an answer. Then they do cycles of testing, interpretation, and new creative to go into higher and higher orbit as fast as possible—called their "Rapid Continuous Improvement System."

ResultsLab is so confident of its persuasion technologies that it welcomes getting paid only on proven results, so they have a vested interest in beating the control email by a significant amount. But they have another reason to want highly valid testing: They live on the philosophy that "whoever learns fastest wins." So they start by testing a whole bunch of very different strategies. Then in subsequent waves they combine the winners and try variations, and then cycle again.

We got Ron to describe some of their tricks for quickly measuring and interpreting results.

Using True Split Runs

Ron encourages his clients to run pure split-run testing just as they should with direct postal mail. To make it pure, they divide the email list into randomly matched groups. Then they send a different email treatment to each group of people, making sure that everyone gets the email at about the same time.

Since all the recipient groups are matched, the differences in results from each group are due to the email treatment they got, and nothing else. Because this method has such strong validity, they can measure differences with higher confidence and after sending fewer emails.

Ron finds that ResultsLab must control every aspect of the test to prevent email distribution supplier stumbles such as strange format changes, not matching the lists, time delays, even their changing the email copy or links so they don't work. You know, the well-intentioned "improvements" that in fact disable a subtle, underlying persuasion psychology.

Clients who want interpretable results and want to avoid retesting delays will welcome the scientific approach by a quality control-obsessed organization like ResultsLab.

When You Can't Do Split Runs, Watch Your Spikes

Ron says, "A great thing about email, besides the potential for 20 percent response rates, is that most of the response typically comes in within two days, creating a very noticeable spike. But we and our clients have a whole list of understandable concerns about whether spikes are caused by some other random event."

Whether your bottom-line metric is to prompt a lot of pageviews for a day or two or to improve clickthrough responses, registrations, or sales, response can vary each day due to random causes.

ResultsLab built a mathematical model showing daily random background spikes, proving that, although random spikes sometimes double and sometimes halve your results, they happen only on a random one or two days a month. So the chance the spikes will happen exactly in the days immediately after any chosen email broadcast day, or drop day, is small. Ron calculates a 5 percent chance that a spike in your response will be a random event and not due to your brilliant campaign.

No problem, Ron simply repeats the test of the winners. He says they should be retested anyway, along with prior controls.

Testing carefully is critical. What do you test? Everything.

Start Simple: Test the Format

This is the easiest test, because you can do it yourself. Install the most popular email software packages and start sending yourself messages. You're looking for strange characters, odd line breaks, and general readability.

Do the HTML versions work? What happens if you change the settings to proportional fonts? What happens if you narrow the email application window? How do the lines break? Do your URLs break in the middle and become unclickable? Or does the email software take care of that for you?

If you don't have a usability testing lab at your company or access to a lot of different computers and software, round up the friends and family or create a new Customer Advisory Council (and hand out the T-shirts to participants). Ask them to be on the receiving end of your formatting tests.

Then test your format for pass-along readability. If one email system adds a tab to the beginning of each line, another adds a gray bar down the left column, and another adds a greater-than sign, what happens to your delicately designed document?

Test Whether *They* Like the Format

The first test is important to make sure your message is readable. The next question is which format gets the best response. All marketers we spoke with send both HTML and ASCII versions and they all say those who opt for the HTML version are fewer in number but higher in response. Do you get the same results?

This is also one of the simpler tests you can run because there's not much to it. Those who signed up for the HTML version get HTML, and those who signed up for the ASCII version get ASCII. There's not a lot you, your service provider, your list manager, or your Webmaster can do to mess things up.

You just have to be sure there is a measurement mechanism in place.

The easiest test that anybody can implement is using alternative URLs. One test segment is asked to click through to one page and another group is asked to click through to another page. Count up the pageviews of each one from the server logs and you have your answer. Just make darned sure those two pages are exactly the same. Why does it matter?

Galileo is generally given credit for being the father of the scientific method. As the *Encyclopaedia Britannica* put it, "Even while Bacon was philosophizing, the true method was being practiced by Galileo, who, with a combination of observation, hypothesis, mathematical deduction and confirmatory experiment founded the science of dynamics."

One of the most important tenets of the scientific method is control over variables.

To test each of these email campaign elements in the purest form means ensuring that all other things are equal. If you want to be sure there really is a difference in response caused by your message being in ASCII or HTML, then everything else, including the landing page, must be exactly the same.

That's how it works in an ideal world. In the real rough-and-tumble world of competitive scrabbling and political maneuvering, one often finds oneself changing three or four factors at once. While that's normally accepted, it's hardly scientific. If you really want to get a handle on how one tiny change can alter a response, you need to go to the laboratory.

Test the Subject Line

Try a dozen—why not? See which pull better, which sell more, which are most memorable three months later. You might just come up with a whole new branding slogan for your company.

Test the List

Quite simple. Mail exactly the same message to different lists at exactly the same time. What's different here is that you are looking for more than just response rates.

How many of your messages bounced, coming back as "no such address"? That's going to tell you how good that particular list is, and it has a decided effect on the results tabulation. If you send out 100 and get a 10 percent response, that's great. But if 10 percent bounced, then you really got an 11.11 percent response.

How many people unsubscribed from that list after your last posting? This is a tough piece of data to reconcile with the rest of your marketing plans. They might have unsubscribed because the list broker set you up with an inappropriate cluster of people and they didn't like getting something so off-topic. They might have unsubscribed because you sent out an HTML posting to an ASCII-only list. Or they might have thought your message was just the straw that broke the camel's back.

Which list pulls best for you? If you're promoting tax preparation services, you definitely want to send that to people who have clicked the Tax Preparation box when they were selecting opt-in categories. But you might find interested parties who clicked on Investing, Stock Brokers, Venture Capital, and even Commercial Real Estate.

Test the Details

Here's where the scientific method becomes important. You have to be aware of all the different elements that might have an effect on your results. That way you can isolate them and determine which elements are actually at work.

If 40 percent of your response is the result of selecting the right list and 40 percent the result of creating the right offer, then some attention should be paid to the latter.

The Offer

Your offer can be changed in subtle ways. *Lots* of subtle ways.

If you're offering 10 percent off, try offering 15 percent off and see if you get a big increase in response.

If you're offering something for a limited time, try changing the amount of time your target audience has to think about it. You wouldn't think about sending out a direct mail piece that had an offer that was good for only two days. You have no control over when the post office will deliver. But you *can* send out emails that have a very short shelf life.

If you change your offer for free installation, will you also throw in free delivery if the client will give you a referral? There's a lot of room to maneuver with your offer. Get creative.

The Price

How will changing the price in your offer change the response? We could write a book! Fortunately, other brave souls have gone before us:

Webster's Marketing Bibliography: Marketing Services, General Product Issues, Books on Products as a Controllable Variable, by Frederick A. Webster (Historical Press, 1986)

The Impact of Price Promotions on a Brand's Market Share, Sales Pattern, and Profitability, by Leigh McAlister (Marketing Science Institute, 1986)

Price Competition, Advertising, and the Evolution of Concentration, by John Sutton (MIT Press, 1991)

Price Wars: How to Win the Battle for Your Customer, by Tom Winninger (St. Thomas Press, 1994)

Total Relationship Marketing: From the 4Ps—Product, Price, Promotion, Place—of Traditional Marketing Management to the 3Rs, by Evert Gummesson (Butterworth-Heinemann, 1999)

The Lead

What if you send the same offer to the same list and changed only the first couple of sentences? You'd have a big impact on your results. People won't spend a lot of time on an email solicitation—even one regarding a subject they care deeply about—unless it grabs them. What grabs people? Start testing.

The Length

The long form or the short form? Hook 'em and reel them in? Or drop the whole anchor on their heads and just wait for them to float to the surface?

The Tone

Is your style rigidly set by the corporate communications department? They should produce some guidelines to protect the company brand, but you should also have a little latitude in this area. Same offer, same list, but some of the recipients get a message that is all business and some get one that's fun, funny, and upbeat. Which draws more?

The Day and Time

Monday? Friday? Sunday? First thing in the morning? Midmorning? Afternoon? Evening? You can make some guesses. You can even survey your customers and see what they prefer. But you'd still only be guessing, when you could be testing.

The Response Mechanism

Does it make a difference what sort of call to action you use? You can have people reply to your message via email, you can have them give you a call, or—the most popular and most logical—you can have them click through to a landing page on your Web site.

Now it gets interesting.

What happens on that page? How is the customer walked through the buying process? Here's another place you can run an A/B split. You can run an A/B split of your entire Web site if you have the time and money.

What if the landing page has a single-button to accept the offer? What if there are survey questions they need to fill out first? What if you're taking the order of a new customer? Just how many hoops do you make them jump through for best results? Try some and see.

The Number of Sign-up Questions

If the response you are looking for is to get people to answer questions, how many do you ask?

And what do you promise them in return? Yahoo! has a whole page dedicated to "rewarded surveys" (see Figure 8.1).

The rewards range. Answer a few questions and see the results online; get entered in a drawing for $25, a $50 gift certificate for jeans, $300 worth of health care books; or get a free animation cel from Teenage Mutant Ninja Turtles. Go figure.

The Brand Impact

This is one that most people don't get, but it's important. People outside the walls of your company have an opinion about your company. That opinion will range from those who think your firm is evil and out to squash all other software vendors (or small, mom-and-pop home-goods stores) to those who think you make the best ice cream (or skin care products) in the world in an environmentally sound and socially conscious way. These brand images are strong enough that you know who we're talking about without even reading the names.

For most of us, the brand image in the minds of the vast majority of the public is "Who?"

When you send out an email that has no impact, the public's opinion is not going to change. You'd like it to change for the better if possible. But how can you tell?

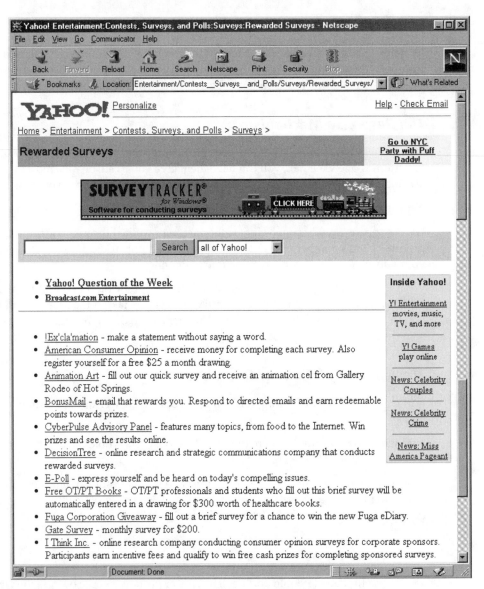

Figure 8.1 Yahoo! has more than a dozen surveys listed that want to give you something for your trouble.

As the director of research and strategic planning at Blue Marble ACG, Jeffrey Graham works with clients such as General Motors, Procter & Gamble, and Capital One to analyze, develop, and evaluate their online marketing and business strategies. Formerly a faculty lecturer in Internet Research at New York University, he writes the occasional column for ClickZ. Here's Jeffrey's take on banner ad branding. Everything he says applies directly to email ad branding:

COMMON SENSE BRANDING RESEARCH

In my last article, "The Cult of Click-Through," I explained why we couldn't rely on click-through rates to determine whether our advertising is effective. So how do you measure branding success?

Truth is, there are a number of tools on the market designed to test effectiveness. But making sure you use the right one takes a solid understanding of research principles, knowledge of Internet technology, and a healthy dose of common sense.

Copy testing, which is the most common tool for testing advertising effectiveness, was once considered groundbreaking research. In offline copy testing, researchers expose consumers to advertising in malls or focus groups and then immediately ask them about the advertised brand. Such testing is supposed to test how compelling the advertising is.

The problem is that people know they're being set up and react accordingly. Imagine this: "Look at this ad for Joe's Hot Dogs!! . . . Now, what hot dog brands come to mind?" Besides, measuring the immediate effect of advertising doesn't take into account the cumulative effect of advertising over time.

This flawed testing model has migrated over to the online environment. Instead of being recruited in front of Sears, respondents are recruited off of banners or pop-up windows. But the methodology is the same: Getting an immediate reaction in the context of an artificial environment.

Fortunately, the Internet has allowed us to explore a different approach. Two years ago, the Internet Advertising Bureau led the way with a study to measure the effectiveness of Internet advertising. When people on certain web sites requested a page on the site, they were asked to take a survey.

One half of the surveyed respondent pool was served the page they initially requested, along with a brand advertisement (test). The other half got the same page with a "dummy" ad (control). A few days later, both groups were queried by email about their attitudes concerning the brand advertised, and results between the control and test group were compared.

This study was a good step in the right direction. By using the power of the Internet to segment people and serve them a customized message, the study could employ the classic experimental (control/test) design.

It was blind; it tested the impact of ads without revealing to respondents what was being tested. The methodology wasn't prohibitively expensive (as a segmented, control/test method would be offline). And best of all, it showed that Internet advertising was effective.

But the IAB study wasn't perfect. The biggest problem was that respondents were exposed to only one ad. Advertisers have known for a long time that multiple exposures are optimal. Most importantly, the study couldn't compare results based on varying levels of exposure.

Online research has come a long way since then. Now, we can keep track of just what ads people are exposed to and when, and compare this information with the answers they give us in surveys. We can tell which ads are most effective in promoting certain attitudes among specific groups of people. We can measure and calibrate the cumulative effect of advertising. And we can do it in real time, allowing us to optimize our campaigns based on exactly which elements of our advertising are best meeting our client's specific objectives.

In order to craft this type of research, you need to understand the ins and outs of cookies, IP addresses, and database management. But what is even more crucial is to know how to customize the research around the needs of your client. Branding research needs to answer the questions most relevant to your client, and every client has different needs.

That's why it's not about choosing the right tools, but being able to use those tools in order to craft the right research plan.

We can use branding research not only to inform and improve our campaigns, but also to make online advertising more accountable. Clients like that. Come to think of it, it's only common sense.

You can test all of the preceding and more. But what does it take to understand the test results? You use a stopwatch, a yardstick, a rain gauge, a postal scale, a calculator, an accountant—any measuring and tabulating tool you can think of—to tell you if it's all been worthwhile.

Measuring Response

Response comes in various shapes and sizes. You're going to need a map. Here's the simplest way to map out a game plan and some results.

The Testing Map

A testing map will help you keep track of what you're trying to accomplish and remind you to keep your efforts simple.

Here's a testing map from a ClickZ article by Nick Usborne (see Table 8.1). He was wondering how soon to send a thank-you email to customers, and how many to send. Seeing that we're all a little thin on experience, the correct answer was to create a testing map showing three different emails sent to 12 different groups of customers at different times. The point is to be as rigorous as possible.

Table 8.1 Days After Purchase for Response

	EMAIL 1	EMAIL 2	EMAIL 3
Cell One	1	1	1
Cell Two	1	5	10
Cell Three	1	10	21
Cell Four	1	21	none
Cell Five	7	10	14
Cell Six	7	14	21
Cell Seven	7	21	none
Cell Eight	7	none	none
Cell Nine	14	21	28
Cell Ten	14	28	42
Cell Eleven	14	42	none
Cell Twelve	14	none	none

Table 8.2 Testing Three Leads against Three Subject Lines

	LEAD 1	LEAD 2	LEAD 3	TOTAL
Subject 1	285	275	456	1016
Subject 2	126	134	157	417
Subject 3	304	332	468	1104
	715	741	1081	

In Table 8.2, three leads are being tested against three subject lines. Subject line number 2 was clearly the worst bit of copywriting and lead 3 was the best of the batch. But subject lines 1 and 3 are just too close together in response rates to be statistically different. Time to test them against something else.

Settling on lead 3, you test subjects 1 and 2 against three different lists. The results come out looking like those shown in Table 8.3.

This is where meticulous testing pays off. The overall totals show that list 3 pulled better than the others. But closer inspection reveals that list 1, using lead 3 and subject 1, was a runaway hit.

So far, you've been sending out 10,000 test messages per run. Now that you've found a combination that will outpull the next best by 15 percent, it's time to run with the big dogs and send out the 200,000 mailing.

The preceding results are good results. But what do they represent? Sales? Clicks? It turns out there's quite a bit to choose from when you're looking to count, measure, weigh, take a temperature, or calculate your results.

Openings

You went to so much trouble to get the right message in front of the right people at the right time. Did they even bother to open the darned thing?

An HTML message will call back to the server when it's opened to grab the graphics files it needs to display. When it does, it's very easy to tell that Internet Protocol address X opened email Y that called for graphic Z. The next test segment had an email that called the server for graphic ZZ and that's how we can tell them apart.

Table 8.3 Testing Two Subjects against Three Lists

	LIST 1	LIST 2	LIST 3	TOTAL
Subject 1	572	326	476	1374
Subject 2	354	246	497	1097
	926	572	973	

Clickthroughs

Did you get them to the front door?

It's easy enough to tell if they actually clicked. Same as above. The email client they're using sends a request to the registered browser, which, in turn, sends a request to your server for the specified Web page.

The server hears the call and sends the appropriate page to the particular machine making the request. That particular machine is identified by a specific IP address. Something like 199.201.128.24. You don't know who's using that machine and the chances are excellent that the number was assigned to the prospective customer dynamically by AOL or MSN or any one of hundreds of local Internet service providers. But you *can* tell if they've been here before with a cookie.

If you're mailing to your own list, you can embed a user ID into the URL, which will tell you just who it was that came knocking. But there's a big difference between knocking and coming in.

Jack Hojnar is director of campaign management at yesmail.com and often finds himself explaining these finer points to clients. "If you're working with an opt-in list company, make sure they can tell how many people clicked, and how many people landed. Lots of times people click on a link, change their minds and hit the Back or the Stop button. Your server records that a request was made, but a special bit of programming is needed to tell if the request was fulfilled."

Length of Visit

So you know they clicked and they found their way to the landing page. Now what? Did they stop there or did they stick around a while? Did they sniff around only a little or did they spend a nice long time bonding with your brand?

Depth of Visit

It's nice that they stayed a long time, but did they go deep? How many pages did they look at? How did they get there? Did they click straight to the contest registration form and then leave? Or did they dig deep to read the intricate details about your products?

Just how far did they get in the optimal site path? You know which pages you *wanted* them to look at. You know which buttons they *should* have clicked and which forms they *should* have filled out—that's your OSP, your optimal site path. But what if a large number of visitors went all the way to your shopping basket and then bailed out? What if they read the money-back guarantee and decided not to buy? What if they scrolled down to the final price including tax and shipping and handling and processing fees and notification charges and support tariffs and never came back?

Repeat Visits

Did they ever come back? Was there enough magic between the original offer, the client, and the Web site to establish a relationship that was more than fleeting? Did your site live up to or exceed the expectations you set in your first email? Did visiting make them feel like a member of the community you're trying to foster?

You can measure the number of people who return, how quickly they return, how long they stay, how deep the click on each visit, and how many of them came back— all to determine the value of one email message over another.

Leads

At some point, you have to declare the casual visitor to your site an actual, qualified lead. Somebody who has all the makings of a genuine customer-to-be. These are the people you want talking to your salespeople. These are the people you want to get the next email offer that tries to close the sale.

Contacts

How many people replied to the message you sent out? Not responded to as in clicked on the link and followed instructions, but hit Ctrl-R and replied to your message with one of their own?

The measurement here is not merely one of quantity, but also of tone. How many wrote back to ask for clarification? How many wrote back to tell you your message changed their lives? How many wrote to tell you they were hanging you in effigy and would you like to see some digital pictures on their Web site?

Instigating a conversation usually indicates you've done something right. Whatever you said caused people to want to reach out to you. Plus, it gives you a wonderful opening to engage them in a conversation. It means you have ample opportunity to convince them to buy from you. Being properly prepared for that conversation is another matter.

Conversion

Jackpot. This is the pot of gold at the end of the rainbow. For those of you selling herbal remedies and office supplies, this can happen in the click of the mouse. For those selling kitchen cabinets, this may take a while. But this is certainly the most significant metric there is.

Getting to this point may involve dozens of steps and hundreds of variables. There are only a few industries where you can actually count all of them, track all of them, and have a meaningful impact on all of them to increase sales. But you can try to get a handle on a handful of the most important ones.

In some sales offices they have a bell mounted on the wall and when a purchase order comes in they ring that bell. In some companies it takes 100 purchase orders to make that bell ring and in some, the sales office is simply an order-entry facility where the orders are pounded in all day long. However you value each individual sale, pay attention to some of the finer points as well.

Time to Close

If subject line 1 went out to list 1 with lead paragraph 3 and got the most people to the order page where they actually placed the order, did those people order products any faster than the folks who showed up from subject line 2 on list 2 with lead paragraph 3?

You can see how quickly the variables become multivariate and the permutations preposterous. But the issue of speed-to-close can be very important to a company running a just-in-time factory with limited stock on hand. It would be nice to know, as Amazon does, just how many orders to expect in what time frame after an email campaign hits the Net.

Size/Value/Repetition of Sale

Did different combinations of variables cause the purchase of different items? Did some people buy more than others? Did they buy things with higher profit margins? Did they come back and buy more often than other emailings?

Lifetime Value of Account

If they did buy sooner, more profitably, and more often than others, are you tracking their lifetime value to the company? Because there comes a time when it's more important to be good to the customers you have than it is to go out and find new ones. Unless, of course, you're selling mausoleums.

Keeping the Peppers and Rogers theorems in mind, if it's cheaper to sell something to a current client than it is to find somebody new, then losing a current client is the costliest mistake of all. How costly? Take annual revenues, minus cost, times retention rate, account for variable costs and net present value. In other words, download a spreadsheet from www.1to1.com (see Figure 8.2).

As long as you have this wonderfully rich accumulation of information about how you found a given customer, how they were convinced to buy, what they first purchased, and what they've purchased since, it only makes sense to make the most of it to sell them more. How do you do that? By building a learning relationship.

Building Loyalty and Trust

The huge opportunity of permission marketing is in client retention. As your clients become linked more closely to you and your company, you learn more about them and are able to serve them better. Are you making inroads forging and maintaining profitable, loyal, one-to-one relationships with your most valued clients? Has your repeat business increased?

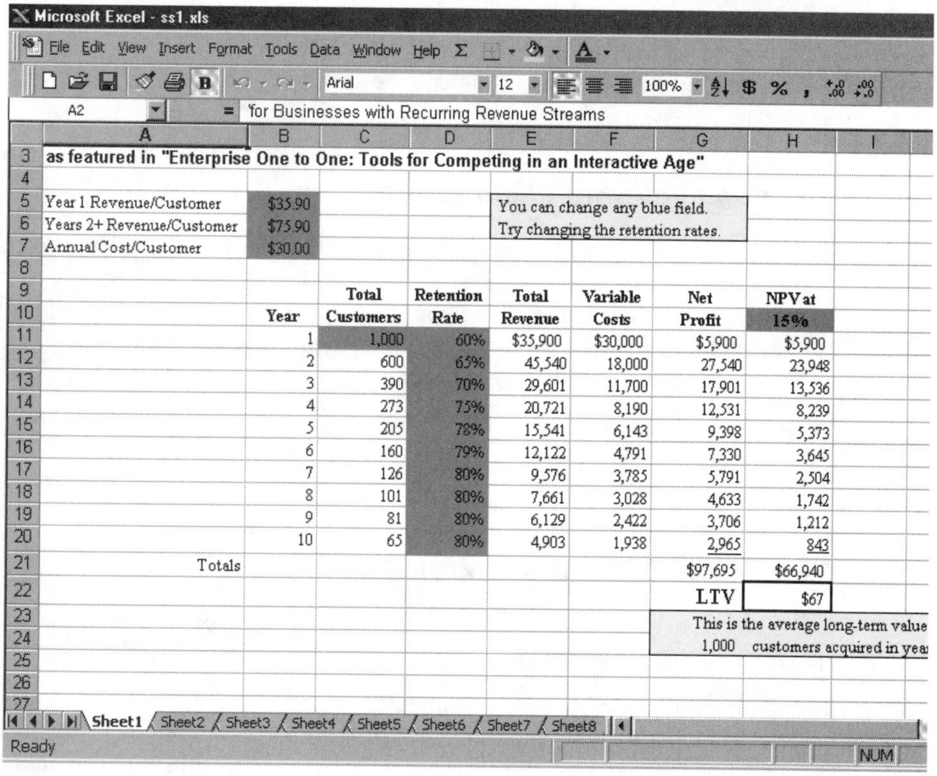
Microsoft Excel - ss1.xls

File Edit View Insert Format Tools Data Window Help

A2 = for Businesses with Recurring Revenue Streams

as featured in "Enterprise One to One: Tools for Competing in an Interactive Age"

Year 1 Revenue/Customer	$35.90
Years 2+ Revenue/Customer	$75.90
Annual Cost/Customer	$30.00

You can change any blue field.
Try changing the retention rates.

Year	Total Customers	Retention Rate	Total Revenue	Variable Costs	Net Profit	NPV at 15%
1	1,000	60%	$35,900	$30,000	$5,900	$5,900
2	600	65%	45,540	18,000	27,540	23,948
3	390	70%	29,601	11,700	17,901	13,536
4	273	75%	20,721	8,190	12,531	8,239
5	205	78%	15,541	6,143	9,398	5,373
6	160	79%	12,122	4,791	7,330	3,645
7	126	80%	9,576	3,785	5,791	2,504
8	101	80%	7,661	3,028	4,633	1,742
9	81	80%	6,129	2,422	3,706	1,212
10	65	80%	4,903	1,938	2,965	843
Totals					$97,695	$66,940
					LTV	$67

This is the average long-term value
1,000 customers acquired in yea

Sheet1 Sheet2 Sheet3 Sheet4 Sheet5 Sheet6 Sheet7 Sheet8

Ready NUM

Figure 8.2 Download a series of spreadsheets from the Peppers and Rogers Group Web site.

Don and Martha's Excellent Adventure

Developing and sustaining relationships is an ongoing process. Don and Martha (Peppers and Rogers) start the process with four steps.

- **Identify**
  Do you remember them from visit to visit and can you determine if they are profitable customers or drains on your resources? Can you tell them apart?
- **Differentiate**
  Do you have a way to treat them differently according to their needs and dissimilar value?
- **Interact**
  Actively learn from them. Why are they buying and how can you use that knowledge to sell them additional products?
- **Customize**
  All of your customers are unique. Can you customize your products to meet their unique needs and keep their business for as long as they're buying?

How are you nurturing your relationships with your clients? Are you using the appropriate Web strategies to build long-term relationships (such as opt-in email, online communities, newsletters, telephone and A/V conferencing, client support services)?

Gathering Relevant Client Information

Pertinent and useful client information is like gold. Have you acquired the information about your prospects or clients that you need to serve them better? Do you know your clients better now than before you started using permission marketing? Do you know who they are, what products they like, their interests? If not, incorporate some additional methods of collecting information beyond what you're doing now.

What have you provided your clients to make them feel that they are benefiting from the relationship? What reason have you given them for wanting to continue to communicate with you?

Focusing on Your Target Market

Market focus helps you expand your Web clientele. Are you achieving higher conversion rates because of better targeting?

The wealth of knowledge you have about your current customers can act as your radar system to help you find additional customers. The more you know about the people who buy from you, the more you'll be able to find others like them. Have you been able to attract and retain more clients through permission marketing than traditional direct mail? Have you improved profitability client by client by focusing on those who receive and return the best value? What ways have you leveraged your marketing costs with this model?

Reckoning ROI

By adding up the campaign's planned costs, the permission marketer can figure out in advance the needed break-even response rate. By carefully analyzing past campaigns, permission marketers can steadily improve their performance.

For elementary ROI comparison of direct mail to banner ads to email marketing, head over to www.yesmail.com (see Figure 8.3).

Compare the expenditures for list rental, the physical materials necessary, the graphic arts talent, and the postage and you can see how fast the costs add up. Some quick divisions by number of respondents and sales give you a quick look at the cost per conversion to customer and the total return on investment.

For a more detailed approach, it's time for the Email ROI Builder (see Figure 8.4).

Nothing happens in a vacuum and it's monstrously hard to calculate the number of people who bought your product who received the email offer within two days of

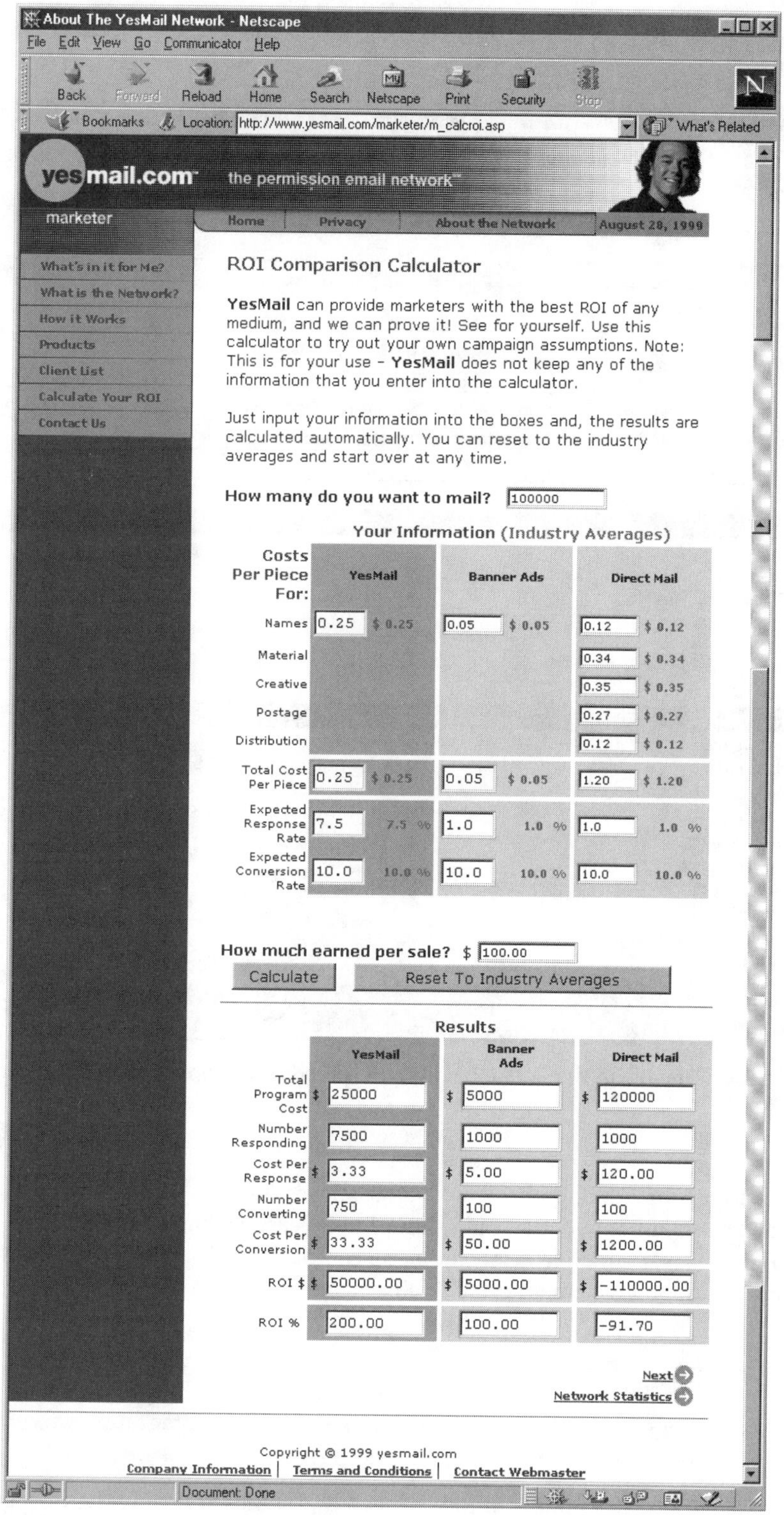
About The YesMail Network - Netscape
File Edit View Go Communicator Help
Back Forward Reload Home Search Netscape Print Security Stop
Bookmarks Location: http://www.yesmail.com/marketer/m_calcroi.asp
What's Related
yesmail.com
the permission email network
marketer
Home Privacy About the Network August 28, 1999
What's in it for Me?
What is the Network?
How it Works
Products
Client List
Calculate Your ROI
Contact Us
ROI Comparison Calculator
YesMail can provide marketers with the best ROI of any medium, and we can prove it! See for yourself. Use this calculator to try out your own campaign assumptions. Note: This is for your use - YesMail does not keep any of the information that you enter into the calculator.
Just input your information into the boxes and, the results are calculated automatically. You can reset to the industry averages and start over at any time.
How many do you want to mail? 100000
Your Information (Industry Averages)
Costs Per Piece For:
YesMail
Banner Ads
Direct Mail
Names 0.25 $ 0.25 0.05 $ 0.05 0.12 $ 0.12
Material 0.34 $ 0.34
Creative 0.35 $ 0.35
Postage 0.27 $ 0.27
Distribution 0.12 $ 0.12
Total Cost Per Piece 0.25 $ 0.25 0.05 $ 0.05 1.20 $ 1.20
Expected Response Rate 7.5 7.5 % 1.0 1.0 % 1.0 1.0 %
Expected Conversion Rate 10.0 10.0 % 10.0 10.0 % 10.0 10.0 %
How much earned per sale? $ 100.00
Calculate
Reset To Industry Averages
Results
YesMail
Banner Ads
Direct Mail
Total Program Cost $ 25000 $ 5000 $ 120000
Number Responding 7500 1000 1000
Cost Per Response $ 3.33 $ 5.00 $ 120.00
Number Converting 750 100 100
Cost Per Conversion $ 33.33 $ 50.00 $ 1200.00
ROI $ $ 50000.00 $ 5000.00 $ -110000.00
ROI % 200.00 100.00 -91.70
Next
Network Statistics
Copyright © 1999 yesmail.com
Company Information | Terms and Conditions | Contact Webmaster
Document: Done

Figure 8.3 This YesMail ROI calculator can help you convince the boss of the value of an email campaign.

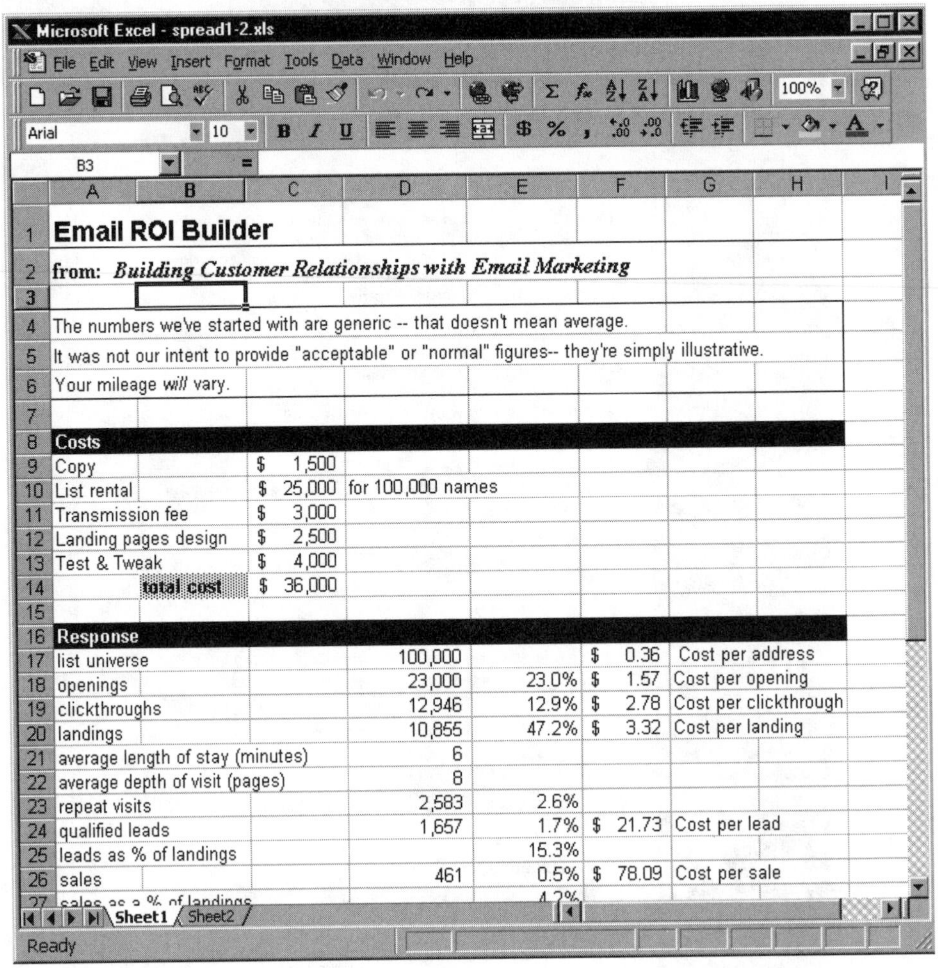

Microsoft Excel - spread1-2.xls

	A/B	C	D	E	F	G
1	**Email ROI Builder**					
2	from: *Building Customer Relationships with Email Marketing*					
3						
4	The numbers we've started with are generic -- that doesn't mean average.					
5	It was not our intent to provide "acceptable" or "normal" figures-- they're simply illustrative.					
6	Your mileage *will* vary.					
7						
8	**Costs**					
9	Copy	$ 1,500				
10	List rental	$ 25,000	for 100,000 names			
11	Transmission fee	$ 3,000				
12	Landing pages design	$ 2,500				
13	Test & Tweak	$ 4,000				
14	total cost	$ 36,000				
15						
16	**Response**					
17	list universe		100,000		$ 0.36	Cost per address
18	openings		23,000	23.0%	$ 1.57	Cost per opening
19	clickthroughs		12,946	12.9%	$ 2.78	Cost per clickthrough
20	landings		10,855	47.2%	$ 3.32	Cost per landing
21	average length of stay (minutes)		6			
22	average depth of visit (pages)		8			
23	repeat visits		2,583	2.6%		
24	qualified leads		1,657	1.7%	$ 21.73	Cost per lead
25	leads as % of landings			15.3%		
26	sales		461	0.5%	$ 78.09	Cost per sale
27	sales as a % of landings			4.2%		

Figure 8.4 Download the Email ROI Builder spreadsheet from www.yesmail.com/book.html.

having seen your poster on the side of a bus, heard your ad on the radio, and dropped by your booth at the trade show. But at least we have a shot at knowing which people responded to a specific email campaign and so we can calculate the specific return on investment pretty well.

Figure Your Cost

List all the things you plan to pay for along the way. In an integrated marketing campaign this type of preparation is done for each medium you use.

The numbers already plugged into the Email ROI Builder are only there as a guideline. Once you've been through this process once or twice, the numbers you use are historical rather than theoretical.

Writing the Copy

It's only email. It doesn't cost anything to write an email. I can do it myself.

That's true. It's also true that you can write a radio spot yourself. You can write a sales letter yourself. You can write an entire series of direct mails, brochures, Power-Point presentations, proposals, and sales contracts yourself. That doesn't mean you should. Plan on going to an outside copywriter with some email experience and spending some money.

List Rental

You can expect to spend around 25¢ per name for most rented lists. If you're running this mailing against your own list, don't forget to add charge-backs from your information systems department or the extra time it takes to sort and search through your database.

Transmission Fees

Sometimes a list owner works with a service bureau. The list owner collects the names, and the service bureau does the database work. When that happens, you might find an additional charge on your bill. Be sure to ask.

Landing Pages Design

When people click on the link in your email, they're going to end up somewhere. You're going to have to create those pages. There should be several, offering alternative methods of persuasion and acquisition. The first page for each campaign will be the costliest; the rest will simply be variations on a theme.

Test and Tweak

If you're rolling out a large, sustained campaign, you're going to want to spend some time and effort (read: money) on solid testing techniques. Budget for multiple runs against different lists. Budget for expert help in getting just the right mix of offer, tone, copy, and price.

Adding it all together is a little daunting the first time. After all, this email stuff is supposed to be cheap, right? Take another look at the YesMail ROI calculator to remind yourself about the comparative cost of reaching this many people using other means. Once you've rolled out your campaign, it's time to read the results.

Count Your Response

Within minutes of an email campaign hitting the Internet, you begin to see results rolling in. Like dot-com start-ups watching their stock price on the first day of IPO trading, excitement mounts as more email is delivered, opened, and clicked. Here's how to make it all make sense.

List Universe

For all of these calculations you need to know the total cost (see previous discussion) and the number of people who reached various response thresholds. The very first calculation you get is cost per address. The list rental company charges you 25¢ per name, but you have more invested into it than just the rental.

Openings

How many people tore open the envelope? Answered the phone? Accepted the flier handed to them on the street? Read your email? This is where you find out if your subject line is a hit or a miss.

Clickthroughs

How many showed up? And to narrow it down, how many actually made it all the way to the landing page without hitting the Back or Stop button? Now you can determine how much it cost you to get somebody to your Web site using email. All the rest of the calculations tell you how good a job the Web site does at closing the sale.

In many companies this is the great continental divide between marketing and sales departments. The marketing people are tasked with getting the leads, and sales is responsible for qualifying and closing. Just as the Internet has lowered the barriers so we can communicate more closely with our customers, so has it raised the necessity for us to communicate more closely within the organization. The handoff between marketing and sales has become a hang-together proposition.

Length of Stay, Depth of Visit, Repeat Visits, and Qualified Leads

These metrics are very valuable for more complex, multivariate calculations. These dimensions help measure the pulling power of your promotional efforts. Just as you created a Testing Map for subject lines, lead paragraphs, and lists, you should create a Results Map showing which combinations of messages drove people deeper into your Web site and resulted in the most sales.

The first question is how many pages did the people who got message 14 look at compared to those who got message 9? The next question is how many sales were caused by these two messages? What if we discovered that the number 9 group bought twice as much as the number 14 group? Should we stop sending out message 14? Not necessarily.

Maybe the goal of the mailing was a corporate name change. Yes, it's good that people buy your products, but the intent was to make a branding statement. You set out to get people to understand the new company direction, catch the excitement of the new possibilities, and become familiar with the new brand you're trying to build for the firm.

It's great that so many people came in to buy the deeply discounted digital camera with the new corporate logo on it, but the purpose was to get them to bond with the new brand. You can't simply assign a dollar value to these goals. All you can do is keep track of which combinations of offer, tone, copy, and price are producing the best intended results.

Sales

Here's the payoff. Branding's nice, but sales is where the action is. We're not in this for our health, we're in it for the money.

First up: How many sales did you make? That's a wonderful way to tell how well you're doing. Did you make more sales than the last mailing you did? Can you figure out why? However, just like the aforementioned lengths, depths, repeats, and leads, sales aren't as cut and dried as they seem at first glance. It's not solely a question of quantity. It's a question of profits.

So cost of sales and profit margins come into play. If you sell 100 items for $10, that's not as good as selling 50 items for $25. If you sell 100 items for $10, it's not as good as selling 75 at $10 if you bought the first batch at $5 and the second at $3.50.

Gather the numbers and plug them in. They will not all be hard-and-fast numbers. Do not be discouraged when your sources give you a range of costs and margins. The real world isn't as neat as a spreadsheet.

Figure Your Return

Now you have enough information for meaningful numbers to pop up in the ROI cells of your spreadsheet. Three data points are going to bring it all together: total profits, total return, and return as a percentage of the expense.

Take all of the sales you made with this one particular mailing and add them up. Subtract the total cost of sales. What's left goes to the bank. That's nice. Profit is good. Profit is our friend.

Now it's time to see how much of that profit figure went toward the emailing that was used to generate that profit. If you sell an item for $10, having paid $7.50 for it, you have $2.50 left over in profits. If you spent $1 in promotions to make that sale, your return is $1.50, or 50 percent.

Fifty percent is a nice round number, one that anybody would be pleased with. Especially with interest rates below 10 percent for more than 10 years.

If your marketing efforts are profitable, then you get to keep your job. If they're very profitable, you get a promotion, a pay raise, and a parking spot next to the CEO for a month. Promotions and parking privileges are important, to be sure, but profits are best. Even better: the ability to take the numbers in hand and use them for a process of continuous improvement.

Who's counting? You are. You can only improve the things you measure.

Email Campaign Data Reporting

It comes in fast and it comes in high. The minute you launch an email campaign, you start getting responses. More and more people are at their desks on a permanent line to the Internet and when your email shows up, they're happy to click. You'd better be ready to record their actions, respond to their needs, and figure out the value of it all.

YesMail serves up results reporting as soon as you launch your campaign. Links embedded in your email messages are funneled through YesMail's analysis systems and turned into online reports for instant viewing.

Starting at the top, YesMail reports hierarchically. In the first screen (see Figure 8.5), Brian's Pet SuperStore is running a Summer Blowout Special campaign, which includes a program called HousePets. There were 25,000 addresses selected for this campaign, which isolates the same list across multiple programs and multiple offers within those programs.

YesMail is tracking four distinct steps for both the Dog and the Cat offers (clicks, landings, conversions, and downloads). The Dog offer got 3314 people to click on the

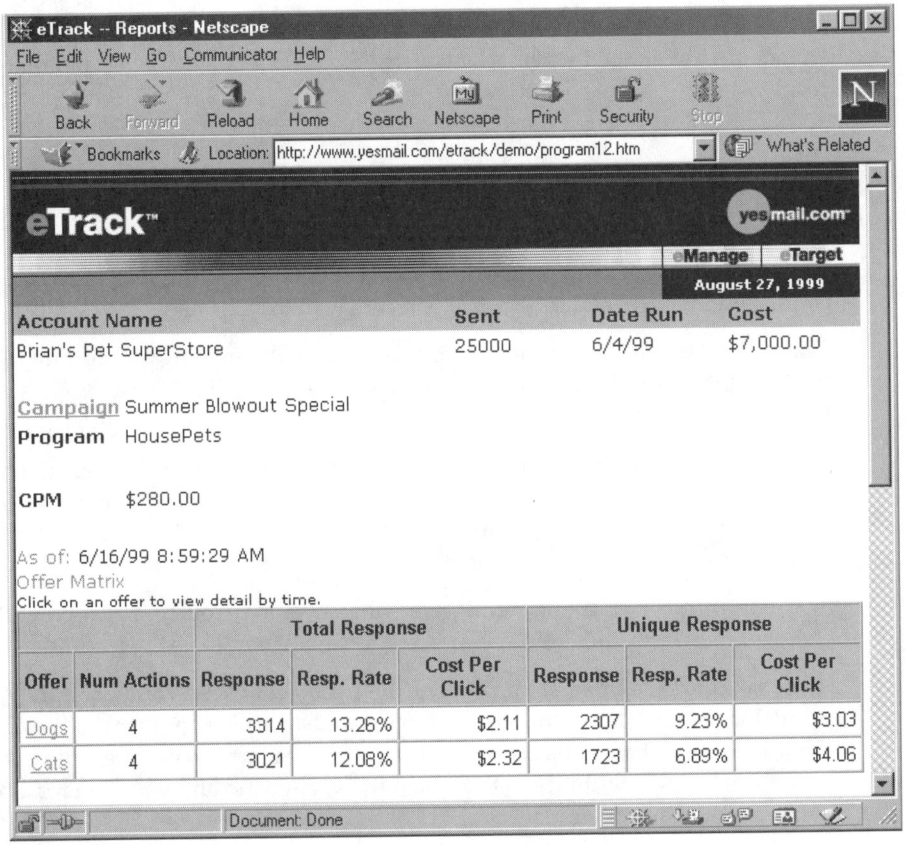

Figure 8.5 YesMail's reporting tools show response rates overall, plus unique responses.

embedded link, which represents a 13.26 percent response rate at $2.11 per response. That's *total* response. A little more than a thousand people clicked on the link more than once. A total of 2307 unique individuals clicked on the link, a rate of 9.23 percent for a total of $3.03 per unique person.

Looking at the Unique Responses in the lower part of Figure 8.6, we drill down to see what sort of numbers we recorded per action. Of the 1611 who made it all the way to the page, 1080 made a purchase and 776 took the time to download Brian's Pet Super-Store screen saver. These numbers are reported via bar charts as well (see Figure 8.7).

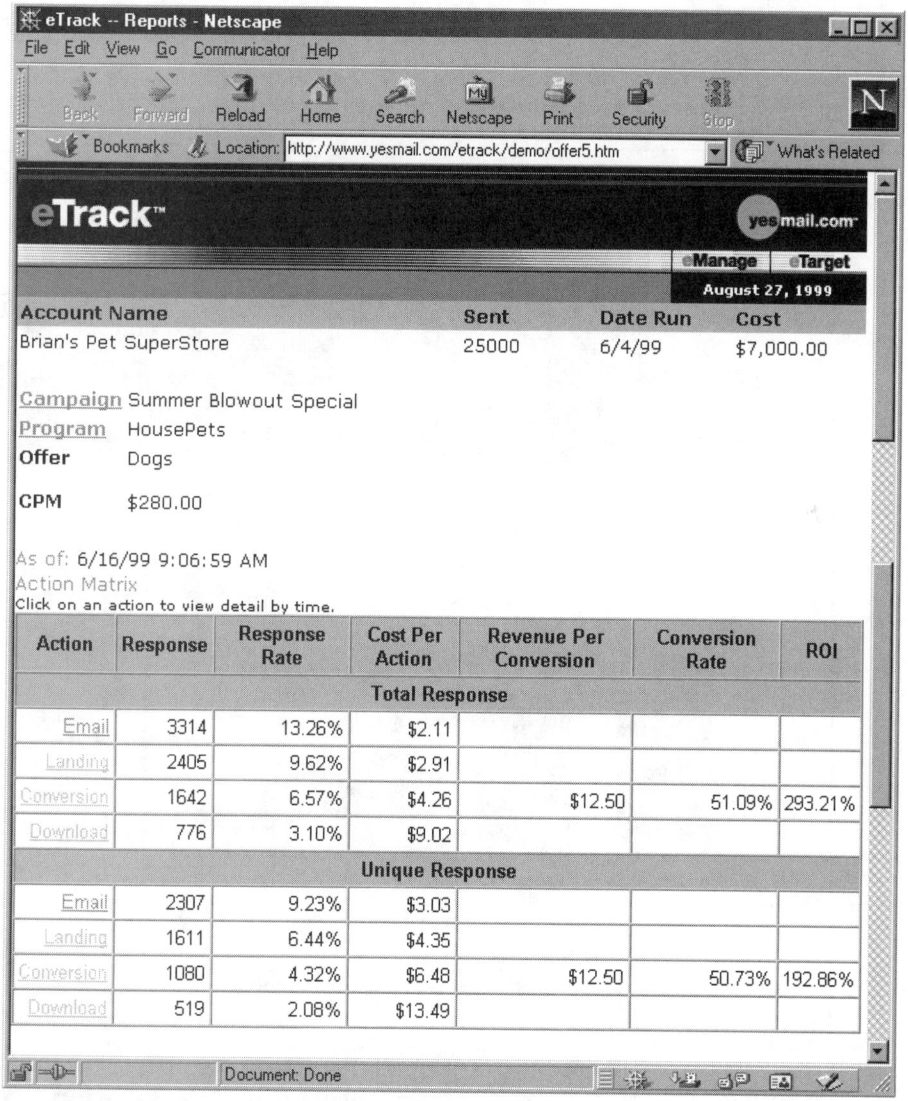

Action	Response	Response Rate	Cost Per Action	Revenue Per Conversion	Conversion Rate	ROI
Total Response						
Email	3314	13.26%	$2.11			
Landing	2405	9.62%	$2.91			
Conversion	1642	6.57%	$4.26	$12.50	51.09%	293.21%
Download	776	3.10%	$9.02			
Unique Response						
Email	2307	9.23%	$3.03			
Landing	1611	6.44%	$4.35			
Conversion	1080	4.32%	$6.48	$12.50	50.73%	192.86%
Download	519	2.08%	$13.49			

Figure 8.6 How many people got to the Web site, made a purchase, and downloaded a file?

The Time Period report (see Figure 8.8) reveals how long it took for the responses to show up. Some of yesmail.com's clients track this on a daily basis. Some track it hourly.

When it comes to the technical issues of measuring and managing the email on your own servers from your own database, the choices are many and varied. Given the speed with which the tools are created and altered, reviewing them here would not serve you well.

Instead, we can point to some excellent resources for learning more about the different types of software packages you'll need. Some of these Web sites require free registration.

Having tools on the back end to capture customer activity is key. But you also need to plan for when prospects and customers want to talk to people—human beings—*you*.

Answering Your Mail

The speed of marketing on the Web is vastly different from that of more conventional means. Selling through the mail can take days, weeks, or even months. Selling by

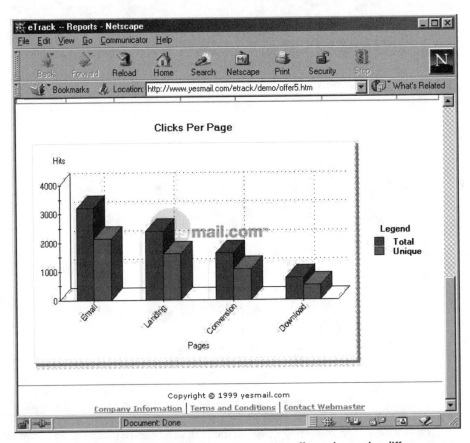

Figure 8.7 A visual display of Brian's Pet SuperStore efforts shows the difference between unique visitors and repeat visitors.

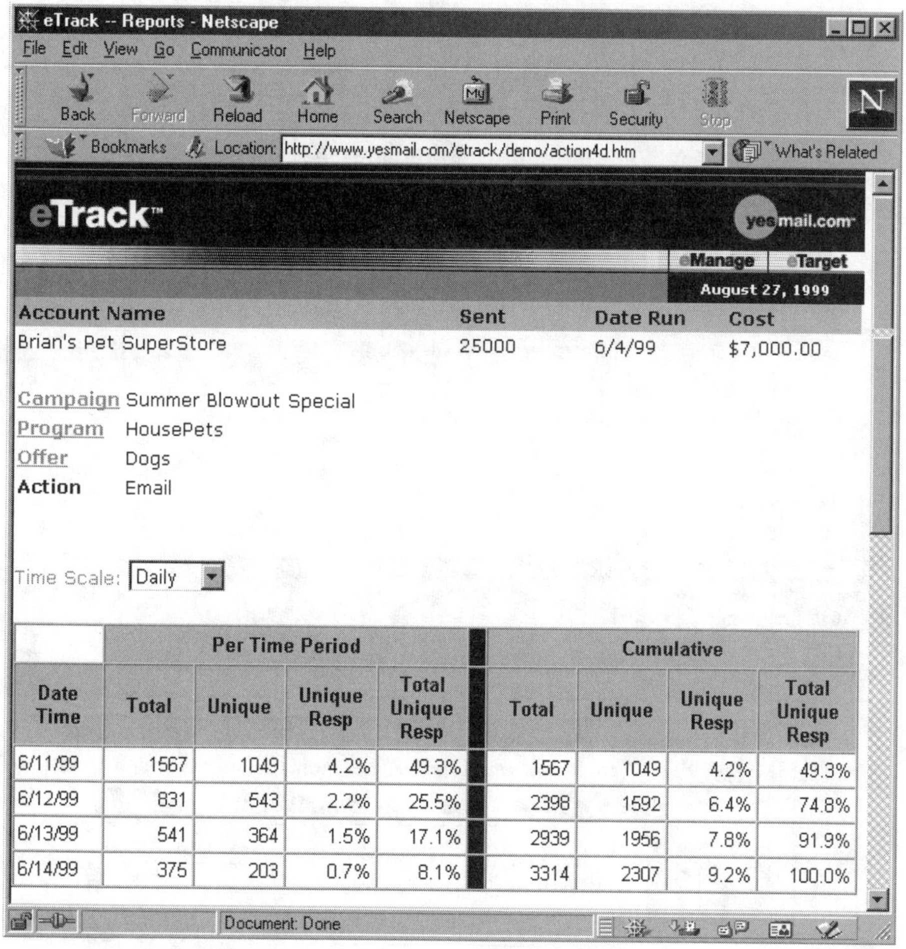

Figure 8.8 The majority of responses will always come in on the first day and taper off from there.

direct email can happen instantly, or it could take several messages back and forth between you and a potential customer before you get the sale. If you are going to market a product by email, be prepared to respond to your customer's questions immediately. Internet buyers are impatient buyers. They expect answers to their questions and concerns the same day they ask them.

Webmaster Bill McLain has become an Internet legend because he answers his email. Yes, you answer your email, too. But Bill's email is defined as anything sent to webmaster@xerox.com. He answers all of it—even the wild and weird questions that have no reason for going to Xerox. Questions like *Do Fish Drink Water?*

That's the name of the book he's published (William Morrow, 1999) about his experiences at the Xerox keyboard, which have earned him the title, "The Wise Old Man of the Web." He's been at it for four years and isn't about to stop. Especially now that he has three people on his staff to answer questions like the following:

Email Tools

Planet IT at CMP's TechWeb

www./planetit. com/prodreviews/internetwk/intweek2

select: Email Clients and Servers

A technology tutorial on this product type

Internet.com's AdResource

www.adresource.com/html/new/mail/index.html

Email Today

www.emailtoday.com

(See Figure 8.9.)

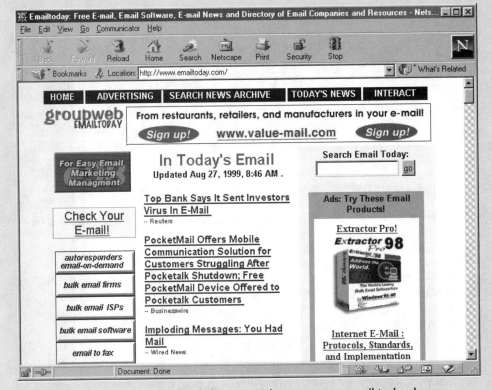

Figure 8.9 Email Today provides daily news and resources on email technology.

How long would it take to vacuum the state of Ohio?

What is the world's fastest roller coaster?

What does the information on a United States penny represent?

Web Server Tools

ZDNet

www.zdnet.com/products/networkmanager/server.html

WebServer Compare

webservercompare.internet.com

(See Figure 8.10.)

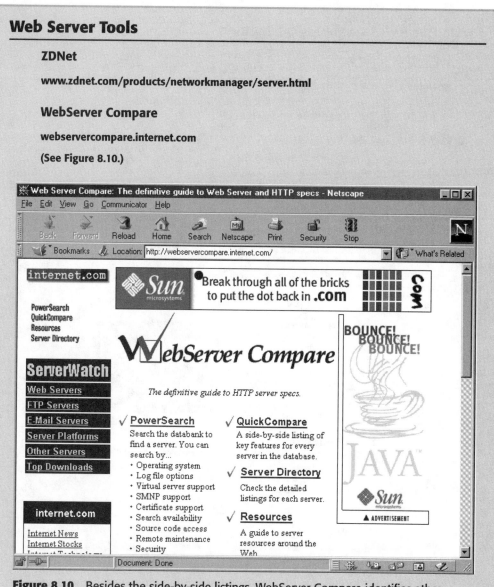

Figure 8.10 Besides the side-by-side listings, WebServer Compare identifies other resources for Web site administrators.

What makes peppers so hot?

How did grapefruit get its name?

What is the book the Statue of Liberty holds?

Why do they drive on the left side of the road in England?

You get the idea. Or do you? Bill and his team have been known to get up to 1000 messages per day. Are you up to that kind of commitment to your customers? Can it be worth your while to answer every email?

Customer Relationship Management Tools

Internet Product Watch

ipw.internet.com/e-business/e-commerce/index.html

MarketPlace 1to1 (Peppers and Rogers)

search.marketplace1to1.com/Mktplace

(See Figure 8.11.)

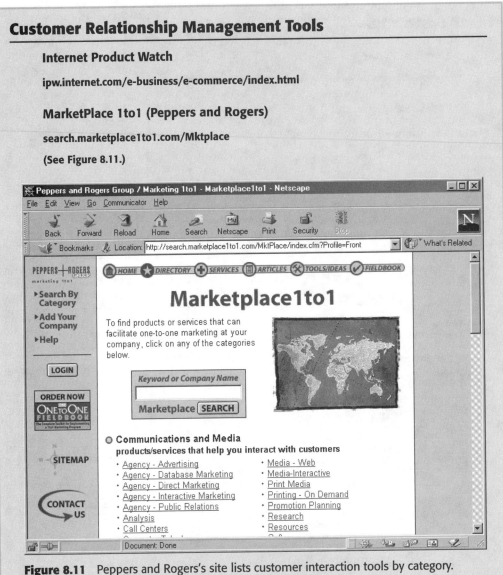

Figure 8.11 Peppers and Rogers's site lists customer interaction tools by category.

Hit 'Em with an FAQ

Dr. Ralph Wilson feels a good Frequently Asked Questions document can go a long way to cut back on the amount of mail you get—and have to answer. He covers eight straightforward steps:

1. Capture the questions.

2. Sort the questions.

3. Rephrase the questions.

4. Answer the questions.

5. Arrange the questions.

6. Make your FAQ easy to navigate.

7. Link to the FAQ from your homepage.

8. Hyperlink your answers to action pages.

For the details on each of these, read the whole article at www.wilsonweb.com/articles/faq.htm.

Make the Computer Do the Work

In addition to posting information on your site for people to get at themselves, you can hire three people like Bill McLain, or you can implement some tools that will help ease the email load.

Email tools run the gambit, but they basically fall into three groups: autoresponders, filters, and intelligent responders. Autoresponders act like fax-back systems, filters help your staff control the incoming deluge, and intelligent responders choose the right response and reply without being touched by human hands.

Autoresponders

Every email system is capable of sending a "vacation" message. This is where you write up a quick note that says, "I'm out until the beginning of next week. If you need something, please contact Gertrude." You then flip the software switch and anytime an email comes to you, it sends your "I'm on vacation" message back.

Marketers quickly realized the fax-back quality of this feature and have been using it to great advantage in print, in banner ads, and on their Web sites. They give people the ability to quickly get information back based on which email address they use when they send a blank message.

Also referred to as *mailbots,* autoresponders bounce back a prewritten, preformatted reply to anybody who sends a message of any kind. Send a blank message to info@realtrains.com and get a nice little introduction back. Send an email to iriinc_info@mailback.com and the Industrial Research Institute will fill you in about benchmarking the best research and development management practices.

There are autoresponder services or you can run your own. Chances are excellent that your ISP can set you up with a mailbot program. Yesmail.com will set you up with an entire campaign program. The day after an opt-in visitor checks out your site, they get the "Thanks For Coming By" message. Three days later, they get the "Don't Forget About Our Specials" message. After two weeks, if they haven't been back, they get the "We've Missed You" message.

To put this sort of system into high gear, the first message you send can include instructions on how to click the embedded links back to your Web site or reply with a different instruction in the subject line for different documents to be returned immediately. Think of it as a fax-back system and you'll understand exactly what it does.

(And please implement some sort of tracking mechanism that won't send the same message to somebody who hits the Reply button. It happens all the time.)

Filters

When sorting a large volume of email gets to be more than one person can handle, it's time for a proper and dependable tracking system, a database to store email messages and email addresses, an automatic email acknowledgment or autoresponder, and sophisticated reporting.

Emailrobot for Exchange/SMTP from GFI Fax & Voice (www.emailrobot.com) is one of those tools that can simplify your strategy for handling the rewards of marketing. Emailrobot is an email management tool that helps companies track, reply, archive, manage, and automate their corporate/generic email.

First of all, companies should be able to keep track of their emails. Since Emailrobot archives all generic email (sent and received) into a central ODBC database, your staff can track emails by searching for names, keywords, or tracking numbers. For instance, in case of a telephone inquiry, staff can instantly see whether an email has been received, whether it was answered, and what the answer was, even if it was answered by someone else. Furthermore, complete customer communications histories can be viewed, including a complete string of emails exchanged with a certain customer, which can be very useful in the case of a complaint.

It is critical that your staff members act on leads while the customer's interest is still high. Quick response times of corporate and Web site email are essential to the success of any business. Therefore, keeping an eye on the amount of email received and average response times is an important part of email management. With Emailrobot's reporting module, you can view average response times and the amount of email received per mail agent and department. This way you can determine whether your Web site is producing enough feedback, whether your mail agents/departments are responding quickly enough to their email, and whether their workload is still manageable.

Sending your customers personalized acknowledgments after receiving their email gives your company a professional image and lets customers know that their email has been received. This acknowledgment includes important information about when the email was received (useful for time differences), who is interacting with the customer, and when the customer can expect an answer. Each acknowledgment also includes a unique tracking number for reference purposes.

Email management entails distributing the email workload evenly. Instead of letting only one person answer all email to a generic address such as sales@yourcompany .com, Emailrobot will distribute this mail among several designated mail agents. For instance, if your company has five salespersons, the generic sales email could be divided among each of them.

Emailrobot can also send out an email a week after a customer orders a product on your Web site, asking whether they have received their product and whether they are satisfied with the service they received. By using merge fields, the email text can include any information that was entered in the Web form. In this way, you can optimize your customer service with hardly any effort on your part. Emailrobot can query your invoice database each month and send a reminder to each company with payment arrears, automatically filling in the outstanding invoice number.

But don't stop there. Let's say you're so good at generating traffic to your site that you receive hundreds of emails, even thousands. If that's your situation, then you need a little artificial intelligence working for you.

Artificial Intelligence Comes of Age

Using adaptive neural network technology, SelectResponse from eHNC Services (www.ehnc.com) analyzes complex inquiries and routes them directly to appropriate content experts. If it can, and you determine the threshold, it will automatically respond by sifting through a database of response fragments.

Finally, and here's the good part, SelectResponse can automatically suggest promotional offerings based on collaborative filtering profiles in its database. That means it looks to see what offers other people with the same questions have accepted. It makes a calculated guess at which offer is statistically more likely to be successful.

For customer service, SelectResponse matches problems to solutions. It's able to cross-reference manuals, Frequently Asked Questions documents, technical notes, knowledge databases, and any other electronic source. Nifty. Not cheap, but nifty.

To get the most out of a system like SelectResponse, couple it with a full-blown customer relationship management system such as eGain's Email Management System (www.egain.com). See Figure 8.12.

A press release on the eGain Web site describes how one customer is making use of their system:

> Cooking.com, the premier online resource for people who cook, is using the eGain Email Management System (eGain EMS) to provide first-class service to its customers. eGain EMS enables Cooking.com to provide fast and accurate responses to customer email inquiries, including information about products and customer order status. By integrating eGain EMS with Microsoft Site Server 3.0 Commerce Edition, customer service representatives can view all customer contact and transaction information from eGain's powerful user interface, rather than having to switch between programs to find data. But Cooking.com goes beyond answering these regular customer communications. The company delivers a unique service by using the eGain system to forward customers' cooking questions to experienced chefs.
>
> "We needed a solution that could enable us to provide the highest level of customer service by giving us a complete view of a customer's interaction with Cooking.com," said Tracy Randall, vice president, commerce, at Cooking.com. "eGain provides us with a solution that is both easily integrated with our back-end [Microsoft Site Server 3.0 Com-

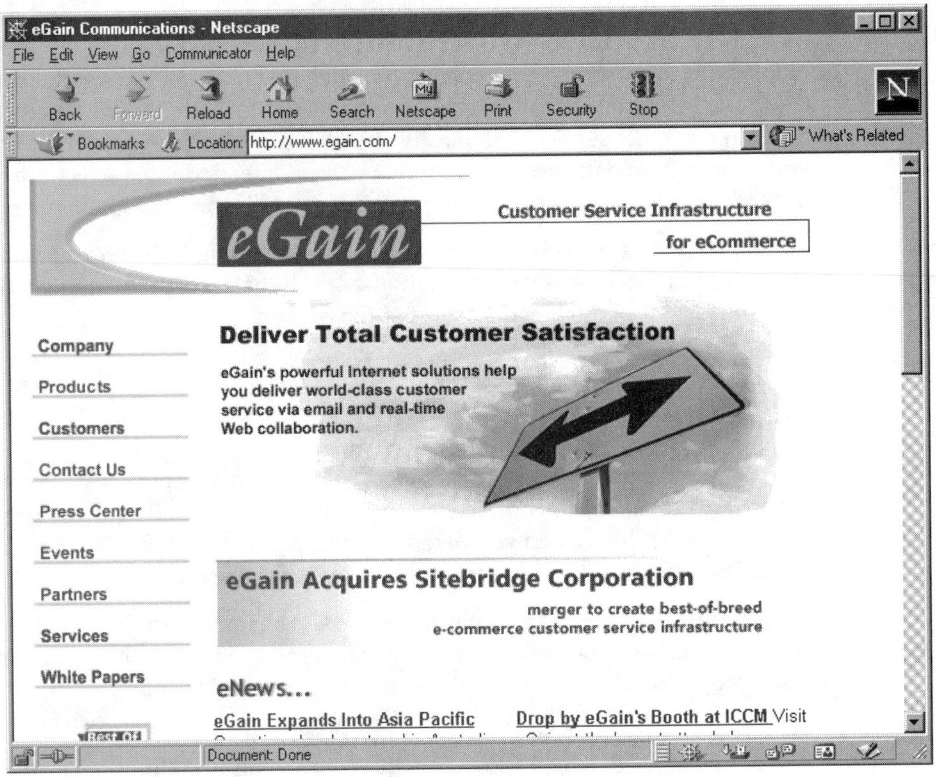

Figure 8.12 eGain's EMS provides email processing and categorization, contact management, autoresponse, and work flow.

merce Edition] and has an easy-to-use front-end interface. It is simple for our outside chefs and customer service specialists to log on to the system and respond to customer questions via the Worldwide Web."

Probably the most interesting thing about eGain, aside from their ability to integrate their system to whatever other contact management, database marketing, or customer service applications you have, is that EMS is not a software package—it's a service. Welcome to the World Wide Web.

The Human Touch

We seem to have wandered away from something very important, something that started with the need to plan for when prospects and customers want to talk to people—human beings—*you*. Shouldn't they be able to reach a human? Nick Usborne thought so in this ClickZ item:

DON'T AUTOMATE THIS
This morning you sent out fifty thousand emails to your in-house, opt-in list.

You included one link in the email to connect them to a page on your site that makes a special offer on a widget.

Over the next forty-eight hours, two and a half thousand people will click on the link you asked them to click.

Over the same period, you will receive two hundred and fifty emails with a question, comment or complaint about this promotion.

"I don't need a widget. Can I get a wodget for the same price?"

"I live in the Keeling-Cocos Islands. Does FedEx deliver here?"

"Is this the same widget you offered last February? If it is, you're pretty stupid."

"Have you read what the American Dental Association has to say about widgets?"

And so on and so on.

With these two hundred and fifty emails in your inbox, here are three things that you could do:

1. Plan on getting to them later in the week. Forget about them until Monday. Figure it's too late to reply. And dump them.

2. Kick in the trusty autoresponder. "Your question is important to us. Please go to the FAQ area on our site and you'll find that you can probably figure out the answer for yourself."

3. Actually employ smart, helpful and knowledgeable people to answer each email one by one.

I'm not aware of too many e-commerce sites that take the trouble to try number three, so I was heartened to read the following at Inc.com.

On a recent afternoon, in yet another grubby and windowless room, Garden.com's customer-service group is meeting. It's a motley yet earnest crew of 30 people. In peak season they collectively receive as many as 1,500 Email messages a day, and they respond to them all. "We stay away from the automatic response," says the group's manager, Kristen Herron.

Good for them. When you take the trouble to reply to inquiries one-on-one, you're very likely to convert the recipient into a more responsive prospect next time.

People really do seem to be delighted when they stumble across a real person at a web site. And a delighted person who has been touched by a living, breathing soul is more likely to become a loyal customer.

What the article at Inc.com didn't explain is what happens to those 1,500 emails a day—after they have been answered.

I would hate to think that they end up in a virtual shoebox.

Why? Because there's gold in those questions.

When a customer asks a question and the answer is at the top of the list of your FAQs, it's tempting to dismiss that customer as stupid. And, truth be told, one may come across the occasional customer who is a few bytes short of a mouthful.

But when that question is asked five times a day, you have to consider a more likely explanation: your FAQs are hard to find or poorly explained.

Inbound emails—particularly those that ask questions or complain—are one of your best sources of user feedback. This is how your visitors let you know about your site.

Fifteen hundred emails a day? Fantastic! After replying to the individual messages, what you have in your hands is an incredible snapshot of your visitor's "user experience." That's better than a dozen fancy usability studies. It's based on what is actually happening, right now.

Of course, to take that snapshot, you have to have some people analyzing the emails. What management needs is a report that highlights areas that need improving, opportunities that are being presented and problems that have still not been solved.

All of a sudden, all those pesky customer emails that come in each day are looking quite valuable.

First, you'll have the opportunity to convert each sender into a loyal customer by touching him or her with a personal reply.

And then you'll be able to mine all this feedback to get a clear picture of the user experience at your site.

So. Don't automate this.

The personal touch does, indeed, convert prospects into customers. Just ask Richard Davidson, the head of the Ski-Europe Web site (www.ski-europe.com). He swears by email as a sales tool (see Figure 8.13).

"It didn't take long to figure out that people wanted to talk to us about their vacation plans," Davidson says. "And it didn't take long after that to do the math. Of all the people who came to our site, the ones we engaged in an email conversation were three times more likely to book a trip with us than the rest. Case closed."

People still want to talk to people. If you have visions of your site running by itself and you're letting the Web server do the selling for you, you're missing a lot of sales. People have questions. People still buy based on emotion and that emotion can be greatly influenced by a caring person on the other end of an email exchange.

There's no question that you should use email in nonspam ways to bring people to your Web site. But once they show up, you *must* be prepared to respond to their questions.

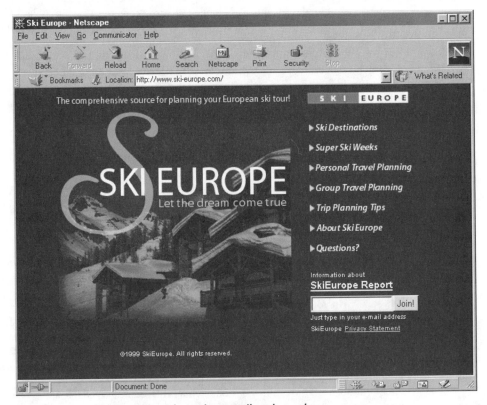

Figure 8.13 Ski-Europe found out that email makes sales.

In January 1999, Brightware (www.brightware.com) released the results of a survey they performed during the previous weeks. They sent an email to each of the Fortune 100 companies with one question, "What is your corporate address?" The results were shocking.

Texaco, Albertson's, CostCo, and Aetna all responded in less than five minutes. These were the heroes of the day. They took the time and the resources to have their email desks properly staffed to handle whatever traffic came in. The appalling part was that 33 of the 100 did not respond at all.

Smaller business can do much better. For example, take Lexmark International (www.lexmark.com) and Zebra Technologies (www.zebra.com). They both sell printers, and people promptly get peeved when their printers are impaired. Both companies have committed to a two-hour response time for email.

Email is a new way to communicate. Yes, it takes additional resources to manage the traffic. Yes, that means spending money. Yes, that means hiring people and training the ones you have.

Now You Know

If you do all of this right, the rewards are many. You now know everything you need to know to get started using email for marketing.

It's a good thing humans have the ability to learn, adapt, and grow by watching the examples of others. That's what the next chapter is all about.

CHAPTER 9

Stories from the Front Line

S ome of these are firsthand accounts. Some of these have been previously published. Some of these are complete with results stats and comments from the marketers who ran them, and a few are just plain weird. All of them are instructional.

Retail

Business to business, small groups of like-minded discussion hounds, and even huge groups of consumers are good targets for opt-in email, as evidenced in these stories. These are companies that use email marketing to sell stuff. They're not selling bits, they're selling atoms.

They're trying to promote new products, unload overstock, and drive traffic to their stores both online *and* offline. It's working.

Macys.com

Kent Anderson, president of Macys.com, said in a *New York Times* article that they send 12 to 15 emails a year to hundreds of thousands of customers. The article quoted him as saying, "We can take demographic elements and say, 'Give me everybody who looks like this customer,' and test different offers, so the odds are much better they'll respond." The results? Customers who click through to Macy's Web site buy five to seven times more often than people who showed up through search engines, banner ads, directly typing the URL into their browser, or any other way.

J. Crew

According to J. Crew's director of new media, Brian Sugar, in an article in the *New York Times*, they send out a message to their customer email list ("in the millions") every Thursday night. In it, they tell their shoppers what to look for in the way of special sales in the coming week—specials that won't hit the Web site until Friday at high noon.

The second type of message goes out once a month or so and sends very specific offers to very tightly selected people. Between demographic information and a database of past purchases, J. Crew finds what they hope is just the right offer for just the right person. If there's no purchase history, the happy subscriber might be on the receiving end of a certificate good for $20 off of any $80 purchase.

Sugar said that J. Crew was forecasting much better response and conversion rates from its email campaigns than from its offline direct mailing efforts. "With our ability to slice and dice the data," he said, "we can send personalized offers to women buyers, men buyers, or men buyers who only buy black medium-sized shirts—and the cost is so much less, we can focus on more personalized offers like that."

Powells Books

Powells Books is up against the big guns of the Internet. So when they describe themselves, they choose a very particular niche:

> You won't find a larger selection of used, rare, and out-of-print books anywhere. Period.
>   Shop at Powell's once and you'll never want to settle for an ordinary New-editions-only bookstore again. Why? Because at Powell's, not only do we carry books by all your favorite authors and on your favorite topics, we let you choose between Hardcover and Paperback, used and new. And every book we sell is completely guaranteed for quality—maybe that's why so many readers scour our Used titles to fill their wish lists.

David Weich writes fiction. But he also writes the *PowellsBooks.News* newsletter. It's touted as being the insider's guide. "A note to nonsubscribers: Beware that the features, special deals, and contests—and the links to each below—may no longer be available. False advertising? No. If you subscribed to *PowellsBooks.News*, you'd have received this edition before Web surfers even knew the features existed."

They chose David to write the newsletter so that it would be more than just news. It would a small piece of literature people would look forward to. It includes not only book specials and event notifications, but quotes from current books and old favorites. The result? It works. It's well matched to readers' erudite interests, and sales are markedly higher the day after each issue goes out.

Powells Books uses the Lyris list server (www.lyris.com) on their own computers for a list that has grown to more than 60,000.

Internet Shopping Network

With 160,000 active shoppers, the Internet Shopping Network (www.isn.com) and its First Auction site (www.firstauction.com) receive 50,000 emails a month from shoppers. They mapped out a plan that had them hiring handfuls of new email answering clerks. Then they started using eGain's Email Management System to track, route, and, in some cases, answer incoming email.

ISN cut their projected need for clerks by 60 percent, and chopped the time people waited for replies by 50 percent. Only 5 percent of the incoming messages go longer than 24 hours for a reply. Not only are customers better served, but ISN lowered operational costs by 60 percent.

Virtual Vineyards

Cyndy Ainsworth, VP-marketing at Virtual Vineyards, thinks email is one of their key customer retention tools.

Email is "a way to keep Virtual Vineyards top of mind," Ms. Ainsworth said in an *Advertising Age Interactive Daily* article (April 19, 1999). "In our experience, people are very open to getting the newsletters."

Every two weeks, 37,500 opt-in recipients get the HTML version and 37,500 get the text version filled with product specials from Peter Granoff, Virtual Vineyards' cofounder and master sommelier (see Figure 9.1). He used to be the chief cork dork, back in the days when it was hard for anybody to take the Internet seriously. Virtual Vineyards has carefully crafted Peter as the voice of the Web site. He's the one with the knowledge. He's the one with the experience. He's the one with the sense of humor.

VV News is enjoying a 10 percent clickthrough rate and people are buying. More important, they aren't just buying the specials. They're drawn in by the specials and are shopping throughout the site.

Virtual Vineyards is working their database to send different product mixes to people who have purchased different wines. They'll even send individual messages to their better customers, offering wines they don't have for sale on the site.

"Virtual Vineyards tested the idea of offering sampler sets in addition to single bottles of wine," read the *Advertising Age* article. "Because the sampler sets generated a 12 percent higher response rate, the company began offering more samplers in its email messages. In one case, a three-bottle set of robust red wine accounted for 20 percent of all the clickthroughs in that particular email."

Software

One of the things that sets software apart from other products is that you can either download it for instant delivery or click over to the Web site for a demo. Software

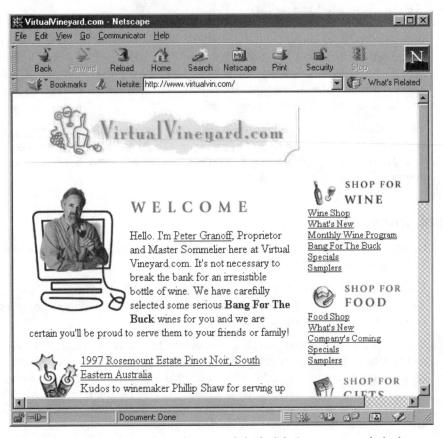

Figure 9.1 Virtual Vineyards credits a good deal of their success on their site to being personal—this is Peter's Web site.

marketing is unlike most others. But the lessons learned are applicable across the board.

Alexa

Alexa (www.alexa.com) is a free, advertising-supported Web navigation service. It works with your browser and accompanies you as you surf, providing useful information about the sites you are viewing and suggesting related sites.

Even though Alexa had a very pervasive banner ad, an affiliate program, and a solid linking strategy in place, the results of the email campaign were quite noticeable. Darian Patchin, Alexa's marketing manager at the time, said, "This has been one of our most successful advertising campaigns."

```
Date: Mon, 2 Nov 1998 10:34:16 -0600 (CST)
From: YesMail <subs@my.yesmail.com>
Subject: A Better Way to Search the Web..and It's FREE!
```

```
----------------------------------------------------------------------
This message is brought to you by YesMail. We appreciate your member-
ship. To modify your member profile, please see "Member Services" below.
----------------------------------------------------------------------
Close your browser windows on those rusty old search engines. Alexa wel-
comes you to a higher level of intelligent navigation on the Web.

Alexa http://www.alexa.com/download/gobeyond1/index.html is a FREE Web
navigation service that helps you surf the Web smarter, faster and eas-
ier. Use Alexa's statistical and factual web site data on your desktop
to determine the value of the web sites you visit as you surf the Web.
Alexa will even suggest relevant links of where you might want to go
next based on the page you are visiting.

Alexa has also added the Encyclopaedia Britannica and the Merriam-
Webster Dictionary to its navigation tools to provide you with a fully
integrated desktop reference wherever you go. And you can use the EBlast
search engine through Alexa no matter where you are on the Web.

This FREE "surf engine" works with Windows95/NT and runs in conjunction
with Netscape or Microsoft Internet Explorer as a toolbar application.
So, get Alexa today (in just seconds!) and always know where you are and
where to go next on the Web.

http://www.alexa.com/download/gobeyond1/index.html
----------------------------------------------------------------------
*MEMBER SERVICES*
To unsubscribe from the YesMail Network send an email to
subs@my.yesmail.com with the word "unsubscribe" in the subject line.

Feel free to forward this email to interested friends, family and asso-
ciates. To find out more about the YesMail Network, visit
http://www.yesmail.com .
----------------------------------------------------------------------
```

Alexa went to yesmail.com to get more people to come to their Web site and download their software (see Figure 9.2). The direct email campaign was sent to 300,000
subscribers over the course of one to two months, across varying categories. Alexa
received a 32.7 percent conversion rate. That is, for every 1000 visitors, 327 downloaded the software. That compares quite favorably to a conversion rate of 3.1 percent
for banner advertising.

Alexa has done several emailings since and knows the secret is in testing. In one campaign, they tested a list of 1000 addresses before unleashing their promotion on the
remaining 149,000. That one was in the form of an advertorial written by the *Locker-
Gnome* technical newsletter and it garnered a 35 percent download response.

Another emailing went out to 1 million eTour.com and Xoom.com addresses after a
small test containing a strong benefit message. These messages were cobranded with
the two list holders and garnered a 25 percent response.

Then they tried another 1-million-address mailing to Webmasters and technologists
through a cooperative project with a marketing partner and fell on their face. Why

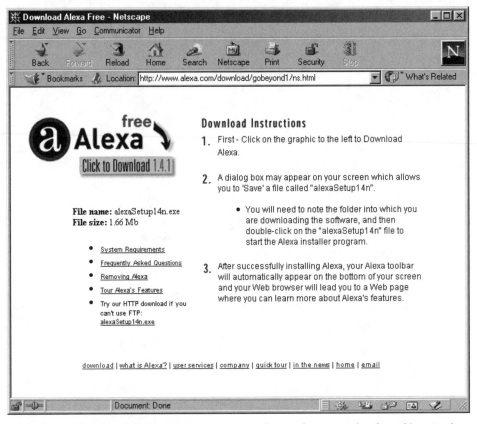

Figure 9.2 The Alexa landing page simply gives the product away for the asking. Registration happens after you install and launch the software.

didn't this one work? Patchin says the list wasn't really their audience, the message was watered down with four other advertisers in the same email, and, he stresses, they didn't run a test beforehand.

eShare

Mark Swanson manages the email marketing at eShare, a firm that makes Web-based customer service and support, customer self-service, live conferencing and events, distance learning, community chat, threaded discussion forums, and custom integration tools. 1800flowers.com uses eShare software to engage Web site visitors in live chat sessions to answer their questions.

As product marketing manager, Mark's efforts included several emailings and he was quite generous with his strategy, tactics, and results.

HISTORY OF ESHARE PROMOTION MARKETING EFFORTS

While eShare dabbled in direct mail and targeted print ads, for the most part, our primary spending focussed on banner advertising and search engine key word purchases. Even though we won an award for one banner that pulled a 13% response rate, for the most part we saw our response rates fluctuate between .5% and 3%, averaging about 1.5%. To get higher response rates, we relied on "teaser" type messages that achieved higher click-throughs, yet did not necessarily translate to increased product sales. It wasn't enough to draw traffic. We wanted a way to qualify our visitors better.

We played around with key word searches, buying the word "chat" for months at a time (you can buy certain search engine key words from Lycos, Yahoo, etc. so that when someone types in "chat" or "customer service," eShare comes up) but found this to be fairly expensive with marginal results.

We learned that in the banner world, if you get a 2% response (clickthrough rate) you're doing well. But this was not good enough for us. Banner ads as a marketing vehicle simply do not enjoy the high response rates that they once did!

Then we discovered opt-in email. It was great to discover YesMail. They provide a dedicated account manager who does list management, list selection recommendations, email copy feedback, as well as results tracking.

EXAMPLE #1: SPRING FOR CHAT PROMO

Here are the lists and email used for the Expressions Spring for chat promo. Naturally, we chose lists that related to the verticals we were trying to sell the product in—in this case, eShare Expressions, our chat and message boards software. The email was sent out to exactly 16,382 "opt-in subscribers" to topic-related lists. (These lists have been strategically selected through analysis of past promotion response rates.)

Lists

Internet Consulting (3,000) New list

Internet: Intranet (2,000) New list

Internet E-Commerce (8,494) 9.88% response rate on test file of similar list

Web Site Owners Ref Tools (2,000) 2.55% with other names on same list

Chat Server Software (888) 27% response rate on same list used 4 months prior

Email

Subject: Get FREE Chat Licenses During Our Spring for Chat Sale!

We're Springing for FREE Chat Licenses During Our Spring for Chat Sale!

Jumpstart your web community this Spring with our award-winning eShare Expressions chat and message boards software. Do it now, during our Spring for Chat Sale and we will "Spring" for up to 250 FREE chat user licenses! Just Point your browser to:

http://www.eshare.com/promo/springpromo.asp?ref=3

It's no wonder PC Magazine awarded Expressions, "Editor's Choice" -- look what you can do: Increase web traffic by over 50%, Build live community among users, Hold meetings and conferences, Conduct distance learning and training, Host guest speaker events. Best of all, it works with any web browser and through corporate firewalls.

http://www.eshare.com/promo/springpromo.asp?ref=3

```
Join thousands of satisfied customers like AOL, Lycos, GeoCities, Sony
PlayStation, and Columbia University that rely on eShare Technologies
for web-based, real-time interaction software.

But Hurry. Our Spring for Chat Sale ends March 31st at 8pm ET! So click
your browser on http://www.eshare.com/promo/springpromo.asp?ref=3
```

CONCLUSION

Naturally we were pleased with average response rates between 3–9%—and one very targeted list (chat server software) that did 27%!

WHAT WE LEARNED

GIVE RECEIPIENTS AN IMMEDIATE CHANCE AND MULTIPLE CHANCES TO CLICK ON LINK: email recipients should have several chances to click on the SAME URL LINK! Don't make the recipient scroll down through 3 or 4 paragraphs before link is seen!

LINKS SHOULD ALL GO TO ONE LOCATION: In the past, we had included the link to our web site as well. But this gave the recipient the chance to click to somewhere else. You should steer them to ONLY ONE LOCATION where the promotion can be explained in more detail.

BREAK UP CONTENT SO IT IS READABLE: We found that 3 or 4 paragraphs consisting of 5 lines each was a good rule of thumb.

CALL TO ACTION ON EACH LINE IF POSSIBLE: You want the recipient to click on the link, so instruct them to do so each time with phrases like: "So click your browser to: http://www.xyz.com" or "Go directly to: http://www.xyz.com."

TRACK EACH LIST WITH ASP PAGES: Special URLs were assigned to each list source and contained an asp reference number that was passed upon form submission to a database file. In this way we were able to identify which lists performed the best.

ASP (Active Server Page)

This is a page that is not static HTML, but is built from a database on the fly. When the surfer clicks, the server looks in the layout database for the format of the page, and the content database determines what information and graphics should be displayed within that layout.

ASP systems can also query other databases such as customer files to create personalized content.

EXAMPLE #2: STICKY PROMO Q2 '99

Here's an example of the steps we took for one of our promotions:

1. Ran mini promotions for several months to see which lists had the best response rates (each list had 3–5 thousand names).

2. We used the lists that pulled the best response rates with the test file, and rolled to much larger numbers on those lists.

3. We were very successful with one promotion called "Sticky Promo Q2 99."

DESCRIPTION

Email blast to 50,000 names from 13 lists encouraging prospects to evaluate Expressions to make their web site more "sticky."

As incentive to fill out form, we gave away popular book, "Customer.com," Also supported by GeoCities Banner and web site banner.

Population: 50,000 list of emails

Response Rates: Highest performing lists pulled 7%, 6.5%, 4.18%, 3.10%, 2.93%

Form submissions: 814 form submissions!

Became Opportunity: 45

EMAIL

```
Subject: FREE best seller "Customer.com" helps you get "Sticky"

Does your site have "Stickiness"?

Holding your web visitor's gaze through live interaction is what makes a
site achieve "stickiness." And the stickier your site is -- the more
likely your visitors will turn into customers! That's why you need the
industry's hottest selling interactive chat, message boards, and web
tours software -- eShare Expressions(R).

Inquire now, and get a FREE copy of best-seller Customer.com while sup-
plies last -- no purchase necessary. Get "sticky" now at:
http://www.eshare.com/springpromo1.html

It's no wonder PC Magazine awarded Expressions, "Editor's Choice" --
look what you can do: Increase web traffic by over 50%, Build live com-
munity among users, Hold meetings and conferences, Conduct distance
learning and training, Host guest speaker events. Best of all, it
requires no downloads or plug-ins and it works through firewalls! Get
"Sticky" now at: http://www.eshare.com/springpromo1.html

Join thousands of satisfied customers like AOL, Lycos, GeoCities, Sony
PlayStation, and Columbia University that rely on eShare Technologies
for web-based, real-time interaction software. Hurry, and you'll receive
a FREE copy of best-seller, Customer.com while supplies last! Get
"sticky" now at: http://www.eshare.com/springpromo1.html
```

The eShare landing page (see Figure 9.3) reminds surfers that there is a free book involved.

CONCUSION

814 form submissions is incredible!

WHAT WE LEARNED

IT'S NOT ENOUGH TO GET THEM TO THE PAY-OFF PAGE: You have to structure the pay-off page in such a way that the visitors are inclined to leave their contact information. We found that it is best to put the form on the same page! The more clicks it takes to get to the form, the less likely you will be to capture their information.

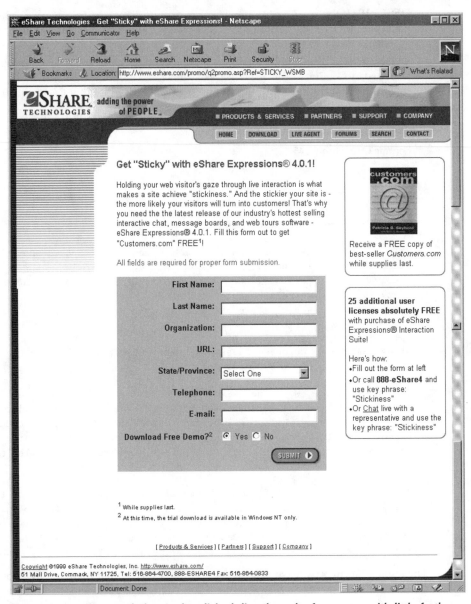

Figure 9.3 eShare took those who clicked directly to the form page with little further selling.

GIVE SOMETHING AWAY RELATED TO PRODUCT: FREE incentives like white papers or FREE books or a FREE download or demo get visitors to spend time leaving their contact info. The giveaway should be related to the product in some way to ensure that the lead is more qualified. If you give away a Frisbee, you may capture contact information from kids who are not really interested or able to buy your product. No kid would spend time filling out a form to get an industry white paper on Community building. Potential customers will.

PROMOTION MAY TRIGGER OTHER INBOUND ACTIVITY: We saw a significant correlation between inbound telephone activity and our inbound chat room traffic and our email campaign. So even if visitors decide not to leave their contact information they still may pick up the phone or speak with a live agent. In this case, marketing should instruct visitors to use a "key word" so that marketing can track the lead back to the promotion.

SUBJECT HEADLINE SHOULD FEATURE BENEFIT UPFRONT! If your subject headline is long, an email recipient may only see the first four or five words (depending on how much horizontal space he has allocated for the subject). Therefore, it is smart to put the benefit up front—for example, "FREE best seller helps you get Sticky" instead of "Get Sticky with a FREE best seller."

USE VISTOR MONITOR MODULE TO CAPTURE MORE VISITORS! eShare is planning on using its own software (eShare NetAgent) to monitor live web visitors. In this way, we can proactively engage all visitors clicking on the promotional URL within their email in a live text-based conversation. Because they made it to the special URL, we know they're interested. With eShare NetAgent, we can pop up a dialogue box that says, "May I help you," giving visitors the option to immediately speak with a live agent. Most of the time visitors may click away before leaving contact information, but by giving them an option to speak with a live agent, a company is more inclined to capture the visitor and even close a sale at the time of decision.

In the long run, eShare also found out that email marketing was the most effective promotional tool in their tool chest. It got the highest response and was responsible for the most sales (see Figure 9.4).

Figure 9.4 Email outperformed every other technique eShare used.

Event Marketing

Like software, events are a product that doesn't come in a package. There's a serious time dependency to events—they are perishable if not sold.

ClickZ

The often-quoted *ClickZ Today* newsletter and ClickZ Forum discussion group became the focus of two different case studies of their own in the summer of 1999. The first was an effort to boost readership of the newsletter and participation in the forum. The second was a straight promotion on behalf of a software vendor, but using Andy Bourland as the spokesperson.

ClickZ Forum

In July 1999, ClickZ Forum moderator Richard Hoy ran a campaign to draw more people into the discussion. He arranged to have Martin Lindstrom, coauthor with Tim Frank of *Brand Building on the Internet* (Hardie Grant Books, 1997), act as a week-long "live" guest on the discussion list. People were invited to ask questions and mix it up with Martin. Here's how Richard described his promotional experience:

Hey all,
   In the sharing spirit of ClickZ, I wanted to share with you all the strategy and results of the campaign I ran to promote Martin Lindstrom's appearance on the list last week.
   I did a few smart things and a few stupid things. And maybe a few more stupid things that you'll tell me about after you read this. But overall, I was happy with the results.
   So here we go:

GOALS:

drive new subscriptions

generate awareness among existing members

provide useful content around which we could build discussions

TARGET AUDIENCES:

existing forum members

subscribers to ClickZ's text newsletter

those interested in Internet marketing

TACTICS:

for existing forum members—announcement offering a free chapter from Martin's book and solicitation for questions

for subscribers to ClickZ's text newsletter—6 line, 60 character per line text ad at the top of newsletter; URL linked to a jump page

those interested in Internet marketing—Postmaster Direct list of 20,000 email addresses of those interested in Internet marketing; URL linked to a jump page

METRICS:

for existing forum members—# of responses to free chapter offer, # of questions generated

subscribers to ClickZ's text newsletter—clicks on URL, sign-ups to list

those interested in Internet marketing—clicks on URL, sign-ups to list

MEASUREMENT METHODOLOGY:

for existing forum members—asked prospect to reply via email; asked prospect to send in question

subscribers to ClickZ's text newsletter—unique URL that led to a custom jump page; form on jump page had a hidden field labeled "source" to let me know which subscriptions came from what form

those interested in Internet marketing—unique URL that led to a custom jump page; form on jump page had a hidden field labeled "source" to let me know which subscriptions came from what form

EXECUTION (AKA WHAT REALLY HAPPENED):

```
Subject: New from ClickZ -> CLICKZ FORUM - Sign Up, Get Free Branding
Info

What, you say?? You're not a member of The ClickZ Forum yet? Well, hell.
You should be!

In fact, this week (July 19 - 23) Martin Lindstrom, co-author of the
book "Brand Building on the Internet," is answering questions from mem-
bers about creating and building an online brand. He is just one of
dozens who you can tap for raw online marketing advice each week.

Click on the URL below to sign up to The Forum. It's fast. It's free.
And you get a chapter from Martin's new book for your trouble.

http://www.clickz.com/list/book/post072099.html

Once you've signed up, fire up your typing fingers and send in a ques-
tion. See if Martin really knows his stuff about online brand building.

The ClickZ Forum is THE place for generating debate and discussion among
online marketing professionals. It's the latest offering from one of the
most trusted sources of practical online marketing advice - ClickZ.
```

Ok, so far so good. I figured out my goals, strategy, tactics, metrics and measurement methodology. But I ran short on time and missed a few deadlines. Things got out later than I would have liked. And we had some database problems that wiped out about one third of the tracking data. 105 of the 378 subscriptions I can't attribute to a specific source.

(If those last few sentences don't sound familiar, then you've been reading about email marketing and not doing it. The course of true e-promotion never did run smooth.)

So the results are given as a range. I know the minimum subscriptions each campaign generated, but I can only guess at the maximum. Despite this, there is still useful information here.

existing forum members

chapter requests	=	139
questions for Martin	=	11

ClickZ's text newsletter

minimum subs generated	=	38
maximum possible	=	143

postmaster mailings

minimum subs generated	=	235
maximum possible	=	340

----

unaccounted for	=	105

----

total new subscribers	=	378

existing forum members
(595 total members)

response rate	=	23.4% (139)

ClickZ's text newsletter
(~14,000 total addresses)

CTR (clickthrough rate)	=	2.66% (372)
conversion	=	.27% – 1.0% (min: 38; max: 143)

postmaster mailings
(20,000 total addresses)

CTR	=	2.95% (590)
conversion	=	1.2% – 1.7% (min: 235; max: 340)

COMMENTS:

I broke up the Postmaster mailings into three sets—two sets of 5,000 addresses, which were mailed out on 7/15 (a Thursday), and one set of 10,000 addresses, which was mailed out on 7/20 (Tuesday). Thursday is a bad day for sending email. I got 30% more response in the Tuesday mailing.

I did an experiment to determine if offering the chapter without the obligation to join the list would increase sign-ups. The thought is that you are perceived as more sincere. This is why I split the Thursday mailing into two batches of 5,000—one pitch required you to join to get the chapter, the other didn't. The conclusion is that it made no difference. In fact, requiring sign-up to get the chapter did a little better.

The CTRs were very close between the text ad on the ClickZ newsletter and the mailing to the Postmaster Direct list. This surprised me because the text ad is mixed in with other content. My guess would be that the response would be dramatically lower in that case. But on the flip side, the conversion rate is much higher with the Postmaster mailing. Yet another glaring example of why you should never judge success on CTR alone.

I need to also point out that in the Tuesday Postmaster Direct mailing, I made some alterations that I think influenced the response rate. On the first mailings, I set the FROM address to richard@clickz.com instead of Postmaster Direct's address. In retrospect, I think this was a bad decision. When that email hit people's boxes, there is no indication UNTIL YOU OPEN the mail that it is from Postmaster. Since the relationship is with Postmaster in those cases and not me, there is a good chance that people thought it was spam and deleted it. I also changed the subject line from:

THE CLICKZ FORUM - Sign Up; Get Free Online Branding Info

to

New from ClickZ -> CLICKZ FORUM - Sign Up, Get Free Branding Info

I think the second leverages the ClickZ brand better.

If this were a true formal study, I would need to measure those variables separately, of course, before I could say timing was the major factor in increased response.

But, for what it's worth, here is some advice I'm going to follow in the future:

—I'm always going to split the mailings up into blocks. It is the only way you can tweak response.

—I'm going to do my direct email early in the week, preferably Tuesday, without fail. Rosalind Resnick, founder of Postmaster, once said that the best campaign they ever did went out on a Tuesday at 10:00 AM eastern time so it would hit people's mailboxes around lunchtime, when many surf.

—I'm making the FROM line the address of the list provider. The recipient will likely recognize the list provider before they recognize me or ClickZ.

—I'm bundling a freebie with all future email solicitations.

—I need to do more cross-selling to the ClickZ newsletter lists. It is a free source (to me, anyway) I haven't nearly tapped yet.

—Fix that freakin' database so we don't lose info!

If you want to see the creative, you can visit the jump pages at:

postmaster 7/15 mailing; get chapter, join if you want
www.clickz.com/list/book/post071599b.html (see Figure 9.5).

same pages, just renamed: postmaster 7/15 mailing; join to get chapter
www.clickz.com/list/book/post071599.html (see Figure 9.6).

ClickZ text list ad www.clickz.com/list/book/clickz071699.html

postmaster 7/20 mailing www.clickz.com/list/book/post072099.html

ClickZ Today on Behalf of Andromedia's LikeMinds

The following message arrived in the mail "from the publisher" of *ClickZ Today*. The publisher, Andy Bourland, is a well-known figure in the world of online advertising. He also writes the occasional article for ClickZ, as well as some of the conference coverage. Given the subject line, the sender, and the lead, it looked like an article that escaped from the standard ClickZ format and arrived on its own.

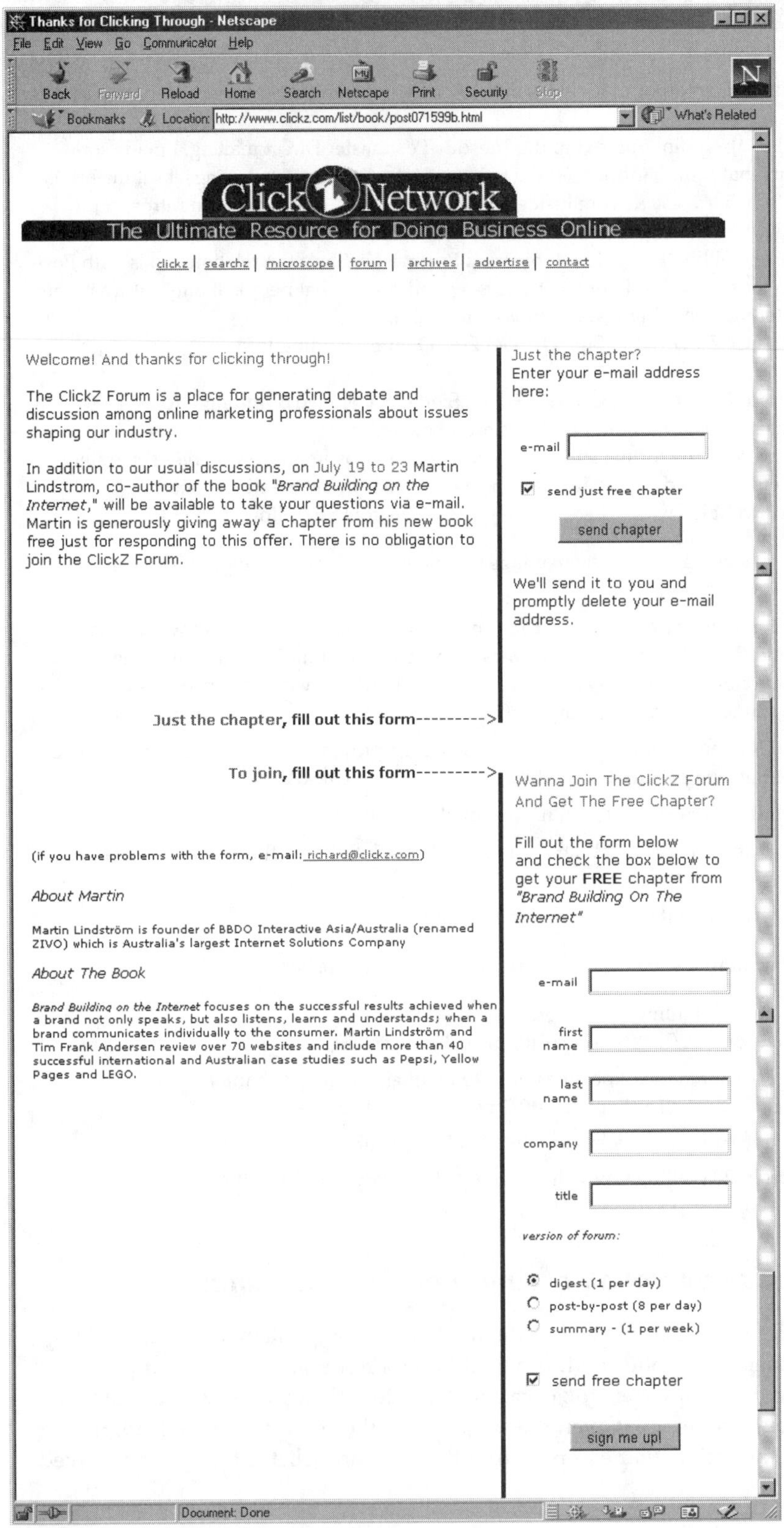

Click Network

The Ultimate Resource for Doing Business Online

clickz | searchz | microscope | forum | archives | advertise | contact

---

Welcome! And thanks for clicking through!

The ClickZ Forum is a place for generating debate and discussion among online marketing professionals about issues shaping our industry.

In addition to our usual discussions, on July 19 to 23 Martin Lindstrom, co-author of the book *"Brand Building on the Internet,"* will be available to take your questions via e-mail. Martin is generously giving away a chapter from his new book free just for responding to this offer. There is no obligation to join the ClickZ Forum.

Just the chapter, fill out this form--------->

To join, fill out this form--------->

(if you have problems with the form, e-mail: richard@clickz.com)

About Martin

Martin Lindström is founder of BBDO Interactive Asia/Australia (renamed ZIVO) which is Australia's largest Internet Solutions Company

About The Book

Brand Building on the Internet focuses on the successful results achieved when a brand not only speaks, but also listens, learns and understands; when a brand communicates individually to the consumer. Martin Lindström and Tim Frank Andersen review over 70 websites and include more than 40 successful international and Australian case studies such as Pepsi, Yellow Pages and LEGO.

Just the chapter?
Enter your e-mail address here:

e-mail [   ]

☑ send just free chapter

[send chapter]

We'll send it to you and promptly delete your e-mail address.

Wanna Join The ClickZ Forum And Get The Free Chapter?

Fill out the form below and check the box below to get your **FREE** chapter from *"Brand Building On The Internet"*

e-mail [   ]

first name [   ]

last name [   ]

company [   ]

title [   ]

version of forum:

◉ digest (1 per day)
○ post-by-post (8 per day)
○ summary - (1 per week)

☑ send free chapter

[sign me up!]

Document: Done

Figure 9.5
ClickZ set up one landing page with two forms . . .

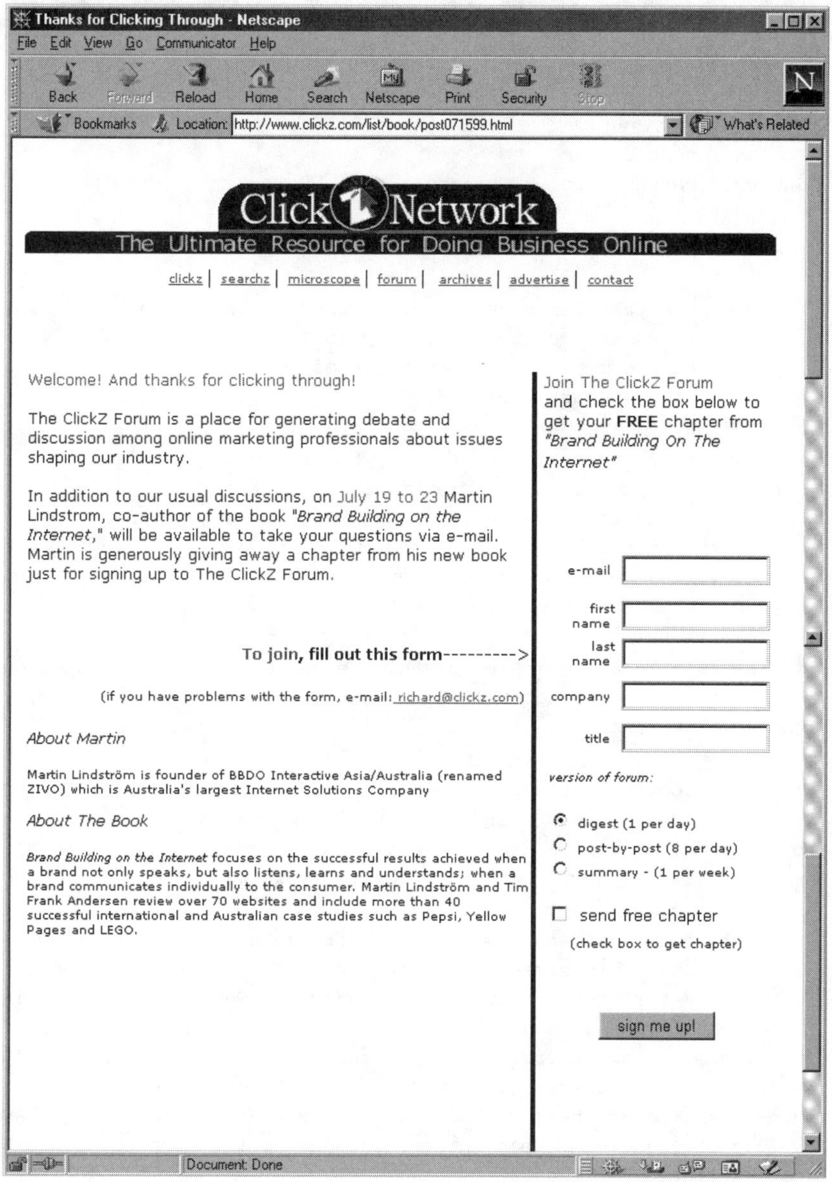

File Edit View Go Communicator Help

Back Forward Reload Home Search Netscape Print Security Stop

Bookmarks   Location: http://www.clickz.com/list/book/post071599.html   What's Related

Click Network

The Ultimate Resource for Doing Business Online

clickz | searchz | microscope | forum | archives | advertise | contact

Welcome! And thanks for clicking through!

The ClickZ Forum is a place for generating debate and discussion among online marketing professionals about issues shaping our industry.

In addition to our usual discussions, on July 19 to 23 Martin Lindstrom, co-author of the book *"Brand Building on the Internet,"* will be available to take your questions via e-mail. Martin is generously giving away a chapter from his new book just for signing up to The ClickZ Forum.

To join, fill out this form--------->

(if you have problems with the form, e-mail: richard@clickz.com)

About Martin

Martin Lindström is founder of BBDO Interactive Asia/Australia (renamed ZIVO) which is Australia's largest Internet Solutions Company

About The Book

Brand Building on the Internet focuses on the successful results achieved when a brand not only speaks, but also listens, learns and understands; when a brand communicates individually to the consumer. Martin Lindström and Tim Frank Andersen review over 70 websites and include more than 40 successful international and Australian case studies such as Pepsi, Yellow Pages and LEGO.

Join The ClickZ Forum and check the box below to get your **FREE** chapter from *"Brand Building On The Internet"*

e-mail

first name

last name

company

title

version of forum:

- ● digest (1 per day)
- ○ post-by-post (8 per day)
- ○ summary - (1 per week)

☐ send free chapter

(check box to get chapter)

sign me up!

Document: Done

Figure 9.6 ...and another with one form containing check boxes.

```
Date: Thu, 5 Aug 1999 16:48:18 -0700
From: Andrew Bourland <ClickZ-gtmail@clickz.guesttrack.com>
To: jsterne@targeting.com
Subject: Personalize or Perish
```

A letter from Andy Bourland, CEO & Publisher of ClickZ...

Did you know that tests show that browser-to-buyer conversion and repeat purchase rates are, on average, very low? Only about 2.7% of visitors buy from an e-commerce site, only 15% of buyers ever return to buy again. Is that pathetic or what?

Fact is, those numbers dramatically improve when the site employs personalization technology. Levi Strauss, utilizing Andromedia's LikeMinds technology increased repeat visitors by 27%, lengthened shopping times from 4 to 7 minutes, and increased number of products viewed from 6 to 10 per visit. So offering a personalized shopping experience can make a huge difference to smart emerchants...

You haven't begun to implement this technology yet? The clue phone is going ring! ring! ring! Hello-o-o! Better get with the program. Your competitors are!

I am not about to attempt to explain this technology to you, but you can attend "Personalize or Perish" -- a highly informative seminar presented by Andromedia, iXL, and Sun Microsystems -- and learn everything you ever wanted to know about personalizing your web site.

Who should attend: Anybody whose job it is to maximize traffic and/or sales online. This seminar will be invaluable to anyone responsible for e-commerce strategy, e-marketing management, Web technology or interactive media. This will not be a technical event, but rather a seminar by marketers for marketers, demonstrating the technology that's driving today's most successful e-commerce sites. Attendees should have a basic understanding of the business uses of Web and e-commerce technology, and should have active responsibility for developing strategy for a Web site or e-commerce business.

Here is the schedule:

```
LONDON, U.K.          NEW YORK              CHICAGO
Thursday,             Tuesday,              Wednesday,
September 9           September 14          September 15
8:30 AM - 1:00 PM     8:30 AM - 1:00 PM     8:30 AM - 1:00 PM


ATLANTA               LOS ANGELES           SAN FRANCISCO
Thursday,             Tuesday,              Thursday,
September 16          September 21          September 23
8:30 AM - 1:00 PM     8:30 AM - 1:00 PM     8:30 AM - 1:00 PM
```

```
Interested in attending? You can get more information by linking to:
http://www.andromedia.com/personalize/clickz or calling: 1.800.833.1439
or emailing: MAILTO:personalize@andromedia.com

It's worth the half-day away from the office folks. Let me know how you
like it.

Andy


------------------------------------------------------------------------
andy bourland, ceo/publisher
the clickz network -- http://www.clickz.com/
ph:978.749.3737 || fx:978.749.3187 || andy@clickz.com
------------------------------------------------------------------------
ClickZ Forum - http://www.clickzforum.com/
marketing discussion with attitude - come join us!
```

The URL linked to a tell-all, sell-all page with one link off to a formal registration page and three links to each of the sponsors (see Figure 9.7).

The message cost $7500 to send to 47,000 subscribers, a Cost Per Thousand (CPM) of about 16¢. Andy wanted to be clear about the downside as well as the upside. "In the interest of full disclosure, I should also point out that I got 100 unsubscribes and an equal number of critical emails versus emails asking for more info. I have a feeling they'll be getting a pretty good response."

Richard Hoy posted a thought or two about the experience to the ClickZ Forum:

> I think I might know in at least one circumstance where using a long pitch will work.
> If the list's normal content is editorial in nature (i.e., a newsletter), then a long pitch sent to out by the list owner will get you good results.
> If the list's normal content is advertising, short pitches are the way to go.
> Here is why I think that.
> At my previous company we had two content sites with companion email newsletters—one dealing with tennis and one dealing with the Year 2000 computer issue. We would send sponsored mailings to the lists regularly. The response rates would bury anything you would get with lists from a broker. Once an advertiser said jokingly that he would never advertise with us again because the response overwhelmed his call center.
> This phenomenon repeated itself a few weeks ago here at ClickZ. Andy Bourland, publisher of ClickZ, sent a "publisher's letter" pitching a conference out to our mailing list of about 43,000. This is the list that normally gets our "ClickZ Today" newsletter. We had never tried a direct email piece from Andy before, so we didn't know what to expect. I don't have permission to give exact numbers. But I can say, in generalities, what happened. We got lots of unsubscribes and upset people. But we got far more positive responses. I mean a lot more—like several times more.
> When we first got the negative feedback, we planned to dump the publisher's letter concept. But after getting the positive results, we re-evaluated the situation.
> Basically, I think our mistake was one of expectation. We never set the expectation that when you subscribe to "ClickZ Today" you could get direct email ads like the one we sent out. This is something we did do at my previous company. We are going to correct that by letting people opt-in to getting these mailings in addition to the newsletter.

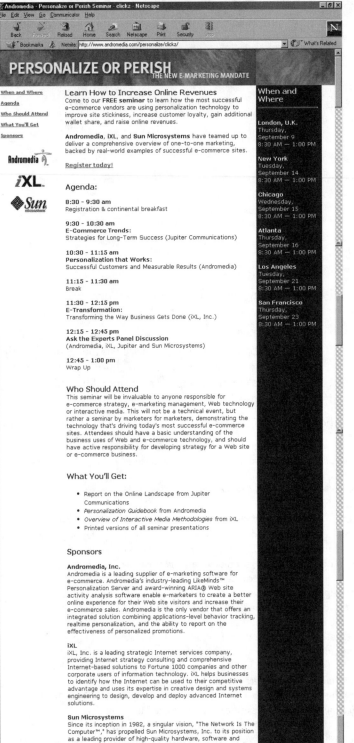

Figure 9.7 The Andromedia seminar landing page was light on graphics and heavy on information.

We are also, of course, going to be selective about what companies we let advertise in this manner. You have to be because the list members trust you as the list owner to only offer things of genuine value. The relationship is with us and the list audience, and that is what the advertiser is leveraging.

The final word, of course, comes from Andromedia. They were pleased.

According to Linda Della, director of marketing at Andromedia, they used a variety of sources to generate registration for their Personalize or Perish seminar tour:

We found that email marketing was the most responsive by far. For example 'outbound email' (including sources such as Click Z, Iconocast, and so on and so forth) promotions had nearly 4 times the response rate of any other vehicle including direct mail and banner ads.

We ran *no* print ads on the seminar. When you review the higher response rate at the fraction of the cost, email marketing clearly stands out as the efficient and effective choice. However, traditional 'reach' is the problem with email marketing. There are still very few quality email newsletter or list opportunities. You want to avoid situations where you cross over into SPAM. Thus email marketing should be a priority. But you can't rely on it solely.

Iconocast Web Attack!

Another from-the-horse's-mouth case study comes from Michael Tchong, writer for *Iconocast*. Breaking out of his text-only persona, Tchong launched a well-publicized conference called Web Attack! He described it this way:

JUST SAY NO TO BORING CONFERENCES! Web Attack!, The Ultimate Internet Marketing Event, will be held on June 17–18 at Fort Mason in San Francisco. Think of it as ICONOCAST Live! Two highly entertaining and inspiring days brimming with on-the-edge interactive marketing issues, including offline branding, closed-loop marketing, desktop branding, email marketing, women on the Web, plus awesome schmoozing!

Within a week of the conference, Tchong shared his marketing experiences with his readers in this *Iconocast* issue.

Spreading the ROI Religion

Iconocast, 6/24/99

One of the benefits of being exposed to Internet media is that more marketers are beginning to demand results that can be measured from other media. To show how **ICONOCAST** was able to draw a large crowd to its first event, here's a complete analysis of our marketing campaign [competitors, we're sure you'll love these insights].

■ Viral marketing—Perhaps the most cutting-edge element of the Web Attack! marketing campaign was a viral "Alert a Friend" program. A total of 4,408 postcards were sent from the site, resulting in 5,433 postcard views from people clicking on the email URL. Grand

Continues

Spreading the ROI Religion *(Continued)*

prize winner Charles Malouf, who'll receive a Sony MiniDisc player, single-handedly generated 2,085 passalong clicks!

- Banner advertising—i33 created a number of superb banners that contributed greatly to Web Attack!'s brand image. In all, ad banners generated a 0.5% clickthrough, on par with the industry average.

- Unicast Superstitial—Demonstrating an uncanny ability to generate clickthoughs, a Unicast Superstitial running on the ICONOCAST site drew a 17.5% clickthrough rate, the highest of any promotional medium used.

- Email advertising—Email was the most effective tool for signing up registrants, generating 85% of trackable registrations. One Media Synergy email announcing Dennis Rodman generated a 12.2% clickthrough rate.

- Rich media email—A Media Synergy "Aloha" multimedia object attached to an email garnered the highest email clickthrough rate (16.8%), equal to 6,637 clickthroughs. The 404KB Aloha attachment elicited 30-odd complaints from disgruntled users, most of whom appeared to be lacking sufficient bandwidth. [We promise to investigate technology that will make these attachments much smaller in the future.]

- Print ads—Not surprisingly, print advertising did worst in terms of ROI, with less than 1% of trackable registrations. However, it's unclear how print affected brand recognition and how many users ignored those lengthy response URLs, used to track print ads.

- Direct mail—Like offline media, conventional direct mail suffers from an inability to accurately monitor response due to the uncertainty of correct URL use. However, both postcards and brochures were self-liquidating while contributing materially to the Web Attack! branding efforts.

In addition to all the above, ICONOCAST mailed a very impactful poster, a "sandvertiser," and a millennium clock sponsored by 24/7 Media, and received radio spots and press mentions that contributed to lifting response in other media. And while banners generated a low CTR, prospects frequently cited them as seen. The lesson is: Catch prospects whenever and wherever you can.

The other lesson? "Email was the most effective tool for signing up registrants."

Sandvertiser (noun)

This is a small, plastic puck filled with purple "sand." When turned over, the sand falls through the cutout words, *Web Attack.* When inverted, the sand falls through the cutout words, *Alert a friend,* leaving black words in a field of purple. Compelling executive toy. Collector's item. Not yet spotted on eBay.

Joke-of-the-Day

Can you really get a response that's comparable to other marketing media by sponsoring a *joke?*

This is proof that advertising on Other People's Email can be a happy event. This is from an article called "Email: The Internet's Secret Weapon," posted on the Joke-of-the-Day Web site. It was written by Eric Targan of Joke-of-the-Day.com.

At JOKE-OF-THE-DAY.com, we do extensive testing with direct marketers determining what works best. And time and again, email conversion rates have been significantly higher than those from banner advertising.

JOKE-OF-THE-DAY.com was part of an advertising campaign for Paramount Studios/Atlas Editions earlier this year. Their objective was to get customers to sign up for a free trial offer where the customer paid shipping and handling. Atlas, a top direct marketing firm, measured every aspect of the campaign and compared web to email advertising. For people who clicked through from general web based banner advertising, Atlas received a 13% conversion rate of orders placed.

On JOKE-OF-THE-DAY.com's email campaign—where the ads followed the daily joke, Atlas received a 40% conversion from those who clicked through to the site, 200% higher than through the web banner campaigns. Several other direct response companies we work with have found similar responses as well.

Just Plain Weird

From *Full Sterne Ahead,* 6/99
www.targeting.com

I was heading to the Houston airport when I saw a billboard depicting the face of a classic male model along with the words, "robert@cKone.com." That was it.

So, overcome with curiosity, I sent a message:

Hi Robert—

I'm an Internet marketing consultant and a writer for various Internet-related magazines. I was giving a lecture to the Houston Business Marketing Association on Thursday and saw your billboard on the way back to the airport.

I'd like to interview the person/people who dreamed up this campaign, find out what the motivation was and what the response has been so far.

Whom should I talk to?

I never did hear from a human. Instead, I was added to Robert's mailing list. Every two weeks or so, I get a message from Robert. They are chatty, personal, and follow along as Robert finds his way in the world. They are not deep. They are not revelatory, they simply keep one up to date.

Things like this:

Continues

Just Plain Weird *(Continued)*

Slowly but surely, this city is starting to get inside my blood. I've never been a tremendous fan of Paris for the simple fact that, in previous visits, I've invariably found myself thrust into the role of the gauche tourist. But Erika's been great. She's been showing me all the hidden-away restaurants and dive bars that the locals would rather keep to themselves.

Truth be told, I'm actually starting to feel a tad guilty about enjoying myself so thoroughly. Patti is still livid, so I've been putting off calling her. I did manage to speak with Tia the other day and was surprised to find she's also furious with me. Apparently, she had been expecting a call to discuss the producing gig. I simply had no idea. To make matters worse, her father's taken ill. Rest assured, I was suitably penitent.

In any case, the city lights are beckoning. And so, au revoir.

R.

If you'd rather not hear from me again, title your reply "get lost" and I most certainly will.

And this:

Comment ca va? Paris is—how you say?—*magnifique.* Met a stunning mademoiselle yesterday. Actually, she's British but who's counting? I am all agog. Nevertheless, nothing scandalous to report.

Yet.

R.

If you'd rather not hear from me again, title your reply "get lost" and I most certainly will.

Simply the ramblings of a hunk on a billboard.

Will this sell more CK One scent for men? You betcha it will. I'm sure there are thousands of girls and women all over the United States (the world?) who are buying bottles for their boyfriends in hopes of turning them into Robert. Or at least smelling like him. Thousands of young buffs are shelling out hard cash so that they can pretend to be a screen-writing photographer on permanent vacation in Paris. Now that's what I call branding.

Call for Stories

The content of this book lives on at the yesmail.com Web site. The long-term goal is to create a new edition in one year's time. The intermediate goal, and the one you can get the most out of, is to host additional stories of ongoing learning.

If you've experienced the thrill of victory or the agony of defeat, we want to hear from you. Your anecdote will become part of an important encyclopedia of email marketing.

Head over to www.yesmail.com/book.html to join others who are learning more about using email for marketing every day.

CHAPTER 10

A Look toward the Future

The state of the art is transitory by definition. This book is great for getting you started and keeping you out of trouble.

While you're headed up to the front lines, here are a few things we've picked up on radar that might be useful. Things to look for, things to look out for, and things to count on.

We'll Get Smarter with Experience

This is new. The best among us have less than five years of experience. When you're up and running at the head of the pack, let us know what marketing is like up there at the front lines and we'll do our best to pass along the news.

In time, some of what you have read here will seem old hat, outdated, and overcome by research. Keep your eyes on the magazines, the ezines, the newsletters, and the conference podium. Ground is being broken before your very eyes. You're breaking some of it.

Email as Prevalent as the Phone

Look at any projections and you see the curve. The Internet is the most quickly adopted technology yet. Email is the most used part of the Internet. The question about whether your customers have email or not is moot.

At the beginning of 1999, the Gartner Group predicted that enterprises will receive 25 percent of all customer contacts and inquiries through Internet email messages and Web forms by 2001. Have you checked your calendar recently?

You wouldn't consider doing business with a company without a fax machine. Very soon, you'll be surprised when somebody offers to send you a brochure. Why not just email a link to the Web page?

We predict that the tyranny of voice mail will be broken by the tyranny of email. At least with email you don't have to listen to each message in sequence. Will voice mail go away? No, it has its uses. But just as companies have more and more sophisticated systems for managing their telephony, they will acquire more and more sophisticated systems for managing their email.

Plan today for more email traffic tomorrow. Plan today for email marketing to get more competitive. Plan today for email marketing response rates to fall—for a while.

Response Rates Will Fall

Gartner, Forrester, and Jupiter all say the same thing. People will become overwhelmed with incoming email and start ignoring it. Even the opt-in stuff. Why? Two reasons: mediocrity and forgetfulness.

Can you consistently crank out outstanding promotions? Great. Give us a call. We can use all the help we can get.

Mediocre. Average. Commonplace. These are not words you'd like associated with your marketing materials. But you stand just as much of a chance of being better than average as you do of being worse. That's why they call it *average.*

Couple the blah marketing that reaches your desktop with the growing number of companies that are going to be using this new medium to get their word out, and you are simply going to end up with too much to read. You will, therefore, ignore it.

But you wanted it, didn't you? Maybe at some point, but not anymore. You were dreaming of winning that vacation, or you wanted to take a look at that white paper, or you just wanted to see how they formatted their newsletter. You entered the contest, saw the white paper was about something else entirely, and weren't impressed with the design. And so you did nothing.

One week, one month, three months later, a surprise comes to your in-box. What's this? It looks formal. It says you subscribed to it. But since you don't recall, you hesitate to send a "remove" message, figuring they're just collecting spamming fodder. The junk email grows.

On the marketer's side of the screen, all they see is a decline in response rates. They still get lots of people opting in and the unsubscribe rates aren't bad. But gradually their readership is losing interest. Those days of 23 percent response rates are dwindling.

The same thing happened with banner ads. The first ones caused a lot of excitement and people clicked like there was no tomorrow. Then tomorrow came and brought a thousand new banners and the thrill was gone.

The more a list database knows about each member of that list, the more those names can be sliced and diced and served up fresh. That means people's tolerance for bad email will go down as their expectations rise.

Infinitely More Specific Personalization

Their expectations will rise because it will be more possible to more tightly target people with a more finely honed offer.

In their report, *Opt-in Email Gets Personal,* Forrester says, "Today's A/B split of a million-name list will give way to efforts consisting of 10,000 cells of 100 people each." We are moving into an era of one-to-one marketing. When the cost of storing information is falling as fast as the cost of processor power, it only makes sense that list databases will accumulate rich information about interests and preferences. That will make selectability more of a science and less of a crapshoot.

People will opt out of lists that don't offer value. Some are doing it already by abandoning old addresses and registering new ones. The only opt-in lists they'll stick with are the ones that really deliver. As a result, response rates will go back up.

Response Rates Will Rise

Response rates will rise over time as list managers become more selective about what they send their special lists.

Better Targeting

If you want to send everybody in Columbus, Ohio, a message about your new carpet-cleaning business, it won't cost very much. There also won't be a lot of people on that list. A geographical list has very little value. List managers won't find it worth the effort because nobody is especially interested in a list defined as "new service announcements in Columbus."

Vendors who manage lists like Macintosh Users in Columbus Who Use PhotoShop and Macintosh Users in Columbus Who Use Tektronix Color Printers have a hot commodity on their hands. The intersection of these lists leads to lots of marketing possibilities for the right vendor. But in order to continue offering lists that are that well refined, the list vendor is going to have to work hard to ensure that the people on that list continue to enjoy getting what they're sent.

In the long run, it'll work just like controlled subscription magazines do today. List recipients will answer lots of questions in return for getting only the information that interests them. Marketers will be able to narrow their depth of field in order to target just the right people—for a price.

With that higher-priced, better-identified market, those advertisers will work overtime to get the best offer out there. They'll learn to do it within the scope of an integrated marketing program.

Better Marketing

Marketing campaigns will streamline to draw prospective customers to a specific purchase page on the marketer's Web site. Television ads will drive traffic, radio commercials will drive traffic, direct mail will drive traffic, and signs on buses in traffic will drive traffic.

When that email piece arrives as a culmination of all the other marketing messages, the recipient will be compelled to click and follow the bouncing cursor to the logical conclusion.

Soon, that conclusion will include formal orders—transactive content is coming.

Legal Email

Digital signatures have been in the works for years. When they suit the purposes of enough large companies, special interest groups will see to it that the government signs them into law as proof positive.

If you fill out the form on a Web site with your name and credit card number, it's a formal purchase order. But if you want to send an electronic invoice, most firms haven't adopted Web technology on the spending end of the spectrum. After all, who wants to go to the trouble of implementing a whole new Web process just to ensure that invoices come in faster?

But with the advent of digital signatures, email becomes just as legal as letterhead or facsimile transmission. The digital signature confirms that you were the actual sender of the document and that the document hasn't been altered since it left your desk.

Digital signatures mean legally signed documents. They mean email-based order processing. When a customer can click the Order button on your email message or hit the Reply button and put an X in the Yes box to place the order, email becomes a formal business instrument.

Email from Everything to Everywhere

Everything with a microprocessor and a battery is going to end up with an Internet address, and everything is going to end up with a microprocessor and a battery. You'll also be able to get your email wherever you are.

Email from Everything

Your car sends an email asking to have its tires rotated.

Your swimming pool sends a message asking for more chlorine.

Your digital camera wants fresh batteries.

Your refrigerator adds milk to your personal digital assistant (PDA) because the milk carton was not returned to its shelf this morning.

Your PDA sends an email asking if you want it to reset your alarm clock so you can make your early morning flight.

Oh, by the way, your car wants you to know that if you get an oil change along with the tire rotation, the shop will give you a 10 percent discount. If you reply yes today, and make the appointment, they'll make it 15 percent.

Oh, by the way, the pool supply company will include a month's free supply if you sign up now to have them deliver it to your home on a monthly basis for a year.

Oh, by the way, identify which of the current pictures are your favorite and the local photofinisher will print them up as big, glossy 8 × 10s if you'll answer this survey.

Oh, by the way, if you buy the gallon of milk instead of the half-gallon, the milk company will download a recipe for omelets.

Oh, by the way, the airline will award you 100 extra frequent-flier miles if you check in at the gate more than 45 minutes before the flight.

Oh, by the way, there are suddenly an infinite number of cooperative marketing partnership promotional opportunities. Are you ready to kick it into high gear?

Connected Everywhere

From *Full Sterne Ahead*, 5/99

www.targeting.com

I'm currently hosting a study group on the PlanetIT Web site http://www.planetit.com and a question came up about designing your site to cater to the bandwidth of your audience.

   Having just been exposed to the inimitable Jack Powers, chief speaker-selector at Internet World and producer of the Internet Appliance Database (which should be up soon) (http://www.in3.org), I couldn't help but ponder the Web page formatting dilemma we'll all be facing soon. I wrote:

   We also have to look out for the various ways people are going to view our sites. It's not just Mac or PC anymore. It's not just three versions of Netscape and Internet Explorer. Soon, more people will be surfing our sites from:

Continues

Connected Everywhere *(Continued)*

television sets (www.webtv.com)

desk telephones (www.hightech-store.com/unidenp200.html)

mobile phones (www.nokia.com/phones/9110/index.html)

pagers (www.PlanetWeb.com/products/consumer/index.html)

and, yes, even refrigerators (www.electrolux.com/screenfridge; see Figure 10.1)

Hold onto your hats, kids, we're going for a ride! Make sure your seatbelt is low and tight across your lap and your pages are truly cross-platform.

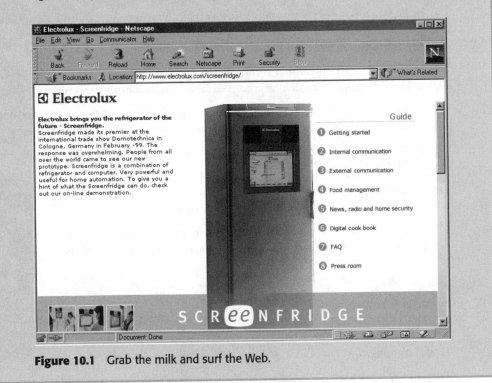

Figure 10.1 Grab the milk and surf the Web.

To Everywhere

Email isn't just going to be everywhere because people in all parts of the world are getting wired. Email is going to be everywhere because people in all parts of the world are getting wireless.

What do you get when you cross a Palm organizer with a mobile phone? The Qualcomm pdQ (see Figure 10.2).

You've gotten used to having a phone with you. They're no longer anchored to a desk by a cable. It's time to get used to having your email with you. It's no longer anchored to an application in your PC.

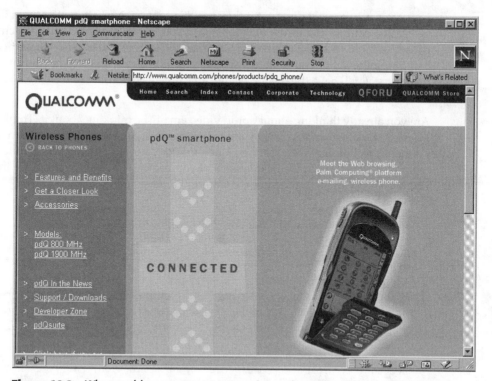

Figure 10.2 Why would you *not* want your voice and email on the same device?

What does that mean for marketers? It means your prospects and customers are just as likely to get your emails in the car, on the golf course, and at the dentist. It means you're going to have to allow them even more flexibility over when and how they receive their offers.

We're used to having a separate phone number for our mobile phones, but that's history. Teenagers today who want their own phone lines simply sign up for the 1000-hours-a-day plan and take their phones with them. They have only one number. The rest of us will follow suit in time. We're here; we're there; we get calls. Same with email.

So customers are going to want to be able to click the box that says, "Only send me this newsletter between 6 a.m. and 10 a.m. on Sundays." Or the one that will send it only to their pager if the stock hits a 52-week high. Or the one that only sends them a message that there is a special on house linens if the cell phone tracking system notices that they are within five miles of one of the stores.

Broadband Confuses the Issue

Finally, get ready for the world to change significantly when broadband rolls out to the masses. It'll take a while, but make sure you keep broadband in mind when doing your long-range planning.

Give them a 10 percent discount if they use this coupon. No? Then offer them the 10 percent off coupon and throw in that batch of special attachments if they watch the entire 7-minute video commercial. Still no deal? Okay, last offer. If they'll participate in a 45-minute online roundtable discussion focus group with three of your product managers, you'll have the device *and* the attachments delivered to their door for a free 10-day trial.

Are you already thinking about opt-in video email? Be thinking about it. Think infomercial on demand. Yes, we want to see the latest developments as presented by your chief technical officer. Yes, we want a tour of your factory. Yes, we want to know what your plans are for the next version of your product. Yes, we want to see the keynote speech at the conference we wouldn't attend.

```
To: Ernst Bernhard, Antique Glass Paperweight Collector
From: Larry Selman
Re: Four Stankards and a Rosenfeld
Date: June 24, 2004


It's been another busy month for collectors and we have a newsletter
full of special offers, events and auction sightings -- very exciting.
Before we get to all that, it's time to set your schedule for July:

[] Sign up for a personal consultantation with Larry. Appraisals, insur-
ance advice, artistic trends-- It's your collection, Larry can help.
[] Watch the next Selman Special -- four new weights created just for
AGPC members by Paul Stankard. Stankard takes us into his studio to
watch as he designs these four gems and supervises the production.
Recorded in May. 37 minutes.
[] Stream to watch    [] Download to watch later
[] Enter to win a personal e-tour of Ken Rosenfeld's Oregon studio. His
innovative use of color and the rare dimensionality of his lampwork are
open for discussion. Limited in number so Ken can personally answer any
of your questions. Twenty-four years of artistry and you could be one of
the lucky ones to join Larry and Ken for this very personal experience.

Last chance for bids on Auction #42. Ernst, your situation has been sta-
ble for a couple of days, but you know how things heat up right before
the auction closes. Here's what you need to look out for:

Item #4: Extremely rare Clichy moss carpet ground weight Since your last
bid of $14,000, there have been three bids at $15,000, $17,000 and the
latest offer at $18,000.

Item #64: Unique Saint Louis spotted amber greyhound weight Since your
last bid of $3,500, there have been three bids at $4,000, $4,500 and the
latest offer at $4,750.

Given your extensive collection, I felt I should bring this particular
piece to your attention before it goes on auction:
```

Extremely rare Baccarat millfore with animals, signed dated, and the only other one we know of is on your living room mantel: the one you acquired in 1979. *Click here* to chat with me about it before it goes on the block in two weeks.

We've added six new Clichy pages and an update of the David Chihuly section since you last visited on June 7th. Come and take a look and we'll credit your account with 5 more Bonus Bidding Points toward the next auction.

We'd like to give you an additional 10 Bonus Bidding Points if you participate in our video roundtable on June 30.

Come and join the discussion!

Shared Profiles

"I'll show you mine, if you show me yours" has now become "I'll show you mine, if my customers say it's okay." Once they say it's okay, the world of cooperative profiling opens up.

We know something about our customers and you know something about your customers and (business opportunity alert!), if a trusted third party were to come along and do an intersection run on our databases, we could both cater to our already-opted-in customers even better. It's time for some serious cross-referencing.

Imagine a competitive landscape where data cartels roam the earth. It would make sense for big players in the computer industry, for example, to form close ties with big partners. It's not hard to picture the databases of noncompetitive corporations getting chummy. Table 10.1 shows a possible result.

Start looking around to see whom you might like as your data partner. Is it Big Brother? Or is it trying to serve the customer better? The customer will decide.

Value-Added Marketing

When all is said and done, it comes down to two things: knowing enough about each individual customer to know what interests them, and knowing when and how they would like to find out.

Table 10.1 The Big Three Data Conglomerates

	DATA CONGLOM 1	DATA CONGLOM 2	DATA CONGLOM 3
Software:	Oracle	Siebel	Microsoft
Hardware:	Sun	IBM	Intel
Network gear:	Cisco	Nortel	3Com
Telco:	AT&T	Sprint	MCI

If you know these two things, you can use email marketing to keep your customers loyal. You can also use the information about them as a divining rod to point to other customers.

If you get it right and email the right things to the right people at the right time, people will flock to you and remain loyal customers.